WHAT ABOUT THE SOUL?

NEUROSCIENCE AND CHRISTIAN ANTHROPOLOGY

JOEL B. GREEN, EDITOR

Abingdon Press
Nashville

WHAT ABOUT THE SOUL?
NEUROSCIENCE AND CHRISTIAN ANTHROPOLOGY

Copyright © 2004 by Abingdon Press

This book is printed on acid-free paper.

Library of Congress Cataloging-in-Publication Data

What about the Soul? : Neuroscience and Christian anthropology / edited by Joel B. Green.
  p. cm.
Includes bibliographical references and index.
  ISBN 0-687-02345-9 (Binding: pbk. : alk. paper)
  1. Man (Christian theology) 2. Religion and science. I. Green, Joel B., 1956-

  BT702.L66 2004
  233'.5—dc22

                                                                    2003026065

All scripture references unless otherwise noted are from the *New Revised Standard Version of the Bible*, copyright 1989, by the Division of Christian Education of the National Council of the Churches of Christ in the United States of America. Used by permission. All rights reserved.

Scripture references marked (NASB) are taken from the NEW AMERICAN STANDARD BIBLE®, © Copyright The Lockman Foundation 1960, 1962, 1963, 1968, 1971, 1972, 1973, 1975, 1977, 1995. Used by permission.

The Hebraica® and Graeca® fonts used to print this work are available from Linguist's Software, Inc., PO Box 580, Edmonds, WA 98020-0580 tel (206) 775-1130.

04 05 06 07 08 09 10 11 12 13 – 10 9 8 7 6 5 4 3 2 1

MANUFACTURED IN THE UNITED STATES OF AMERICA

CONTENTS

CHAPTER 1

Body and Soul? Questions at the Interface of Science and Christian Faith

Joel B. Green

> When I look at your heavens, the work of your fingers,
> the moon and the stars that you have established;
> what are human beings that you are mindful of them,
> mortals that you care for them? (Ps. 8:3-4)

There is a new image of man emerging, an image that will dramatically contradict almost all traditional images man has made of himself in the course of his cultural history. For instance, . . . it will be strictly incompatible with the Christian image of man, as well as with many metaphysical conceptions developed in non-Western religions. (Thomas Metzinger)

What does it mean to be human? What does it mean to be fully alive as humans? Though rarely asked explicitly in day-to-day conversation these days, these questions and others like them are nonetheless widespread. What is more, what appear to be competing answers to questions regarding the makeup of humanity—from religion on the one side, natural science on the other—are heading for a showdown. If, as Thomas Metzinger insists, new data from the sciences are generating "a radically new understanding of what it *means* to be human,"[1] then those of us in the church had better prepare ourselves for searching questions about the propriety of Scripture and traditional Christian thought in our talk about humanity, salvation, the end time, and more.

Indeed, quantum leaps in our understanding of the brain in the last three decades are rewriting our understanding of who we are, and are of immediate consequence for the centuries-old quest for answers to basic, human questions: Who am I? What am I doing here? Why do I do what I do? After a century of claims that our behavior is determined by our childhood experiences of family (Freud) or by our respective social locations vis-à-vis the means of production (Marx), we now hear repeatedly how nature trumps nurture. Well known in the annals of the relationship between scientific innovation and theology are the revolutionary proposals of Copernicus and Darwin. Today, a further scientific innovation, among neurobiologists, has the potential to be just as sweeping in its effects among theologians and within the church.

What Does It Mean to Be Human?

Increasingly at the turn of the third millennium the question of the nature of the human person has been pressed upon the contemporary public. For most people, exposure to the issue is subtle and indirect. The typical source is not sermon or learned treatise, but works of science fiction, whether at the movie theater or on television or in a best-selling paperback. An earlier generation introduced to Mary Shelley's monster, that "hideous phantasm of a man," the creation of Victor Frankenstein, might have wondered whether humans were simply the sum of their body parts, animated by a powerful electrical charge. Today, the puzzle of what constitutes the human person surfaces more in the realm of cybernetics and the promise of bionic humans.

Perhaps most widely known is the perennial struggle of Data, the android bridge officer from television's *Star Trek: The Next Generation*. If the voyages of the *Star Ship Enterprise NCC-1701-D* are famous for going boldly "where no one has gone before," Data's own journey is consumed by his yearning to become human. But this begs the question, What does it mean to be human? In the episode, "The Measure of a Man," Captain Picard persuades a court of law of Data's right to self-determination. In "The Offspring," Data creates a "daughter" by mapping his own neural nets onto an android body he has fashioned, thus proving himself proficient in a form of procreation. Eventually the recipient of an "emotion chip," he is capable of affective response and in the movie *Star Trek: First Contact* is given, however temporarily, patches of human skin. Finally, in *Star Trek: Nemesis*, Data sacrifices himself for the sake of his friend. Do such attributes as these move Data closer to being "human"?

My own appetite for such questions was whetted in the late 1960s, while devouring the science fiction of Isaac Asimov. Already almost two decades old when I first read it as a young teenager, Asimov's book *I, Robot* portrays robots with traits that others might have reserved for humans. Robbie the robot wants to "hear a story," is "faithful and loving and kind," and is even called "my friend . . . not no machine" by his young companion, Gloria. Gloria's mother is nonetheless clear that Robbie is "nothing more than a mess of steel and copper in the form of sheets and wires with electricity"; "it has no soul," so should never be confused with a human being. Another robot ("Cutie," for "Robot QT-1") possesses intuition, has (or rejects) beliefs, claims that "I, myself, exist, because I think," and even spontaneously generates a religious structure for the universe and so counts it a privilege to serve "the Master." As readers of Asimov will know, robots in the early twenty-first century have a basis for moral thought and ethical activity hardwired into their positronic brains.[2] As precursor to those presentations of androids that would follow (the screenplay for *Bicentennial Man* [1999] traces its genealogy to the work of Asimov), *I, Robot* and other contributions to Asimov's "The Robot Series" press the question of personhood, of the uniqueness of *homo sapiens*. What does it mean to be human?

For Christians, this is a question of some urgency. What distinguishes us from nonhuman animals? What view of the human person, what anthropology, is capable of funding what we want to know about ourselves theologically—about sin, for example, as well as moral responsibility, volition, repentance, joy, and growth in grace? What anthropology is capable of casting a canopy of sacred worth over human beings, so that we are capable of ethical discourse and ethical practices regarding "human dignity" and "sacred worth," not least on beginning- and end-of-life issues? How should we think of issues surrounding healing and health? How should we understand "salvation"? What does salvation entail? Salvation of my soul? If so, does this entail a denial of the world and embodied life, focusing instead on spiritual life and the life to come? What view of salvation, or soteriology, is funded by a given anthropology? How ought the church extend itself in mission? Mission to what? The spiritual/soulish needs of persons? The cosmos? What is the nature of the church? Or, what ecclesiology follows from a given anthropology? What happens when we die? What anthropology is consistent with the Christian belief in life-after-death?

Body and Soul?

For many, and not least for many Christians, the traditional answer to the question, *What makes a human genuinely human?* has been the human possession of a soul. If, beginning already in the second century, the origin of the soul would be debated among Christian theologians,[3] in the postapostolic period it was nonetheless clear to most, as the *Letter to Diognetus* puts it, that "the soul dwells in the body, yet is not of the body" (1.27). Exegesis of the Genesis account of the creation of humanity "in the image of God" generally focused on God's breathing into Adam "the breath of life," with the result that the first human, as with every human to appear subsequently, is a human being by virtue of the soul. "Without the soul, we are nothing," wrote Tertullian, "[Without the soul] there is not even the name of a human being—only that of a carcass" (3.532). Writing in the early fourth century, Lactantius is even more clear: "The body can do nothing without the soul. But the soul can do many and great things without the body" (7.208-09). Dogmatic or systematic theology concerned with theological anthropology, the doctrine of humanity, has traditionally discussed the uniqueness of humanity in two theological loci, human creation in the divine image and the human possession of a soul.[4] Often these two loci are reduced to one, with the soul understood as the particular consequence of creation in God's image.

It is true that, for persons of faith—Christians included, but many others besides—the idea of a soul separable from the body has contributed a great deal. We have regularly appealed to the soul as proof that humans are not mere animals, and so as a foundation for our views of human dignity and the sacredness of human life. Human possession of a soul thus has immediate and far-reaching consequences in the burgeoning and troubled arena of bioethics. Moreover, inasmuch as a dualistic approach to understanding the human person typically emphasizes the mastery of the soul over the body, Christians have derived from the existence of the soul their affirmation of the human capacity to choose between good and ill as free moral agents. Further, since it is with regard to the soul that the divine image shared by human beings comes into clearest focus, the soul provides the necessary (though not sufficient) ground of human spirituality, of one's capacity to enter into and enjoy a relationship with God. Still further, the existence of a nonphysical soul, distinct and separable from the body, is generally regarded as the means by which human identity can cross over the bridge between this life and the next; indeed, traditional Christian thought has tended to regard the body as frail and finite, the soul as immortal.

But it is the human possession of a "soul" that science now questions. When, as neurobiology and evolutionary psychology increasingly urge, the attributes and capacities traditionally allocated to the human soul are conditioned in every detail by biological processes, on what basis can belief in a soul be maintained? Of course, for some, such questions can only lead to the exclamation, So much the worse for science! If science and Christian belief stand at odds on the question of the existence of the soul, then Christian belief must trump science. But this way of thinking begs an important question—namely, whether science ought to be excluded as a source for Christian theology.[5]

8

Christian Faith, Natural Science

How might we negotiate the apparently competing claims of traditional theology and the neurosciences? In the twentieth century, one of the most prominent voices on such matters has been that of Karl Barth. For Barth, natural science has little relevance for theology, but rather presents a competing ideology. Faith comes by means of divine encounter, a view that for Barth led to a polemic against any possibility of discovering, discerning, or encountering God through natural science. The revelation of God was not available through any natural mediation. Rather, although creation makes possible the covenantal relationship between God and humanity, the chasm between Creator and creation disallows humans from making valid judgments about what we may know concerning the Creator on the basis of creation. For Barth, theology and the natural sciences comprise noninteractive disciplines, with each having its own respective magistrate.[6]

In the modern history of the interaction of Christian faith and science, Barth's is a minority position. Indeed, the concept of "two books" became a regular fixture in seventeenth-century English natural theology. Accordingly, science and religion were not antagonistic toward each other, for science was nothing more than investigation into God's creation. True, the materialistic focus of "the new science" could marginalize the need for God, but, it was insisted, this was neither a necessary consequence of scientific investigation nor an appropriate use of science. First published in 1642, Thomas Browne's *Religio Medici* insisted that the physician was not doomed to atheism, for the physician's work leads to God; Scripture and the natural world formed a dual pathway to God.[7] Similarly, Richard Cumberland's *De Legibus Naturae* argued that mechanistic physics need not devolve into unorthodoxy in ethical theory nor into atheism; when atheism was the effect, impiety and not science was to blame.[8] Perhaps most famous was Boyle's *Free Inquiry into the Vulgarly Received Notion of Nature*, which opposed the materialist infidels and insisted that the new, mechanistic science was religion's invincible ally.[9] Thomas Willis (1621–1675) was a key figure in setting the study of the brain and nervous system on its present course. In his preface to *The Anatomy of the Brain*, Willis likened his dissection table to "the most holy Altar of Your Grace," Gilbert Sheldon, Archbishop of Canterbury, and referred to his work as an examination of "the Pandects of Nature, as into another Table of the Divine Word, and the greater Bible: For indeed, in either Volume there is no high point, which requires not the care, or refuses the industry of an Interpreter; there is no Page certainly which shews not the Author, and his Power, Goodness, Trust, and Wisdom."[10]

More recently, Alister McGrath has insisted that the Christian doctrine of creation demands a unitary approach to knowledge. If God made the world, then it is only to be expected that something of God's character would be disclosed in creation. Consequently, for McGrath, there are two modes of knowing God—natural order and Scripture—with the second clearer and fuller than the first.[11]

We can press further in our thinking about the relationship between Christian faith and natural science. Science must be taken seriously, first, on account of our doctrine of creation. This means that, for the Christian, inquiry starts not from "science," but from the Christian tradition in its understanding of nature in its creatureliness. Of course, until the modern era, discussion of science-theology relations was irrelevant since science, philosophy, and religion comprised the same vocation, proceeded from the same intellectual impulses, and focused on the same subject matter. On account of the Christian doctrine of creation, theology is an all-encompassing enterprise, so that the subsequent segregation of science from theology could not mean that science would fall outside the purview of theology. Insofar as science is present as one of the sources for the theological enterprise, theology remains open to the possibility of reformulation on account of scientific discovery. It is not only that our doctrine of creation urges a unitary approach to knowledge, pressing us to account for natural science in our theological work, however. There are also considerations of an epistemological sort—considerations, that is, which focus on how we know what we know. Accordingly, we must account for the reality that natural science is and has always been part of our worldview. The two, science and theology, interact in a more organic way, with the result that it is virtually impossible to extricate the one influence from the other, or to prioritize one vis-à-vis the other. This is true in the "science" presumed of the biblical writers. It is also true of the "science" presumed of biblical interpreters and theologians from the second century onward. We have before us a long history of interpreters of biblical texts who have engaged those texts on the basis of scientific views of the human person pervasive in the worlds of the interpreters.

If the "truth" about the human person was decisively determined by Holy Scripture, what would happen when contravening evidence surfaced from extra-biblical sources, particularly from scientific observation? Twenty-first-century hermeneuts will recognize the naïveté of the question itself, since "what the Holy Scriptures teach" about the human person is always located in a hermeneutical circle (or spiral) with the presumptions brought by the interpreter to the theological enterprise.[12] The question is, then, Will we allow a particular scientific rendering of the voice of Scripture to masquerade as "timeless truth"?

The Present Discussion

Theologians, philosophers, and scientists have brought to the table a plethora of considerations, resulting in a dizzying array of possible solutions to the body-soul, mind-brain problem. These include substance dualism (Swinburne), naturalistic dualism (Chalmers), wholistic dualism (Cooper), emergent dualism

(Hasker), constitutional materialism (Corcoran, Baker), emergent monism (Clayton), and nonreductive physicalism (Murphy).[13] For the noninitiated, the terms of the discussion can be bewildering, and a few definitions may be helpful.

We refer to *nonreductive physicalism* as distinct from the physicalist view (sometimes known as *reductive materialism*) that people are nothing but the product of organic chemistry. Physicalism, or reductive materialism, is well represented in the words of Francis Crick: "'you,' your joys and your sorrows, your memories and your ambitions, your sense of identity and free will, are in fact no more than the behavior of a vast assembly of nerve cells and their associated molecules."[14] In opposition to this *reductive* account of the human being, *nonreductive physicalism* assumes (1) it is not necessary to postulate a second, metaphysical entity, such as a soul or spirit, to account for human capacities and distinctives, and (2) human behavior cannot be explained exhaustively with recourse to genetics or neuroscience.[15] In contrast to these two *monist* positions is a *radical dualism*, according to which body and soul are regarded as separate entities, with the real "person" or authentic "self" identified with the soul; and *functional wholism*, which assumes an ontological dualism (body and soul) that embraces both the functional integration of human life and a disembodied intermediate state beyond death. Only rarely does one find today in serious theological literature a *tripartite* view of the human person, according to which the human being is made up of three ontologically separate entities—body, soul, and spirit. As different people work to account for different aspects of the evidence, they locate themselves on the continuum between radical dualism and reductive materialism. Contributions to this book occupy space toward the midpoint in this continuum.

How does the present collection of essays contribute to the issues we have sketched?

1. Christians often struggle simply to stay current on what we are learning from the sciences. The contributions of Malcolm Jeeves (chapter 2) and Gareth Jones (chapter 3) provide in an accessible form an orientation both to important research in neurobiology and mind-brain (and, thus, body-soul) questions, and to some of the urgent issues that arise from that research. This sort of update is crucial, since it reminds us of the shape of the evidence before us and urges us to account for this data without running ahead of what science has actually opened before us.

2. For Christians, the character of the biblical witness to the nature of humanity is a non-negotiable landmark in addressing the question, What does it mean to be human? But it is the nature of the biblical witness that is itself contested in current discussion. A baseline consideration is how the biblical materials speak of the creation of humanity and address the question, What is a human being? Explicit biblical attention to this question is as important as it is sparse, and the relevant materials are ably explored by Lawson Stone (chapter 4) and Patrick Miller (chapter 5). Some participants in the discussion on body-soul matters

point to specific texts or concepts to prove that the Bible teaches the dual nature of humans, body and soul. Bill Arnold and Joel Green explore two of these contested areas—with Arnold turning our attention to the account concerning communication with the deceased Samuel by the witch at Endor (chapter 6) and Green addressing the nature of the "resurrection body" in the New Testament (chapter 7).

3. William Hasker (chapter 8) and Charles Gutenson (chapter 9) direct our thinking in a philosophical direction, but come to different conclusions. Hasker is keen to work out a view of the human person that accounts for Christian belief in free will and the afterlife, *and* which takes seriously what we are learning about the close mind-brain link from the neurosciences. Gutenson takes up two related questions concerning the continuity of human existence: (1) Should we assume an intermediate state of human existence between death and the general resurrection? (2) What set of conditions or state of affairs assures that some person, who is present in resurrected life, is the continuation of the life of the same person in this life? Hasker's response moves in the direction of dualism, but Gutenson argues that one can take seriously the same concerns that have occupied Hasker without drawing Hasker's conclusions.

4. Though it may be surprising to a wide range of Christian readers, a number of recent works have set forth a strong case for locating a non-dualist anthropology squarely within the Christian tradition.[16] Christian philosopher Nancey Murphy has observed that "all of the human capacities once attributed to the immaterial mind or soul are now yielding to the insights of neurobiology."[17] And the eminent theologian Wolfhart Pannenberg recognizes that recent advances with regard to the close mutual interrelations of physical and psychological occurrences have robbed of their credibility traditional ideas of a soul distinct from the body that is detached from it in death.[18] These conclusions notwithstanding, there is much about Christian practices that remains to be addressed within this emerging paradigm—not least with regard to missions and evangelism, bioethics, pastoral care, and so on. Hence, the contributions by Michael Rynkiewich on missiology (chapter 10), Virginia Todd Holeman on counseling (chapter 11), and Stuart Palmer on pastoral care (chapter 12) are of particular significance.

How these various perspectives contribute to the question of the nature of our humanity, and to the ramifications that follow from how we answer that question, is the focus of a final, integrative chapter, written by neuropsychologist Malcolm Jeeves.

Jeeves may provide the final chapter of this book, but the final chapter in this conversation cannot yet be written. Nevertheless, these essays contribute significantly to the ongoing struggle to clarify and appropriate our faith as Christians in ways that take seriously our theological tradition and the resources, drawn from every corner of inquiry, that continue to be brought to light.

CHAPTER 2

Mind Reading and Soul Searching in the Twenty-first Century

The Scientific Evidence

Malcolm Jeeves

Two central issues confront us. First, how do innovations in neuroscience impinge on our traditional portraits of the human person, and specifically those within the Christian tradition? Second, what implications does this new knowledge have for practices generally associated with Christian life and ministry (e.g., spirituality, evangelism, and pastoral care)? This chapter offers an overview of the challenges of the neurosciences in their twofold aspects. First, we will explore some implications of the mind-brain links for our understanding of a Christian anthropology. Second, we will examine whether and in what ways this may shed fresh light on how meaningful distinctions between humans and other animals are best formulated. Discussions of how the science presented in this chapter might have implications for living the Christian life and the nature and meaning of spirituality will be left to chapter 13.

What, in terms accessible to the nonspecialist, is the evidence that maps out the main contours of the neuroscientific picture of humankind; and in what directions are exciting developments at the interface of neuroscience and evolutionary biology affording new insights into human-animal similarities and differences? For this latter task, the focus will be on the work of evolutionary psychologists whose work, according to Laland and Brown, is "undoubtedly the dominant school of thought" as regards the application of evolutionary biology to the understanding of human behavior.[1]

From "Soul Talk" to "Mind Talk"

The Last Three Centuries

In the seventeenth and eighteenth centuries, "soul" talk, at least among philosophers, changed to "mind" talk. Noting this, Kenan Malik wrote,

> The difficulty in finding a common language in which to talk of the immortal soul and the body-machine led many seventeenth- and eighteenth-century natural philosophers to speak increasingly of the "mind" rather than of the "soul." The mind was not simply a synonym for the soul in a more mechanistic language. Rather, those aspects of the soul's relationship with the world that were amenable to naturalistic explanations—memory, perception, emotions, and so on—were recast as problems of the mind. This transformation helped minimize conflict between theologians and natural philosophers: the soul eventually became the domain purely of theology, while natural philosophers developed the "science of the mind." But it did not resolve the underlying problem of how to talk about an immaterial entity using a language developed for describing machines. It simply transformed the terms of that problem: the question of how the transcendental soul acted upon the physical body became replaced by the question of how the immaterial mind could arise out of fleshly matter. It still remains a central question for the science of the mind.[2]

Since it is generally agreed that Plato was one of the two philosophers who have had the greatest influence on Christian theology, and since Plato argued that the rational part of the soul preexists the body, dwelling in the transcendent role of the Forms, and returns at death, the mind has been closely associated with the soul. It is in this sense among others that developments in neuroscience were seen by Francis Crick as challenging many widely held views of the soul and its relationship to the body. This led him to claim that "the idea that man has a disembodied soul is as unnecessary as the old idea that there was a Life Force. This is in head-on contradiction to the religious beliefs of billions of human beings alive today. How will such a radical change be received?"[3] Saint Augustine's view of the person is a modified platonic view: the human being is an immortal soul using a mortal body. It is René Descartes, however, who facilitated the shift from minds to souls. It is because soul and mind have frequently been used synonymously that changing views from within science of the relationship between mind and body are seen as relevant to historical discussions of the relation of soul and body.

It remains an intriguing puzzle how it was that Vesalius's paper *On the Fabric of the Human Body*—published in 1543, the year after Copernicus's famous paper *On the Revolutions of the Heavenly Spheres*—failed to cause a stir like that of Copernicus. Dava Sobel has observed that Vesalius's work was just as much an affront to Aristotle: "even while Galileo sat writing the *Dialogue* nearly a century later, Aristotelians clung to the heart as the origin of the nerves, though Vesalius had followed their course up through the neck to the brain."[4] As recently as the late eighteenth century, some of the leading physicians in London seemingly saw no causal link between something wrong with the ability to speak and what was going on in the brain. For example, those who attended the famous English lexicographer Dr. Samuel Johnson when he suffered a stroke in 1783 (an event documented in detail in his diaries) prescribed for him the then-accepted treatment of inflicting blisters on each side of the throat up to the ear, one on the head, and one on the back, together with taking regular doses of hartshorn (which we would today call ammonium carbonate). Thus, they "treated" peripheral structures located in the neck and throat, believing that there was the physical basis of speech. Clearly for them, brain events and the mind events involved in speech and language were not linked. Such a view went counter to one of the prevailing views about the physical basis of mind that had competed with others for the previous two thousand years.

In the years following Dr. Johnson's experiences in the late eighteenth century, views changed rapidly. In 1825, Bouillard, a French physician, argued from his clinical observations that speech was localized in the frontal lobes of the brain. His views were supported by Gall, the distinguished anatomist and phrenologist. Shortly afterward, in 1835, these views were expanded by Marc Dax, who argued that speech disorders were linked to lesions of the left hemisphere, views further reinforced in 1861, when Paul Broca reported the case of a patient who stopped speaking when pressure was applied to the anterior lobes of his brain. Thus the notion of cerebral dominance of language in the left hemisphere was enunciated.

In the space of less than a hundred years, the assumption that brain events and mind events were not linked changed to a recognition of the clear link between brain, language, and intellectual function generally. There were also hints of a link between brain and personality, including social and ethical behavior. Such moves did not go unchallenged, however. In the early nineteenth century, Pierre Flourens, a pioneer in techniques of making small lesions in the brains of animals as a way of investigating brain function, published results that were taken to imply that psychological functions are not discretely localized in particular cerebral areas. It was a view championed a century later by Karl Lashley, who put forward a "theory of mass action," contending that the behavioral outcome of cortical lesions depends more on the amount of the brain removed than on the particular location of the lesion inflicted.[5] Although today, as we shall see in a moment, the localizationist view is dominant and well documented, it is for our purposes no more than illustrative of the cumulative trend of neuropsychological research pointing to the conclusion that neural and mental processes are two aspects of one set of physical events.

The Current Scene

During the second half of the last century, and particularly immediately after the Second World War, there was a reawakening of interest in the brain-behavior relationship. Facing the task of rehabilitating thousands of servicemen with circumscribed gunshot wounds, research began to advance rapidly. As sometimes happens in science, the outcome was not so much the discovery of new ideas but the rediscovery of old ones. In this case, the views of some of the nineteenth-century neurologists mentioned above, combined with the development of new behavioral techniques of the experimental psychologists, gave impetus to the development of neuropsychology.

The rapid development of cognitive neuroscience in recent years is generally attributed to the convergence of three previously relatively unrelated areas of scientific endeavor: experimental psychology, comparative neuropsychology, and brain imaging techniques. The cognitive revolution within experimental psychology freed it from earlier, narrowly circumscribed behaviorist approaches to the understanding of mind and behavior. Psychologists could talk freely about mental events and not simply about stimulus-response contingencies. The development of new experimental techniques enabled cognitive psychologists to fractionate psychological processes into their component parts—memory, for example, into long-term memory, working memory, and short-term memory.

In comparative neuropsychology, techniques found useful in studying human remembering and perceiving were adapted and applied to the study of nonhuman primates. Exciting new findings came from studies of memory and visual perception in animals. Other psychologists, following the pioneering studies of Hubel and Wiesel with cats, used single-cell recording techniques to study perception in awake and alert monkeys. At the same time, there were exciting developments in brain imaging techniques, notably nuclear magnetic resonance and, most recently of all, positron emission tomography scanning techniques. These latter developments, combined with cerebral blood flow studies, made possible the monitoring of brain activities occurring when specified mental tasks are performed by normal people.

It is important to set what follows in context. Because the focus is on findings from research in neuroscience and evolutionary psychology, that does not mean that any claim is being made that explanation at these levels are to be regarded as the only or the most important accounts that can be given of the human person.

Each of us is a complex system, simultaneously part of a larger social system and at the same time composed of smaller systems, which in turn are composed of ever smaller subsystems. Any aspect of human behavior and cognition we choose to investigate may be analyzed at these different levels to begin to generate a full account of reality. Each level entails its own questions and calls for appropriate methods in order to answer them. Although the account given at each level may be complete within itself, that does not mean that by itself it constitutes a full account of the phenomena under investigation. Because at one level it is exhaustive does not mean it can claim to be exclusive. Each account complements the others. Take memory for example. Neurologists and neuropsychologists study the cerebral localization of short-term memory, working memory, episodic memory, and procedural memory, as well as the chemical codes and neural networks in which information is stored. Cognitive psychologists investigate the memory in nonphysical terms as a partly automatic and partly effortful process of encoding, storing, and retrieving information. Social psychologists study how our moods and social experiences affect our recall of past events. Recognizing the importance of these multiple levels of explanation does not entail adopting a reductionist position. That is not a part of science. It may be a procedural device or it may be linked with materialist presuppositions held for other reasons. There are certainly great scientific benefits in the reductionist approach as a methodological stance and not a metaphysical one.

Illustrating the Tightening Mind-Brain Links

One of the more consistent findings of research capitalizing on the convergence of experimental psychology, comparative neuropsychology, and brain imaging techniques has been how specific mental processes or even component parts of those processes appear to be tightly linked to particular regions or systems in the brain. Within those regions, moreover, there often emerged a further specificity indicating that certain columns of cells were involved when a particular aspect of the task was being performed.

Sensory Processing of Face Perception

From time to time over the past fifty years, there have been occasional reports in the neurological literature of patients who, having suffered strokes, reported that they could no longer recognize faces, including their own. They could recognize dogs or cats or houses, but not faces. With the advent of brain scanning techniques, it became possible to identify areas of the brain which, when damaged, seemed to result in problems with face processing.

There was already ample evidence of how visual signals arising from the face provide an abundance of social information about an individual's gender, age, familiarity, emotional state, and potentially their intentions and their mental state. Neuroethologists, having studied across many species the information gained by interpersonal face perception, pointed out that the primate face has evolved an elaborate system of facial musculature that helps in producing expressive facial movements. What also soon became clear was that the direction of gaze was of crucial importance. The eyes had of course long held a special interest to humans. They were said to be "the windows of the soul" and normally are one of the first points of contact between infants and their mothers.

Twenty years ago, researchers such as David Perrett of the University of Saint Andrews, a leader in this field, using single-cell recording techniques, discovered that there were cells in the brains of monkeys that responded selectively to the sight of faces.[6] This was a surprising finding since, with further research, the specificity of the links between what the monkey was seeing, such as the identification of the faces, seemed to become stronger with every experiment. One important feature of any face was the direction of gaze of the eyes and the direction the head was pointing.

Cells that were responsively selective for faces were found in the superior temporal sulcus on the monkey's brain. When the researchers changed the color or size of the faces, these cells did not respond. There was a remarkable specificity in the cells' responses to facial stimuli. Among other things, Perrett found that changing head view (that is, its horizontal orientation) had a dramatic effect on the activity of face-responsive neurons. All this suggested to Perrett that one of the key functions of these neurons may be to determine the direction of another's attention. He proposed that the information provided by the eyes, the face, and the body were each selectively processed by particular groups of neurons, all part of a processing hierarchy possibly for attention direction or social attention. Other researchers demonstrated that this was only part of a larger system.[7]

The results of this research with nonhuman primates have since been supported by research on human beings, using techniques such as event-related brain potentials (ERPs), functional magnetic resonance imaging (fMRI), and positron emission topography (PET scans). There has also been a small amount of evidence from patients suffering from very selective brain damage which is consistent with the other research.

Taken together, this research has now made strong links with those whose main interest is the study of autism. The potential link between the amygdala, one of the parts of the overall functional system involved in face processing, and autism has been suggested by the work of neuropathologists studying the brains of autistic individuals. The neurons of particular nuclei of the amygdala are, in such individuals, more closely packed than in normal brains. A small number of neuro-imaging studies of living autistic brains also confirms this research.

Memory

Through the work of experimental psychology, instead of speaking simply of memory, we became able to fractionate memory into its subcomponents. One of the most widely used models is that of Alan Baddeley.[8] He identified three distinct components of what he called working memory: the visuo-spatial sketch pad, a phonological loop, and a central executive. Using brain imaging techniques, Frith and his coworkers showed that the phonological loop involves two separate locations within the left hemisphere of the brain, the visuo-spatial sketch pad is distributed across at least four locations in the right hemisphere, and the central executive depends on a range of locations within the frontal lobes of the brain.[9]

Personality and Emotion

But it is not only cognitive functions that have been localized. A long though patchy history within neurology should have alerted us to the fact that, with changes in the neural substrate, we may observe changes in personality and emotion. The best-known example of this and the one most frequently retold is that of Phineas Gage. Gage survived accidental damage to the frontal part of his brain, which changed him overnight from a conscientious, reliable, dependable, hard-working pillar of society to an unreliable, boastful gambler, unable to devote himself for any length of time to any task. In short, as the result of selective brain damage, a reliable, morally upright, excellent character had become unreliable, morally irresponsible, and a source of little good to the society within which he lived.

A series of similar cases, with damage to the same brain region resulting from disease and vascular accidents, has recently been documented by Antonio Damasio and his colleages.[10] Cautious copy never sells newspapers, however, so it was no surprise that, when reporting Damasio's findings, the *Times* of London, came out with a large headline: "Brain Damage Can Produce Psychopaths."[11] Commenting on Damasio's patients, Frans de Waal wrote, "It's as if the moral compass of these people has been demagnetised, causing it to spin out of control." He continues, "What this incident teaches us is that conscience is not some disembodied concept that can be understood only on the basis of culture and religion." Morality, he claimed, is as firmly grounded in neurobiology as anything else we do or are.[12]

19

Bottom-up and Top-down

Most of the examples thus far are those in which changes have been made to neural substrates and observations have been made of subsequent changes in perception or cognition. This is sometimes labeled a bottom-up approach. One of the contributions of Nobel laureate Roger Sperry was his emphasis on the importance of paying equal attention to the role of cognition in modifying brain processes. This he labeled a top-down effect.

Since the order of magnitude of the events occurring in the brain range from several centimeters in the case of long pathways and networks, down to molecular events occurring in changes in neurotransmitters, we may summarize the evidence underlining the ever-tightening links between brain and cognition by tracing some examples taken from what I have called the bottom-up approach, moving up through the lower levels to the top levels of networks and systems; and then starting at the top levels, selecting top-down effects occurring at successively lower levels. Figure 1 traces out some of these effects, using examples of research reported in the last few years.

Gesch presented evidence indicating that, where offenders consume diets lacking in essential nutrients, this could adversely affect their behavior. This study carried out in a prison showed that, where there was a dietary reduction of vitamins, minerals, and essential fatty acids, there was an increase in antisocial behavior, including violence.[13] Lai and his colleagues identified a gene whose function is thought to be involved in the development of speech and language.[14] Both of these studies concern clearly bottom-up phenomena.

Moving up from molecular levels to systems and maps in the brain, we may refer again to Damasio's studies, cited above, showing the effects of early brain injury on the moral behavior of people in their late teens. Still at the level of systems and maps, but now considering top-down effects, we may recall how Sadato studied people who were born blind and who had been taught braille; in them it was found that the parts of the cerebral cortex normally devoted to vision had been taken over by touch.[15]

Continuing with top-down effects at adulthood, consider another dramatic and widely reported top-down effect in the study of London taxi drivers, by Maguire and others in 2000.[16] Their research built on two facts—first, that one important role of the hippocampus is to facilitate spatial memory in the form of navigation; and second, that licensed London taxi drivers are renowned for their extensive and detailed navigation experience. Maguire, studying structural MRIs of their brains, compared them with those of matched control subjects who did not drive taxis. They found that the posterior hippocampi of the taxi drivers were significantly larger than those of control subjects. Hippocampi volume also correlated with the amount of time spent as a taxi driver. They concluded, "It seems

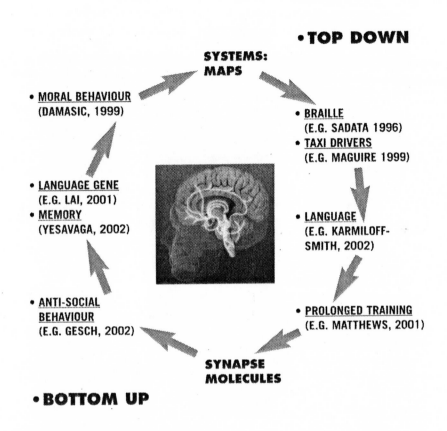

• **TOP DOWN**

SYSTEMS:
MAPS

• MORAL BEHAVIOUR
(DAMASIC, 1999)

• BRAILLE
(E.G. SADATA 1996)
• TAXI DRIVERS
(E.G. MAGUIRE 1999)

• LANGUAGE GENE
(E.G. LAI, 2001)
• MEMORY
(YESAVAGA, 2002)

• LANGUAGE
(E.G. KARMILOFF-
SMITH, 2002)

• ANTI-SOCIAL
BEHAVIOUR
(E.G. GESCH, 2002)

• PROLONGED TRAINING
(E.G. MATTHEWS, 2001)

SYNAPSE
MOLECULES

• **BOTTOM UP**

Figure 1: The dynamic interdependence between what is happening in the brain and what we think and how we habitually believe, identified in recent examples from the neuroscience literature.

that there is a capacity for local plasticity change in the structure of the healthy adult human brain in response to environmental demands."

Again at the level of networks and neurons, we may refer to a paper recently published in the journal *Neurology*, which reported that memory in normal subjects was significantly improved by modifying neurotransmitter processes in their brains using drugs.[17] At the level of synapses and molecules, we may mention the study by Keith Matthews and his colleagues in 2001, which showed that, when rats habitually engaged in particular forms of maze learning, several of their brain neurotransmitter systems, including dopamine and serotonin, were systematically changed in adulthood.[18]

Finally, we may consider a very recent, elegantly designed study by O'Craven and Kanwisher, which beautifully illustrates how the "mind" selectively mobilizes specific areas or systems in the brain. They showed that imagining faces or houses was linked to activity in two different brain areas. Seeing or thinking about faces activated the fusiform face area, whereas seeing or thinking about houses activated the parahippocampal area. The experimenters could actually "read the minds" of their subjects by observing their brain activity. That is, they could tell whether their subjects were thinking about faces or houses by measuring the activity in the fusiform face area and the parahippocampal area.[19] This study also dramatically illustrates the rate of progress in research in cognitive neuroscience. O'Craven and Kanwisher, in their report in 2000, cite a paper by Grabowski and Damasio, published in 1996, where they wrote, "the imaging of the neural correlates of single and discrete mental events, such as one image or one word, remains a most desirable dream."[20] O'Craven and Kanwisher add, "That dream is now a reality."

Some Cautionary Comments

With rapid advances in studies about genes and human behavior, there is an increasing temptation to look for a one-to-one relationship between complex behaviors, such as altruism, aggression, and language on the one hand, and specific genes or locations in the brain on the other. Such a view has, for example, been given wide publicity by Steven Pinker, using data from adult neuropsychology and genetic disorders. Other leading workers in the field, such as Annette Karmiloff-Smith, have argued that Pinker's interpretation of the data is flawed. She points out that it is based on a static model of the human brain which ignores the complexities of gene expression and the dynamics of postnatal development. I agree with Karmiloff-Smith's critique. Head of the neurocognitive development unit at University College London, she used her British Psychology Society Centenary Lecture to give a balanced view of the relationships between specific genes and complex behaviors. She pointed out that "understanding the complex pathways from gene-to-brain-to-cognitive processes-to-behaviour is like a detective story, in which seemingly unimportant clues early in development play a vital role in the final outcome."[21] She argues that comments by distinguished scientists, such as Pinker, repeatedly support assumptions that could imply a one-to-one relationship between specific genes and complex behaviors. Those of such a nativist persuasion claim that human infants are born with genetically specific brains that contain specialized components, not only for low-level conceptual processes, but also for higher-level cognitive modules like language and face processing. She recognizes that, at first blush, there are indeed a number of genetic disorders that seem to fit such a model. Dyslexia is one such disorder with a clear genetic component. Another is

Williams syndrome. Pinker has claimed this as the prime example of impaired and intact cognitive modules directly linked to genes. He compared another disorder, known as Special Language Impairment (SLI) with Williams syndrome (WS), arguing that "overall, the genetic double dissociation is striking, suggesting that language is (both) a specialisation of the brain. . . . The genes of one group of children (SLI), impaired their grammar whilst sparing their intelligence; the genes of another group of children (WS) impaired their intelligence whilst sparing their grammar."[22] By contrast, Karmiloff-Smith argues that "there is no one-to-one direct mapping between a specific gene and a cognitive-level outcome. Rather, there are many-to-many indirect mappings, with the regulation of gene expression contributing to broad differences in developmental timing, the neuronal type, neuronal density, neuronal firing, neurotransmitter types and so on." She concludes "that data from adult neuropsychology and genetic disorders cannot be used by Nativists to bolster claims about genetically specified, modular specialisations of the human brain. We need to understand how genes are expressed through development, because the major clue to genotype/phenotype relations turns out to be the very processes of development itself." This timely and well-informed comment should be borne in mind whenever there is an attempt to deduce genetic determinism from research results in cognitive neuroscience.

Personal Agency

When analyzing human nature from the perspective of neuroscience, it is all too easy to forget the primacy of the role of consciousness and the cognitive agent in all that we do. As medical or basic scientists, we are constantly aware of the risk of so focusing on each new discovery of how this or that aspect of cognition or behavior is embodied in this or that region or system of the brain that we give the impression that we are, after all, "mere machines." We just take it for granted that people recognize that it was someone's personal agency that produced the research. It was undertaken on the personal initiative of someone and that someone had reflected long and hard on the results before writing them up, presenting them at a conference for peer scrutiny, and submitting them to a journal, all indicative of personal agency at work. Without this personal agency, none of the work would have been done.

We can recognize and emphasize personal agency in humans while at the same time affirm rudimentary forms of agency in animals. Whether it is manifest, for example, in nonhuman primates is an interesting scientific question and as Christians we have no stake in the outcome of studies to answer it. To recapitulate: First, we are only at the beginning of our understanding of the complex interrelations between what is happening at the levels of cognition and its neural substrates. Second, there is no simple pattern of when, and under what circumstances, it is the top-down, cognitive, behavioral, environmental factors that are crucial, and under what circumstances it is the built-in, bottom-up, genetic, neurochemical factors that are dominant, and which represent the key determinants of the final outcome of any expressed cognitive capacity or behavior.

We turn now to a second area of research, which some see as having profound implications for our understanding of human nature, particularly as it relates to animal nature. It is also an area of research where some of the most exciting advances are at the convergence with neuroscience research.

Mirror Neurons: A Bridge from Neuroscience to Evolutionary Psychology

Peter Bowler, commenting on how difficult it is for nonscientists, including theologians, to keep abreast of developments in science, notes how in some of their discussions at the interface of science and religion, the writings of some theologians quickly fall into disrepute because their science is several decades out of date.[23] Bowler is doubtless in some instances correct and, therefore, in the present context, it is sensible for me to alert my theologian and philosophical colleagues of the current excitement in scientific circles of the discovery of so-called mirror neurons, since they form a natural link between neuroscience and an aspect of evolutionary biology—namely, evolutionary psychology—and promise to become of increasing importance in the future.

Mirror Neurons, Imitation, and Mind Reading

The mirror neuron story began fourteen years ago, when Giacomo Rizzolatti and his colleagues at the University of Parma reported the discovery of neurons in the frontal part of the brains of monkeys which possessed functional properties hitherto not observed.[24] Their report caused considerable interest among neuropsychologists, while passing largely unnoticed by evolutionary psychologists.

These neurons, located in the area known as F5 in the primate brain, did not respond when the monkey was presented with a conventional visual stimulus. Rather, they were visually activated when the monkey saw another individual, whether the experimenter or another monkey, making a goal-directed action with a hand or, in some cases, with the mouth. The responses evoked were highly consistent and did not habituate. The unusual properties of these cells were that they were active, not only when the monkey itself initiated a particular action, but also when the animal observed another monkey initiating and carrying out the same action. For this reason, they were labeled "monkey see-monkey do"

24

cells. One of the coauthors of Rizzolatti's paper, Vittorio Gallese, speculated that one of the primary roles of these mirror neurons is that they underlie the process of "mind reading," or at least a precursor to such a process.

Roughly speaking, "mind reading" refers to the activity of representing to oneself the specific mental states of others, their goals, their perceptions, their beliefs, and their expectations. Rizzolatti and Gallese comment, "It is now agreed that all normal humans develop the capacity to represent the mental states of others." They believe that there are sufficient examples from the behavior of nonhuman primates to constitute a strong argument supporting the hypothesis that they are indeed endowed with cognitive abilities that cannot be easily dismissed as the results of simple stimulus-response operant conditioning.

Further studies using functional imaging techniques have begun to examine the neural substrates of movement production, perception, and imagery in humans. Results indicate that witnessing real hand movements activate the human brain and the prefrontal cortex in the homologous area to that identified in the monkey studies. Thus, the cells in this area are believed to constitute the neural basis for imitation and for mind reading in humans as well as in nonhuman primates.

The potential importance of this work, according to the high-profile research neurologist and neuroscientist V. S. Ramachandran, was such that, in 1999, he proclaimed, "I predict that mirror neurons will do for psychology what DNA did for biology."[25] This is a truly bold and far-reaching suggestion. Ramachandran believed that understanding these cells may give us a deeper insight into how we understand other people's behavior and how we assign intentions and beliefs to other inhabitants of our social world. In the context of our current discussions, it is of particular interest in that it represents the convergence of state-of-the-art research in neuroscience, evolutionary biology, and psychology. Some will see this as further underlining our common heritage with nonhuman primates, others as removing yet another aspect of human behavior from the list of what might set us apart uniquely from other animals—namely, "mind reading."

Evolutionary Psychology, Mind Reading, and Human Uniqueness

"Mind reading" has its intellectual roots in the research of a group in California, led by Cosmides and Tooby. Initially, they were closely linked with the Harvard group of sociobiologists, but they sought to differentiate themselves from human sociobiology by calling themselves Darwinian or evolutionary psychologists. The main focus of research in evolutionary psychology is the question of how human beings came to be the apparently special animal we are today. That should, at once, relieve anxieties that evolutionary psychology is focused on humans as though they were "nothing but" bodies. It asks, What are the long-term evolutionary influences that made us what we are?

In 1992, Tooby and Cosmides defined evolutionary psychology as "psychology informed by the fact that the inherited structure of the human mind is the product of evolutionary processes."[26] It tends to offer functional explanations rather than causal ones. Some see it as part of the continuing search for the factor or factors that differentiate animals from humans. Past attempts to identify such a factor, such as the proposal by Oakley in 1949, proposed that it was the making and manipulation of tools, but by 1971 this was shown by Jane Goodall to be wrong: chimpanzees could do both of these. More recently, it has been suggested that what differentiates humans is a variety of factors combining to produce the complexities of human behavior that we see today, with the focus moving strongly toward social behavior.

In 1988, Richard Byrne and Andrew Whiten published a collection of papers under the title, *The Machiavellian Intelligence*.[27] This looked at the complexities of the social life of our ancestors as a possible route to understanding the development of our distinctive abilities. In 1997, in a second volume under the same title, they extended their findings, arguing that "intelligence began in social manipulation, deceit and cunning cooperation."[28] Earlier, Nicholas Humphrey had argued that a crucial aspect of human society is the ability to understand and "to read" the mind of another individual.[29] This in turn entails attributing beliefs and motivations to others.

As far back as 1978, Premack and Woodruff had described animals who had the ability to understand the mind of another as possessing a "theory of mind."[30] This term was subsequently taken up by developmental psychologists. According to Whiten and Byrne, "having a theory of mind or being able to mind read concerns the ability of an individual to respond differentially, according to assumptions about the beliefs and desires of another individual rather than in direct response to the others' overt behavior."[31] Earlier, a developmental psychologist, S. Baron-Cohen, had suggested that autism demonstrates what human life would be like without a "theory of mind."[32]

One of the main contentions of evolutionary psychology is that any straightforward separation between cognitive and social capacities is likely to be unsatisfactory. The unprecedented complexity of human beings as compared to monkeys and great apes has come about precisely because these two domains are integrated in mutually reinforcing ways. Evolutionary psychologists also believe that we can learn about human evolution by looking at the behavior of other animals. For example, we may detect possible beginnings of tool use, theory of mind, and culture in chimpanzee societies. However, they are clear that we cannot simply read off implications for human behavior from observations of other animals. Andrew Whiten, writing of his concept of "the deep social mind," argues that what differentiates human society from chimpanzee society is the level of cognitive sophistication at which social integration operates.[33] Reactions to the paper by Premack and Woodruff (above) varied considerably. Some argued that chimpanzees simply learn specific clues in certain situations, while others argued that chimpanzees are indeed capable of mental attribution. A recently published paper by Joseph Call lends strong support to the view that chimpanzees do indeed have a theory of mind.[34] It needs to be emphasized here that, since this is cutting-edge research, the interpretation of some of it remains hotly contested. There are those who question the need to invoke "mind reading" as an explanatory concept, and who argue that an interpretation in terms of simulating behavior is sufficient.

The wider relevance of this for us today is, as we hinted above, that it has implications for our understanding of what constitutes human uniqueness and it warns us against seizing upon "mind reading" as a uniquely human capacity. It also flags for us the need to think carefully when focusing upon the capacity for relationships as a key feature, if not the key feature, in defining what Warren Brown has called "soulishness."[35] The capacity for social relationships is itself, according to evolutionary theory, an evolved capacity, but one that may well have taken a quantum leap when combined with cognitive ability to equip *Homo sapiens* with capacities and achievements so clearly different from those of our nearest, nonhuman primate relatives.

Indeed, as the work of Richard Byrne highlights, in one sense, developments in evolutionary psychology, if anything, accentuate the puzzle of why it is, with our brains so similar in basic architecture to nonhuman primates, and with our nearest neighbors possessing mirror neurons as we do, *nevertheless our cognitive capacities have so outstripped those of our nearest neighbors*. Libraries, symphony orchestras, the scientific enterprise with all its achievements, medicine, all characteristic today of our twenty-first-century society, are completely lacking among apes and chimpanzees. Why? In the past, it is not only religious people who would have invoked the idea of humans possessing a "soul" as this defining difference. But, as we have already seen, insofar as "soul" as traditionally construed is in many ways synonymous with "mind," it is not a separate thing, but rather one aspect of the functioning of a whole. In this sense, animals exhibit "soulishness," albeit in a rudimentary form.

When the research on mirror neurons outlined earlier is brought together with the work on mind reading in nonhuman primates as well as in humans, particular issues that are relevant to our present discussion arise. First, we may refer to the possibility that the existence and the presence of these particular types of neurons may give a clue to one aspect of the possible neural basis of a capacity for social relatedness. Workers in the field of autism have already noted this and are actively exploring whether, in some forms of autism, the mirror neuron system may be absent or malfunctional. The second aspect is that the presence of these mirror neurons in both nonhuman primates and in humans flags another aspect of the close relationship between ourselves and nonhuman primates. Paradoxically, it also underlines yet again the enduring puzzle of how it is that, with so many aspects of our neural apparatus so similar to that of non-human primates, we are yet so different in terms of our culture, achievements, and so on.

The search for how the quantum leap occurred that made humans so different from animals remains a scientific question that will occupy us for many decades to come. It is possible that, as some have suggested, what the physicists called a "phase change" occurred at some point in brain evolution, so that the same basic materials exhibited new properties. Oxygen and hydrogen in appropriate proportions and under specific conditions become a liquid with different properties from gases. Polkinghorne recounts how the seeming irrationality of the superconductivity state made sense only when it was realized that there was a higher rationality than that known in the everyday world of Ohm. After more than fifty years of theoretical effort, an understanding of current flow in metals was found which subsumed both ordinary conduction and superconductivity into a single theory. The different behaviors correspond to different regimes, characterized by different organizations of the states of motion of electrons in the metal. One regime changes into the other by phase change (as the physicists call it) at the critical temperature.[36]

Perhaps this is a useful analogy for what we shall eventually discover produced the remarkable changes between human and nonhuman primates. Another possibility currently being widely canvassed suggests that the rise of modern *Homo sapiens* was crucially defined by our capacity for language.[37] It is argued that the key component of this language ability is focused on the left hemisphere of the human brain, and a specific gene called protocadherin XY is postulated to play a crucial role in this language capacity. It is this gene that can be said to define our species. On this view, the emergence of *Homo sapiens* was not a gradual or continuous process; instead, there is the possibility that 100,000 to 150,000 years ago there was a jump that gave rise abruptly to our species. The jury is certainly still out on judging this recent proposal.

The analogy of superconductivity in physics and the possibility of an explanation in genetic terms should alert any whose enthusiasm for accounting for human uniqueness might lead to proposing a "god of the gaps" approach. Such an approach would entail invoking the injection of a soul at a particular point as a way of defining human uniqueness.

Unity, Interdependence, and Duality

The science presented above should be sufficient to indicate the accumulating evidence that points to the intimate relationships between mind, brain, and behavior. Some of these relationships were bottom-up and some top-down. The emerging consensus is well summarized in the views of a neurologist and a psychiatrist, Antonio Damasio and Robert Kendall. Damasio wrote, "The distinction between diseases of 'brain' and 'mind', between 'neurological' problems and 'psychological' or 'psychiatric' ones, is an unfortunate cultural inheritance that permeates society and medicine. It reflects a basic ignorance of the relation between brain and mind."[38] Similarly, Kendall, past president of the Royal College of Psychiatrists in Britain, wrote, "Not only is the distinction between mental and physical ill-founded and incompatible with contemporary understanding of disease, it is also damaging for the long-term interests of patients themselves."[39]

It is one thing to observe this consistent pattern of the intimate links between mind and brain, but it is an enduring problem to know how most appropriately to conceptualize it. Some talk about a relationship of identity, some of interaction, and still others of interdependence. Interdependence at least has the virtue of avoiding all of the unnecessary philosophical baggage that comes with using such words as dualism, monism, physicalism, mentalism, or reductionism.

Although the evidence from the so-called top-down effects may, in some instances, be helpfully described as showing *interaction*, the warnings sounded by Roger Sperry about the inadequacies of this description should be taken seriously; for this reason, I prefer *interdependence* to interaction. Interaction normally is used to describe causal relationships between events at the same level, but here we are describing relationships between events at different levels. We have no idea how what happens in the mind and through habitual behavior produces changes in the brain, even though, as I have tried to show, there is lots of evidence that it does.

The evidence for interdependence is so widespread, one might also say universal, in all the work that I have described that it seems to be a part of the created order. In other words, we may provisionally describe it as *intrinsic*.

At the same time, as many have pointed out, descriptions in terms of personal agency and at the level of cognitive processes cannot be reduced to descriptions at the level of neurotransmitters and synapses. In other words, the interdependence that we observe is best described as an *irreducible* intrinsic one.

Since there is widespread reference today to top-down effects, a further word is called for in order to avoid misunderstandings. The late Roger Sperry used this term to emphasize the importance, in his view, of the cognitive aspect of behavior. At times he went so far as to talk about mental activity "pushing and hauling" the activity of the brain, thereby seeming to forget his own cautionary remarks about misusing the notion of interaction. It is not necessary to go as far as Sperry went in order to do justice to the importance of top-down effects. As we have indicated, the embodiment of the cognitive in the neural is one of interdependence, an even closer relationship than "pushing and hauling." Donald MacKay preferred to talk about the determinative efficacy of cognitive processes. He wrote, "I would insist . . . on the determinative efficacy of our thinking, valuing, choosing, and so forth. . . . I prefer not to call the link 'causal' because we normally use the term cause and causality to point to relations of dependence within one conceptual level—one physical force causing another."[40]

If one thinks about the overworked analogy of solving a mathematical equation on a computer, it is fair to say that the mathematical equation is efficacious in determining the physics of the computer. However, that does not mean that it is sensible to devote time trying to find elements in the physics of the computer that are "sensitive to" influences from the hypothetical mathematical world. There is, I am suggesting, between the mental and physical an irreducible relationship in the sense that to get rid of either is to tell less than the whole story. This is *duality*, but it is not a dualism of substance.

Philosophers may find hints here of the contributions of Strawson several decades ago.[41] In his pioneering work on the ontology of language, he argued that, from the point of view of the logic of the metaphysics of Western language use, as far as people are concerned, the prime ontological term is "person" as the individual subject of whom we assert two types of predicates—mental and physical. There is duality, but not dualism; the ontological reality of "person" is primary and is neither mental nor physical.

The take-home message is that any view of human nature that fails to recognize the psychosomatic unity of the person is a view that cannot be defended from science. As other contributions to this book make clear, such a view resonates with well-founded theological, biblical, philosophical, and pastoral views of the person. What is today urgently needed is, first, a spelling out of this view as a reaffirmation of the Hebrew-Christian account of the person; and second, a sustained attempt to think through and apply this view to the Christian life both individually and communally. Succeeding chapters attempt these tasks.

A Neurobiological Portrait of the Human Person

Finding a Context for Approaching the Brain

D. Gareth Jones

For most people the brain is a fascinating yet perplexing organ. It is an organ unlike any other in the body, since it is "me" in a way in which my liver, kidneys, and pancreas are not. Our brains appear to make us the sort of people we are, and this is why there is general interest in the brains of people like Einstein. The feeling is that their brains will provide clues as to what made them the outstanding people they were. The other side of the coin is what happens to us as people when something goes wrong with our brains. The harsh reality is that we may be dramatically changed, since certain forms of damage to our brains can have major repercussions for our personalities. The person we knew and instantly recognized as Dave or Megan may no longer be that same person; remnants of the person may remain, but the interactions we cherished and lived for may have vanished.

In one sense, the brain is *only* an organ, like the liver, kidneys, or pancreas; it can be described, dissected, and understood in mechanical terms just like these other organs. In another sense, however, it defies our attempts at simple analysis. Since it is the organ we use to understand ourselves, it is very difficult to separate our knowledge of the brain as a subject of interest and study from who we are as people.

Our view and knowledge of both the world and ourselves are products of our brains. It is because of the organization of our brains that we are able to love and pray, to command and obey, to create and enjoy beautiful things, and even to believe and worship. The development of the cerebral hemispheres allows us to think in abstract terms, plan ahead, and ponder the significance of the past; and it allows us to communicate by both the written and spoken word with those distant from us in space and time. We have values and goals, visions and hopes; we are aware of ourselves and of others, and we know we are transient. Our brains are the one means we have of confronting reality. They also enable us to consider questions at the interface of the brain, mind, and soul!

For neurobiologists, however, there is neither room, nor need, for talk about the soul. Even talk about the mind has dubious overtones, while the subject of consciousness has only recently been acknowledged as a topic to which neurobiologists may be able to make an important contribution. The problem with the mind and soul is that neither can be analyzed scientifically, even in the limited way in which brains can be analyzed scientifically. Limited as scientific analyses are in some regards, they represent the working tools of neurobiologists, tools that have proved extremely effective. Consequently, it would be hazardous to indulge in person-talk or mind-talk without any reference to the brain, even acknowledging that brain-talk is not the same as person-talk.

My aim in this chapter is to trace how far a neurobiological approach can take us in understanding what we are as human persons. I am not suggesting that a neurobiological portrait of the human person can ever provide a complete understanding; that would be to go well beyond the bounds of a scientific analysis. It would also ignore central facets of a Christian understanding.

Alternative Perspectives

Many will not agree with the portrait I am putting forward. For some, the brain is simply another bodily organ; since a scientific analysis of the kidney has no philosophical repercussions, neither does an analysis of the brain. For instance, Moussa and Shannon contend that, since personhood is a social and moral construct, biological realities neither guarantee the presence of, nor constitute the definition of, a person.[1] According to them, a functioning nervous system is a presupposition only of physical activity, with an integrated nervous system being required for intellectual activity. Although it is true that person-hood is more than neural activity, this approach suggests that neural activity is irrelevant. I hope to show that isolating physiological and philosophical perspectives in this manner is doomed to failure.

The vigorous debate of recent years on ethical issues surrounding human embryos has inadvertently brought into focus varying perspectives on the relationship between personhood and the nervous system. According to one position, to be a human being is to be a person, even at the very earliest stages of human existence.[2] Hence, personal abilities—including self-awareness, responsibility, and creativity—are all potentially present from the earliest stages of development. Since there is no indication of a nervous system for the first three weeks of development, this position inevitably leads to the conclusion that a nervous system is never relevant for an understanding of personhood. However, as we shall see, this is counterintuitive since the overall organization of the human nervous system provides significant insights into human self-awareness and creativity.

This same debate has also led in another direction, namely, that a person is not a genetic or biological category. If this is so, neurobiological studies again prove irrelevant in coming to terms with human personality.[3] Instead we are to look to human appearance and identity, since we discover the significance of people by interacting with them and by committing ourselves to them and their welfare. This leads to a realization that particular human beings, including fetuses and the severely handicapped, are irreplaceable. Commitment to persons as proposed by this stance is helpful, although by itself it is too vague. Unless it is informed by neurobiological data, it lacks the precision to resolve conflict between respective treatments for different people.

Yet another perspective starts from the standard position that we are persons throughout our history.[4] Those who lack certain cognitive capacities are regarded as simply the weakest and most needy members of our community. We care for them and about them as we seek to discover in their faces the face of Christ. Like the other examples, this position also bypasses reference to any neurobiological criteria. As such, it escapes the problem of advocating a neurobiologically based concept of personhood, but it fails to recognize any physical criteria for distinguishing between different forms of treatment in ambiguous ethical situations.

All these attempts to omit neurobiological considerations contain within them helpful pointers for ethical decision making, but in my view they suffer because of their reluctance to accept that scientific criteria help direct our moral gaze. Such criteria are required for demonstrating when a nervous system does or does not exist with sufficient material complexity to embody those capacities judged morally pertinent.[5]

In other words, a scientific study of the nervous system by itself will not tell us all we want to know about people and their functioning. And yet, when confronted by a barely functioning brain on account of immaturity at the beginning

33

of life or degeneration at the end of life, neural activity cannot be ignored. The lack of any functioning of the central nervous system, no matter what state one's body may be in, must have implications for our assessment of the meaningfulness of that human life. These extreme situations provide a useful starting point for demonstrating the intimate relationship between brain and person, and it is this relationship I shall now proceed to explore.

Are Brains Machines?

Even this cursory description has forbidding overtones for many people (perhaps especially for Christians) on account of its mechanistic and deterministic overtones. This is because of the underlying dictum that appears to assert that if an individual's brain is changed that individual will be changed. If this is so, does the individual amount to no more than his or her brain? If this is even remotely the case, what becomes of humans as free agents? The impression is readily gained that they have lost all that is special about them; their very essence has disappeared, and the foundation on which their relationship to God is based has been eroded. These are understandable concerns, made all the more formidable by many of the vistas opened up by current neurobiological and neurogenetic developments.

I shall argue that such an approach is at odds with contemporary neurobiology, since a machine-type of model suggests fixity and rigidity. The brain, by contrast, is the antithesis of this, being highly responsive to numerous environmental stimuli at all stages of life. The two-way interactions between the brain, the world internal to the individual, and the world external to the individual, point to the richness of its multidimensional context. In no sense can it be isolated from an individual, in the way in which the heart can be; neither could it be replaced by another brain without destroying the integrity of the individual as the person he or she is known to be. It is erroneous, therefore, to regard ourselves as *composed of* a brain, plus various other organs, and an immaterial something that constitutes the real me (mind or soul).

On the contrary, our brains represent us. They make us what we are only in the sense that we make them what they are. Far from being a machine-based model, this is a person-model. This latter approach is far more amenable to discussions of the brain within a Christian perspective.

Brain Plasticity and the Person

In developing a personal model of the brain we need to look more closely at the brain itself, and in particular at one of its features, its plasticity. Once we do this, we realize that what we are as persons is not laid down once and for all in the genome. Although it is true that the basic ground plan for an individual's brain is specified in the genome, the detailed patterns of its nerve cell connections are fashioned by numerous influences throughout life.

The developmental period is characterized by an initial overproduction of nerve cells. There is massive competition among them, and only about half survive into adulthood. The significant influence here is the external environment, since it is this that determines which synaptic connections (between nerve cells) persist and, therefore, which nerve cells will survive and flourish. For example, the eyes of the newborn must receive visual stimulation from the environment during the early months in order to fine-tune the structure of the visual part of the cerebral cortex.[6] In addition, this stimulation must occur at specified times (the so-called critical periods of brain development), revealing yet again the extensive influence that external inputs have on the end-product that is the adult brain, and hence the adult individual. Any disruption to these extrinsic factors will impact negatively on nerve cell development and may grossly disturb the cytoarchitecture of the brain, leading possibly to long-term neurological deficits. Change the environment, delay when sensory impulses arrive during development, and the resulting brain is different from what it would have been under other conditions. This is why malnutrition, alcohol, and hormonal influences during pregnancy can have such devastating consequences for a child's subsequent intelligence and behavior. In other words, physical influences on the brain affect what the person will become.

It is the specific fine-tuning of the synaptic connections in any given brain that contributes substantially to that individual's uniqueness and personhood. For instance, two people with identical genetic makeup will have different brains, precisely what one finds with identical twins (or possibly with human clones in the future). This is because the organization of the brain depends as much upon soft wiring (influenced by the environment) as upon hard wiring (built in genetically). As the brain develops, the final form of its synaptic connections and neural networks depends upon the environment just as much as it does upon genetic factors. In other words, the environmental influences are not peripheral add-ons, but are integral to the final form of any brain and, therefore, to important features of the person.

Consequently, two individuals with identical genetic backgrounds will vary depending on the spiritual and intellectual culture in which they are brought up, the people they interact with, the books they read, and the religious influences on them. This is made possible by the plasticity of their brains and the ever-changing forms of their brains in response to the pressures of their environments. Very simply, without characteristics like these we would not be human persons. If we lacked these characteristics, we would be unable to respond to God.

Extensive plasticity, such as I have just described, makes possible the enormous range of human beings' intellectual abilities and spiritual gifts. It also opens up exciting therapeutic vistas, since it may prove possible to exploit the newly discovered regenerative possibilities.[7] The extent of this regeneration is far more extensive than anything thought possible a few years ago, leading to optimism regarding ways of treating what up to now have been debilitating neurodegenerative diseases (like Parkinson's disease and even Alzheimer's disease)[8] and trauma (especially damage to the spinal cord). However, care is needed even here, since some erroneously conclude that we will be able to live lives that are both disease-free and of indefinite length. Such expectations are unhelpful and misleading. Although it is entirely appropriate to seek better treatment for debilitating and tragic diseases, the nature of human existence will not be revolutionized. The essence of regeneration is to rectify what has gone wrong, rather than bring about some new (and superior) way of functioning.

Intrusions into the Brain

The plasticity of the brain, such as I have just described, renders the brain amenable to being modified for therapeutic and possibly other reasons. For instance, it is possible to transplant brain tissue from (aborted) human fetuses into patients with Parkinson's disease. Since the aim is to overcome the movement deficits experienced by these patients, the transplanted brain tissue is that responsible for motor control. Results have had limited success in clinical terms, and the approach remains an interesting if experimental one.[9] What is significant for us is whether transplanting brain tissue like this has implications for patients' view of themselves. To date, the answer appears to be "no," at least not when the tissue is implanted into motor regions (striatum). This may not be the case if the regions concerned were to be those with direct involvement in the expression of personality and emotional traits (including the frontal and temporal lobes).

What is emerging, then, is that a nerve cell's significance stems from its functional capabilities and from the connections and circuits of which it is a part. What seems to be important, therefore, are the brain regions being studied, and the character and extent of the nerve cells, growth factors, and transmitters being transplanted, rather than their origin—from other individuals or even from rats or pigs. In light of this, there may be no difference between nerve cells from different species, as it is the environment and context within which they develop and function that determine an individual's ultimate personality.[10]

From the evidence available to date we can say that the presence of another human's nerve cells inside our brains does not make us different people. The pivotal consideration should be whether the individual will be enhanced or diminished as a person by the procedure, not whether the graft comes from human fetuses, or from the brains of young rats or pigs. What this is saying is that it is the person as a self-reflective and self-knowing being who is important, and not what goes to make that person's brain function. If there is no essential difference between the person before and after a neural transplantation operation, I fail to see in what way the transplantation poses a threat to the integrity of what that person is and stands for.

Neural transplantation is just one approach to the repair of the brain, an approach that may turn out to be relatively unsophisticated. Far more precise methods are being actively investigated, including the use of embryonic stem cells, neural progenitor cells, and gene therapy, all of which may be able to contribute in major ways to the repair of brains.[11] For instance, it is now known that damaged nerve cell axons are able to regrow if given a conducive environment, and the production of new nerve cells can take place long after the end of the brain's developmental period. Also, advances in stem cell biology and gene therapy are providing undreamed of initiatives for the replacement of injured or diseased nerve cell populations in the brain.[12] These diverse approaches tell us that what we are as persons is not set indelibly at some early stage in our lives. Our brains are able to change far more than once thought, signifying that what we are as persons is also amenable to considerable change.

However, plasticity such as described here may have a forbidding side to it. With the advent of neurotechnological approaches, neural devices can be implanted in the brain to function as a "second brain." Currently, this technology is being directed toward producing corrective tools for physical disabilities, such as developing microelectrodes that are placed in the visual cortex to electrically stimulate the brain to see scenes from a miniature camera.[13] These attempts at therapy are simply extensions of well-known procedures used extensively to improve the functioning of other body organs, such as the heart and gastrointestinal tract, and by themselves appear to pose no threats to the essential nature of what we are as persons. But would it be possible to use cybernetic transplants, where computer chips would be internalized in the brain? In this way, it may prove possible to increase the dynamic range of senses, enabling people to see currently invisible wavelengths, or to enhance memory, or to enable constant access to information where and when it is needed. Such implants may even have a role to play in moral decision making.[14]

Implants of this nature will become part of the individual in question, and will probably change them in some permanent way. In no sense, though, do these intrusions imperil the close relationship between brain and person. Rather, their ethical and moral acceptability would depend on whether they brought healing and wholeness to the person, whether they assisted that person in relating to God, and whether they improved interpersonal relationships and encouraged all-around fulfillment.

It should now be clear why I categorically dismissed the "brain as a machine" model. The classic view of machines is that they are manufactured according to certain specifications, so that they function in certain predetermined ways. When they cease to function as designed, they are adjusted or repaired so that they again work as required. When I buy a machine (whether this be an automobile, a washing machine, or even a computer), I am provided with the specifications of the particular model, and the only expectation I can have is that the model I purchase will do the things I am assured it will do. The human brain is entirely different from this. My brain was not designed to conform to some predetermined pattern. What I am, and what other people recognize as characteristically me, could not have been predicted at the time of my birth—even by some hypothetical superbeing who had detailed information about the present and future states of my brain. What they could not have known would have been the numerous environments that would influence my (and my brain's) development, and the decisions I would make throughout my life, all of which would influence my brain and my future directions as a person.

The personal model I am espousing reflects these ongoing interactions between what we are as people, the organization and plasticity of our brains, every facet of our environment, and all the relationships of which we are a part. But in what way does this help us resolve the challenges posed by various forms of determinism, and by even more intrusive manipulations of our brains?

The Fear of Neural Determinism

One of the prevailing fears of some people is that of neural determinism—that is, we act in certain ways or are certain sorts of people because of the brains we possess. Taken to its logical endpoint, this position states that the dimensions of some brain area (or brain "nucleus"—a group of nerve cell bodies), or the synaptic connectivity between the nerve cells within a region, determine some aspect of that individual's lifestyle or even beliefs. Confronted by this prospect, the temptation is to move in one of two directions: accept that physical determinism of this order is true, or reject the notion that the brain has anything to do with our thinking or attitudes.

For me, both directions are equally unsatisfactory, since they lead either in the direction of materialism and a rejection of human freedom, or of a brain-mind dualism. In their different ways, neither takes neurobiology seriously and neither is able to retain a holistic view of the human person. What, then, should be our point of departure?

Consider ordinary brain activity, that which takes place when everything appears to be functioning normally. A fundamental working assumption of most neurobiologists is that our thinking and consciousness are embodied in the activity of our brains. What this means is that a change in someone's conscious experience or personality is accompanied by a corresponding physical change in that individual's brain.[15] By the same token, any changes made to the brain (say, by drugs or electrical stimulation) have corresponding effects in conscious experience or personality. The precise effects depend on the brain region affected.

Since it is only through our conscious experience that we learn about anything at all, primacy should be given to the data of our conscious experience.[16] Therefore, although mental activity is embodied in brain activity, it is just as real as brain activity. The two need each other; they are complementary. Consequently, it is appropriate to state that "I am thinking" and "I am deciding." It would be unhelpful to state that "my brain is thinking" or "my brain is deciding," as though my brain is separated in some way from "me" as a thinking and deciding individual. There is no question that "I" need my brain, but "I" am not made redundant because of dependence upon my brain. What I am as a person cannot be reduced to what my brain is, as though my body and personality are simply extensions of my brain.

This two-way interaction comes as no surprise to neurobiologists, since our brains are influenced by everything, from education to the relationships of ordinary life, from simple memory tasks to creative intellectual activities, from years of psychological abuse to being brought up to conform to extremely taxing expectations. While this has been an underlying assumption of brain scientists for many years, it is now relatively easy to demonstrate the relationship between simple tasks and brain activity, using noninvasive techniques like functional magnetic resonance imaging (fMRI), and single-photon-emission computerized tomography. Respectively, these track radioactively tagged chemicals around the brain and monitor the rate of blood flow in the brain (to determine the relative activity of different brain regions).

For instance, the use of such noninvasive procedures can demonstrate which brain regions are functioning when people think about certain events or memorize various tasks. In this way, the performance of patients with neurological disorders can be compared with control subjects. Differences can even be detected between depressed and non-depressed individuals in their response to, for example, "sad" words.

It is well known that specific brain regions control particular functions and responses. By stimulating various parts of the brain, one can identify certain regions that are involved in the generation of needs and desires, the ability to think and speak, and the establishment of a total behavioral repertoire. The relationships between these are both extensive and intricate, demonstrating that the brain is far more than a series of isolated units; indeed, it is the very complexity of the brain that is essential for all we consider normal about human behavior. Even a localized, isolated fault can result in bizarre and terrifying abnormalities of personality.

Is it possible, then, to distinguish between obvious pathology and more subtle personality disorders which are sometimes associated with social deviance? It is relatively straightforward to understand the manner in which tumors, say, give rise to neurological symptoms and signs. These are cases of overt pathology, where a tumor in a particular region presses on a nerve, or increases the pressure within the skull, or compresses a neighboring brain region. The resulting symptoms and signs fall squarely into the neurological category.

What is more difficult is where a tumor appears to give rise to psychiatric symptoms, especially if there is no reason initially to suspect the presence of a tumor.[17] Such tumors are relatively uncommon, and do not constitute the major reason for psychiatric conditions.

In spite of this, the presence of excessive violence has frequently been accounted for in biological terms. In this connection, considerable attention has been devoted to a nuclear mass in the brain, known as the amygdala, and also to parts of the temporal lobes of the brain.[18] There is considerable evidence from animals and humans to show that these brain regions are involved in the expression and control of the emotions. After all, such control must lie somewhere within the brain. What happens, then, when something goes wrong in these regions? Very simply, major changes may ensue, dramatically altering crucial features of our personalities, including our motivation, interest in life, attitudes, and value systems. On occasion, placid people become violent.

Some have argued that extreme violence usually has a neural basis.[19] This, in turn, led to the widespread adoption of psychosurgical procedures, which use surgery to alter behavior (even in the absence of tumors or any indication of a pathological cause). This reached a zenith in the 1950s and 1960s, before people like Elliot Valenstein discredited the notion of a direct relationship between violence and biology.[20]

Psychosurgery marked the beginning of using surgery to modify the behavioral responses of those considered by some to be socially deviant or at the very least socially unacceptable. Surgery, of course, is not the only way of doing this—the use of psychopharmaceuticals is far more widespread. What is relevant for us is that all such approaches represent a biological means of tackling what are usually far wider social problems. One psychiatrist has commented, "Most of the violence in society has little to do with psychiatric or medical disorders per se. Most violence is caused by social factors, such as poverty; economic motives, as in robberies; drug dealing; subcultures of violence; and domestic disputes and child abuse."[21]

Therapy and Enhancement

In spite of this, many people seek ways of improving human brains, and of using various forms of "therapy" to "enhance" current performance. This practice parallels the same thrust in genetics, although it is much closer to reality in neurobiology. The major drive for performance enhancement comes in the form of psychopharmaceuticals, with the desire to find drugs to combat everything from shyness and forgetfulness, to sleepiness and stress. This is the world of what Arthur Caplan has described as "super-Prozacs."[22]

The issue here is how to distinguish between the normal and the enhanced. For example, how much depression is normal? While clinical depression is a recognized clinical entity, what are we to make of the low-grade, subclinical depression with which many people live their whole lives? Is there any virtue in living with low-grade depression, if it can be obliterated? In other words, what is normal? Similarly, should we aim to treat the slight deterioration in memory that accompanies aging for many people (mild cognitive impairment), or hyperactivity in children? Both are treading a fine line between the normal and pathological. But which is which?

The perspective I am promoting is that the use of drugs to assist a person's neural functioning is acceptable, as long as the intended improvements bring those people's capacities within normal biological limits. The aim of therapies is to cure or prevent diseases that have placed someone outside the normal range. By contrast, the intention of enhancements is to change people who already fall within the normal range, bestowing upon them capacities they do not already possess. This distinction does not solve every problem, since it leaves a definition of normality unresolved, but it is a start.

No matter how we argue some of these points, perplexing situations remain, where people's actions appear to be unnervingly dominated by the organization of their brains. I shall confine my attention to two examples.

When the brains of depressed subjects who have committed suicide are examined, it is invariably found that there is a reduction in one of the brains' neurotransmitters, serotonin.[23] This deficiency can lead to a predisposition to impulsive and aggressive behavior, suggesting that the individual is at risk of acting on suicidal thoughts.[24] More specifically, this loss of serotonin is mainly found in the prefrontal cortex (just above the eyes, and having an important impulse-dampening role), and in one brainstem nucleus. It has even been proposed that the more lethal the suicide attempt, the greater the serotonin deficiency.[25]

These data can be viewed from different perspectives. One approach is to conclude that individuals with such deficiencies have little way of escaping suicide. However, many researchers see the situation as being more complex than this, since these serotonin defects do not exist in isolation but are found alongside other deficits in the brain.[26] An alternative approach is to search for tools that will help develop tests for individuals who may be at risk from suicide, so that better treatment strategies can be devised. There may be genetic factors, and yet any predisposing gene or genes have proved elusive so far. And we often do not know which comes first, the serotonin deficit or precipitating social factors. The response of someone whose mother had committed suicide is helpful: "These statistics serve as warnings to me and to others with biological ties to suicide. . . . Perhaps someday science will better understand the basis for such harrowing acts so that families like mine will be spared."[27]

The second example is that of homosexuality, where a neurobiological link has been proposed. In the early 1990s, the idea was put forward that there is a difference between homosexual and heterosexual men in the structure of a brain region called the hypothalamus.[28] The research focused on one group of nerve

41

cells within a particular region of the hypothalamus; this group appeared to be larger in heterosexual men. However, this finding by itself fails to provide any useful clues about whether the difference was present at birth, nor whether it led to the homosexuality or resulted from it (or had nothing at all to do with sexual orientation). Another difference between homosexual and heterosexual men lay in the size of a bundle of nerve fibers (anterior commissure) that connect right and left regions of the brain.[29] Once again, there is no evidence of which came first, nor of whether these differences have the least significance behaviorally. Similar comments apply to a number of other studies looking at differences in hormonal levels and stress during pregnancy, and differing abilities of the different groups on visuo-spatial tasks.

These examples illustrate clearly the issues at stake. Simple conclusions based on brain features alone are unlikely to be helpful. Decisions concerning what is, or is not, normal are not biological decisions alone, but incorporate social, philosophical, and theological considerations. The answer is not to ignore brain differences in any of these cases, nor to argue that the findings are biased. The neural data are part of the overall picture and constitute one important factor in determining what can best serve those involved.

As embodied individuals, we all function with clearly discernible boundaries. Regardless of our strengths, we have limitations (biological and social) and weaknesses (toward one addiction or another). If we knew what to look for, we may well could find within our brains neural patterns corresponding to these limitations and weaknesses. But we would be foolhardy to conclude that these patterns constitute grounds for relinquishing responsibility for our actions (any more than "spiritual" neural patterns would determine the belief systems and faithfulness of Christians). Responsibility and decision making are core markers of the human person, even though the personal history of some individuals makes responsible decision making exceedingly difficult to attain. None of us starts off our lives with a clean genetic or environmental slate. But surely Christians should be the last people to expect this.

The World of Behavioral Genetics

We frequently hear reference to gay genes, IQ genes, genes for aggression, and even of smart mice. Regardless of which gene one is allegedly interested in, the basic message is the same: There are genes that cause us to act in certain ways. The underlying assumption is that there is a direct correlation between genes and disease, or genes and behavior. Although such associations have repercussions for many groups of people, the concern of Christians is that they undermine central elements within our responsibility as human beings. If I have no choice but to be aggressive, say, or I am unable to respond to the call of Christ to be a peacemaker and to love my neighbor as myself, it may even be that the fruits of the Spirit cannot manifest themselves in my life—not because I am being unfaithful, but because I am genetically inclined to be otherwise. How do we respond to these unsettling possibilities?

The link between individual genes and behavior is far more complex than suggested by the "gene for X" scenario. This is because:

- more than one genetic factor usually contributes to a trait; there are usually multiple genetic factors that interact with each other;
- environmental factors generally contribute in a major way to the expression of traits, and these factors also interact with each other;
- there is a complex interrelationship between genetic and environmental factors;
- the proteins produced by genes may themselves be subsequently modified; and
- genes are switched on and off in response to a variety of pressures, both during development and later on in cell life.[30]

Consequently, a gene (or even a set of genes) will rarely be the *only* cause of a particular condition. The pathway between a gene, a particular protein, and an individual scoring highly on an IQ test, say, or having an aggressive personality, is very indirect. This is not to argue that genes have no influence on behavior; they do, and every development in modern biological science leads us to expect them to do so. But the complexity of what we are as human beings is rivaled only by the complexity of our genetic (and environmental) makeup.

The so-called IQ gene is a totally misleading concept with no basis in scientific reality. Why is this the case? To begin, IQ is not a unitary concept, but is influenced by many different genes. If, for the sake of argument, the heritability of IQ is 0.50 in Western populations, and if there are 25 genes associated with this variation, each will be associated with 2 percent of the observed variation in IQ Such a small effect is not easily distinguished from chance fluctuation.[31] Detailed genetic studies comparing groups of children with substantially different IQs have led to the conclusion that "some differences in the frequencies of particular alleles at particular loci have been found between high and average IQ groups."[32] Studies like this open the way to determining how genetic differences might lead to differences in IQ, but this is very far from finding an IQ gene that can be manipulated to increase intelligence.

What about antisocial behavior and violent crime? While relatively few genetic studies have been done in this area, one study on a particular family with a high incidence of violence and serious crime among its male members claimed to find an association. The focus settled on a gene responsible for producing a protein, monoamine oxidase A (MAOA), involved in regulating a neurotransmitter, serotonin, in the brain. The male members involved in aggressive behavior had low levels of MAOA in their bodies, had lower than average IQ, and had a defect in this particular gene.[33] A subsequent study by other researchers investigated this link in a group of five hundred male children.[34] The data of these workers pointed in the same direction, but only if the individuals concerned had also been mistreated and abused as children. What emerges then is that it is probably the interaction between the genetic variant and the environment that is important.

Considerable publicity has surrounded the report of a so-called gay gene, stemming from a 1993 study.[35] This study was based on forty pairs of homosexual brothers with family histories indicating a high rate of homosexuality on the mother's side. There were significant similarities in the genetic markers in a particular region (which contains around one hundred genes) of the X chromosome. These workers found that 82 percent of sibling pairs had shared DNA in this region of the chromosome, significantly above the 50 percent one would expect. In a subsequent study, the same group of researchers replicated the results, but in a lower number of homosexual brothers: 67 percent.[36] However, another group failed to establish the same genetic linkage.[37] Studies such as these tend to suggest that this particular region on the X chromosome may contain genes with a role in sexual orientation in males, although the association is less strong than initially proposed.

Genetic studies on sexual orientation suffer from small sample sizes, the method of recruitment of research subjects, and the definition and measurement of sexual orientation itself. In the final analysis the most likely conclusion will be that a number of genes are involved, along with a host of environmental and social factors.

The world of behavioral genetics points clearly to the conclusion that aspects of our character and personal identity have a genetic basis. This is hardly a surprising conclusion, since we are our bodies, and our bodies are us. Genetic factors are inevitably involved, even at the deepest (some would say the most sacred) levels of what makes us the people we are. But this in no way threatens the conception of a person as a rational being, capable of taking responsibility for ourselves as free agents. Neither does it even hint that we cannot act as God's agents and stewards in his created order.

We are "of the earth," and we recognize that God himself was incarnated to become one with us: to become flesh, with (among many other things) its genetic building blocks. These building blocks, however, are far from unalterable, since what they give rise to is intimately affected by the environment—both internal (down to the levels of cells and tissues) and external to the body.

It is up to us as persons to determine what we do with both our abilities and restrictions (no matter how obviously genetically based some of these may be). We are to use the resources at our disposal, rather than view ourselves as prisoners of our inheritance. "Freedom of action requires that one's reasons play a causal role in what one does. Once this is properly understood the threat of determinism falls away as irrelevant."[38] The information provided by behavioral genetics should be used to increase our repertoire of understanding, so that we can come to terms with the behavioral conundrums with which we are all confronted.

Will this change in a future world if the genetic makeup of individuals is totally known? Genetic "chips" might be available, and these could be used to read out our individual genetic makeup. Theoretically everything that could be known about us genetically would be known; it would just be a matter of reading out and then analyzing our genetic blueprint. Information would be available on the functioning of our kidneys or brain, the chances of our manifesting a whole range of cancers or heart disease, and even our ability to cope with stress, or our proneness to depression.

This is the realm of potential genetic determinism. Some argue that we would have become prisoners of our genes, that we could do nothing but live out what we were predestined to be. On the other hand, even in this extreme situation, genetic determinism would not work out like this. The multifaceted nature of genetic action, as described above, would still apply. Genes would not act in isolation of many environmental forces, and in the end it would be up to individuals to decide what they were going to do with the knowledge available to them. A predisposition for a disease or behavioral trait is not the same as having that disease or expressing that trait.

Brain-talk and Mind-talk

My emphasis in this chapter has been a dual one: the brain and the person. This dual emphasis has been deliberate, since it is impossible to study the human brain in its many dimensions without appreciating the intimate interrelationship between the brain and the human person.

I have indulged in two forms of talk: that which stems from what we are as persons and that which is derived from neurobiology. We know each other not as brains ensheathed in bodies, but as embodied persons. We are people who relate to each other as beings created in the image of God. While neurobiological descriptions have an essential part to play in this, they elucidate rather than undermine what we are as persons. A knowledge of the brain, of what can go wrong with the brain, and of ways of rectifying deficiencies should all be welcomed by Christians, since they have the potential to enhance what we are as people before God. Their potential for misuse is as little or as great as in any other human endeavor. Wise discernment and judgment are always called for. For instance, to take Prozac when one is not clinically depressed is to treat it as a cosmetic, but a cosmetic with substantial implications for our view of life. Taking it under these circumstances says far more about our theology and worldview than about the state of our brains.

I have avoided reference to "the mind," for the reason that I do not find this a helpful concept. When used as a noun, the impression is given that it is an entity of the same type and nature as the brain and existing alongside the brain, with each influencing the other as equivalent but different compartments. Such a notion is foreign to neurobiologists, most of whom eschew any knowledge or interest in such a concept. One has to acknowledge that there are exceptions, of whom the late Sir John Eccles, a very distinguished neurobiologist, was one. He sought to establish a neurobiological basis for dualism.[39] However, others have not followed up this attempt of a few years ago in a productive fashion.

To dismiss the mind like this is not to lapse into materialism, or to deny the existence of mental states. These have been implicit throughout the preceding pages, since they are basic to consciousness, self-awareness, and all thought processes. However, they are capable (potentially at least) of explanation in physical and chemical terms, not in the sense of explaining away their personal significance ("we are nothing but chemical reactions"), but of providing a physical underpinning to what is occurring when we act in human ways. After all, just as we can explain what happens in the gastrointestinal tract when we eat a satisfying meal, we can explain (to some extent) what happens in the brain when we make decisions, pray, enjoy fine music, and show acts of love and compassion.

Similarly, for the same reasons, neither have I made reference to the soul. In no way does this deny a spiritual side to human nature. There is no conflict between the mechanistic explanations of brain science and the spiritual emphases of Christians. The former does not lead inevitably to a materialist stance (excluding spiritual reality), while the latter does not demand a role for nonphysical influences on our brains (the necessity of an immaterial soul). Just as our mental activity is embodied in our brain activity, so are our spiritual awareness and responses. Mental and spiritual realities are not identical with brain activity in the sense that they can only be understood in neurological terms. Neither is brain activity any more real than these other realities.[40] They represent different categories, and are to be assessed on their own terms.

This notion of embodiment also means that all we stand for as people before God will outlive our current embodiment in our present bodies and brains. While we have no assurance regarding precisely what will happen after death, Christians look forward to a "new body" (and new brain?), in the resurrection of the body. Donald MacKay expressed this hope eloquently and provocatively when he wrote, "The destruction of our present embodiment sets no logical barrier to our being re-embodied, perhaps in a quite different medium, if our Creator so wishes."[41]

My argument has been that when we seek to construct a neurobiological portrait of the human person, we are provided with a framework that is entirely consistent with Christian emphases on the wholeness and coherence of the person. Of course, these emphases are provided not by neurobiology but by theology and its myriad contributions to understanding the human person.

CHAPTER 4

The Soul: Possession, Part, or Person?

The Genesis of Human Nature in Genesis 2:7

Lawson G. Stone

From the cowardice that dares not face new truth,
from the laziness that is contented with half-truth,
from the arrogance that thinks it knows all truth,
Good Lord, deliver me!
("For the Spirit of Truth," Prayer from Kenya,
The United Methodist Hymnal, no. 597)

Scientific descriptions of the biochemistry of the brain have raised new questions about the necessity of positing an intangible, self-contained, metaphysical "part" or aspect of human nature called the "soul" to render a penetrating account of human experience.[1] Christian thinkers easily discern friction between these assertions and Christian descriptions of human nature because they seem to deny the spiritual dimension of personhood, traditionally construed in strictly dualist terms. Theological responses to neuroscience and its attendant claims range from hysterical denials, through facile accommodations, to panicked revisionism. But such reactions miss the point. Before tackling the scientific and theological issues we must ask whether notions of personhood dominating Christian discourse deserve privileging as "the Christian view." John Calvin expressed the traditional dualists' distaste for any binding of the soul to the body when he castigated those who chain [the soul] to the body as if it were incapable of a separate existence, while they endeavour . . . to suppress the name of God. But there is no ground for maintaining that the powers of the soul are confined to the performance of bodily functions. What has the body to do with your measuring the heavens, counting the number of the stars, ascertaining their magnitudes, their relative distances, the rate at which they move, and the orbits which they describe? . . . These lofty investigations are not conducted by organised symmetry, but by the faculties of the soul itself apart altogether from the body.[2]

For Calvin, denying the soul's autonomy risks more than error, but "suppress[es] the name of God."

But what theological considerations privilege the partition of human nature into separate physical and spiritual faculties over against an often physicalist neuroscience? Although the Bible is not the sole voice shaping Christian thinking, a theological analysis of human nature requires a convincing construal of the biblical narrative. If dualisms fail here, they forfeit their status as a privileged Christian view and scientific denials of dualism appear less controversial. If dualist readings prevail, then the scientific claims of some species of monist physicalism constitute a more penetrating challenge to the coherence of the Christian vision of human life. Thus if the immortality of the soul and, hence, dualism are essential to Christian thought,[3] then the church should be bracing for an encounter with science far overshadowing debates about creation and evolution.

The Point of Departure

The narratives of Genesis 1–3 provide the *locus classicus* for biblical thinking about human nature.[4] The pivotal text is Genesis 2:7, which reads classically in the King James Version: "And the LORD God formed man of the dust of the ground, and breathed into his nostrils the breath of life; and man became a living soul." In the traditional reading, God took an element of the material creation, dust, and, by a unique act of "special creation," imparted to it a nonmaterial, spiritual essence, the "breath of life," by which humanity became a creature possessing a "soul" or higher spiritual nature. Genesis 2:7 thus exegetes the claim in Genesis 1:26-27 that humanity bears the image and likeness of God; in this case, the "image and likeness of God" is taken as a supernaturally imparted spiritual nature elevating humanity above the rest of creation. As the spiritual essence of personality and identity, this "soul" departs the body upon death, resides in the spiritual domain, and reunites with the body upon the resurrection of the dead in the last day. Early orthodox Christian readings display variations on this précis, but do not deviate significantly from it.[5]

A fresh consideration of Genesis 2:7 cannot merely try to defend or to refute the traditional view. Rather, the encounter with neuroscience should inspire a closer reading of the text, wherever that might lead. The three principal statements of the passage will form the structure of our discussion.

Formed from the Dust

The text first indicates that Yahweh God formed Adam out of the dust of the ground. The text does not say, "God formed a *body* out of dust," but that Yahweh formed "Adam" out of the dust. From the moment of the divine molding, this being is already known as Adam. Although some have denied the normal humanity, especially the maleness, of Adam,[6] the syntax of the usage of the terms for "man" and "Adam," not to mention the plotline of the story itself, requires construing the "dirt creature" as a male human being,[7] who is already named "Adam." Adam already has an identity in the purpose and mind of God, before he is alive, before he has awareness of any kind.

The terminology employed for Yahweh's making of Adam is that of potters shaping their vessels. The same terminology features in Genesis 2:19: "And out of the ground the LORD God formed every beast of the field, and every fowl of the air" (KJV); though lacking the term "dust," the statement specifies a common origin from which God forms animals and Adam. By contrast, God emphatically does not "form" the woman from the ground, but "builds" (*banah*) her from a longitudinal section of Adam. The woman alone merits status as a "special divine creation."

The term "dust" is also pregnant. This word, occurring 110 times in the Old Testament, figures in several charged metaphorical contexts. Dust constitutes the human body. In the curse of Genesis 3:19, God declares,

> By the sweat of your face
> you shall eat bread
> until you return to the ground,
> for out of it you were taken;
> you are dust,
> and to dust you shall return.

For the author of Job 4:18-20, humanity's composition from dust points to its fragility:

> He puts no trust even in His servants;
> And against His angels He charges error.
> How much more those who dwell in houses of clay,
> Whose foundation is in the dust,
> Who are crushed before the moth!
> Between morning and evening they are broken in pieces;
> Unobserved, they perish forever. (NASB)

Strangely, although only Adam was created literally from dust, the author of Job regards every human being as having sprung from the dust, for he says of the wicked, "Behold, this is the joy of His way; and out of the dust others will spring" (Job 8:19 NASB). Continuing to lament the fragility of human existence, Job cries, "Remember now, that you have made me as clay; and would you now turn me into dust again?" (10:9 NASB). Even Elihu declares that if God withheld his spirit, his breath, "All flesh would perish together, and man would return to dust" (34:14 NASB). But human frailty, dustiness, can also call to mind divine compassion. The psalmist declares, "For He Himself knows our frame; He is mindful that we are but dust" (Ps. 103:14 NASB). Still, when God withdraws his spirit, humans return to dust (Ps. 104:29 NASB). Ecclesiastes predictably finds in human "dustiness" a reminder of mortality and the ultimate leveling power of death: "All came from the dust and all return to the dust" (3:20; 12:7 NASB).

The association of dust with fragility and mortality leads naturally to ties with death. Sheol itself is equated with dust in Job 17:16. The psalmist protests, "What profit is there in my blood, if I go down to the pit? Will the dust praise you? Will it declare your faithfulness?" (30:9 NASB). In a remarkably uncharacteristic statement about the final victory over death, Isaiah declares, "Your dead will live; their corpses will rise. You who lie in the dust, awake and shout for joy" (26:19 NASB). The hope of the dead being raised from the dust emerges most clearly in Daniel 12:2: "And many of those who sleep in the dust of the ground will awake, these to everlasting life, but the others to disgrace and everlasting contempt" (NASB). Indeed, many ancient Near Eastern myths characterize the realm of the dead as exceedingly dusty.[8]

Thus when Genesis 2:7 speaks of Adam's being formed from the dust of the ground, it stresses his fragility and commonality with the animals. In addition, ancient readers would know the associations of dust with death. These connotations could not have been lost on the audience. In addition to being similar to the animals, then, Adam's very constitution bespeaks death and the grave.

The origin of Adam's body from the dust of the ground comports well with an affirmation of humanity's basic continuity with the material order. Claims for a "special creation" of humanity in comparison with animals and the material world conflict with the strong assertion in Genesis 2 that, physically (organically?), Adam does not differ from the "beasts of the field."

Those hesitating to recognize this continuity with the material and animal domains should note a similar trend in Genesis 1:1–2:4a. Far from portraying God creating the world, nature, plants, animals, and humanity *ex nihilo* and without any mediation, Genesis 1 surprisingly admits that God's creation took place through intermediary action on the part of the creation itself. In Genesis 1:11, when God says, "Let the earth sprout vegetation," and then in Genesis 1:12, "so the earth brought forth vegetation," the English intransitive verbs mask strong constructions in Hebrew that can and should be rendered, "Let the earth *cause vegetation to sprout* . . . so the earth *caused vegetation to come forth.*" The

Hiphil stem of the verbs "sprout" and "bring forth" locate the ultimate causality in God, but assign a significant immediate agency to the earth itself, which responds to God's command. The Creator did not make a "dead" earth, but indeed, an earth with inherent powers of generativity upon which God calls. Likewise, on the sixth day, the text states God's command, "Let the earth bring forth living creatures . . . cattle, creeping things wild beasts . . . everything that creeps on the ground . . . and it was so." Again the writer employs the Hiphil form of the verb "to come forth." God's word of command is not for the animals to appear *ex nihilo* but for the earth itself to produce these animals: "Let the earth *cause living creatures . . . to come forth*." Then the verse follows immediately with the summary, "*so God made . . . cattle . . . and creeping things*" (Gen. 1:24). In "making" them, God did not cause the animals to materialize out of thin air, but invoked the powers of generativity latent in the earth by his own creative action. In short, God made a maker. In this context, the affirmation in Genesis 2:7 of Adam's physical origins from the earth flows naturally. God shapes the earth that has already produced vegetation and large land animals at his command into the form of Adam.

The Breath of Life

Into this pile of molded dust, already named "Adam" by the text, God "puffs the breath of life." Traditionally, interpreters see here the direct impartation of life to Adam in an act of divine "special creation." But is this the case? Although we do not read of the animals, who are formed like Adam from the ground, receiving this breath in Genesis 2, the very next occurrences of this expression and its variants remove all doubt that the animals also possess the "breath of life" given by God. Three times in the flood story this note is sounded, employing two different idioms. First, we read of the "spirit/breath of life" (*ruakh hayyim*):

> And behold, I, even I am bringing the flood of water upon the earth, to destroy all flesh in which is the *breath of life*, from under heaven; everything that is on the earth shall perish. (Gen. 6:17)
> So they went into the ark to Noah, by twos of all flesh in which was the *breath of life*. (Gen. 7:15)

Another idiom conflates both Hebrew terms for "breath": *ruakh* and *neshamah*.

> Of all that was on the dry land, all in whose nostrils was the breath [*neshamah*] of the spirit [*ruakh*] of life, died. (Gen. 7:22)

How much more explicitly could the text link the "breath of life" to animals as well as humans? The impartation of the "breath of life" does not distinguish Adam from the animals; rather, it binds him to them.

Does this demean humanity, that the same breath that fills its nostrils also courses through animal lungs? Certainly the "breath" in human nostrils does not always speak of dignity. Isaiah castigates his audience to "stop regarding man, whose *breath of life* is in his nostrils; for why should he be esteemed?" (2:22). Several other passages speak of the breath of God as a fiery force of judgment (Job 4:9; Ps. 18:15). Most graphic is Isaiah 30:33: "For Topheth has long been ready, indeed, it has been prepared for the king. He has made it deep and large, a pyre of fire with plenty of wood; The breath [neshamah] of the LORD, like a torrent of brimstone, sets it afire." Other passages use the term "all that breathes" (*kol hannashamah*) to refer to those exterminated by Joshua during the conquest (Deut. 20:16; Josh. 10:40; 11:11, 14). In Deuteronomy 20:16, the law of warfare distinguishes between distant enemies and the cities within the conquest mandate specifically by demanding the extermination of "all that breathes" in the latter. Although this could naturally refer to humans, warfare against distant cities was distinguished by killing only the men, sparing the women, children, and animals. This might suggest that the "all who breathe" provision of the following passage refers to every living thing, human, or animal. Readers must make their own decision whether these considerations demean humans or elevate animals.

Despite the negative connotations noted above, a few passages use *neshamah* to speak of a distinctively divine dimension in life. In these passages, *neshamah* is used synonymously with *ruakh:*

> To whom have you uttered words? And whose spirit [neshamah] was expressed through you? (Job 26:4)
> But it is a spirit [ruakh] in man, and the breath [neshamah] of Shaddai gives them understanding. (Job 32:8)
>
> The Spirit [ruakh] of God has made me, and the breath [neshamah] of the Almighty gives me life. (Job 33:4)
> The spirit [neshamah] of man is the lamp of the LORD, searching all the innermost parts of his being. (Prov. 20:27)

The description of the "breath" as a divine dimension here speaks of an inward aspect of human personality that directly expresses God's creative activity. What is important is that these usages do not contradict the "breath" as a link between humanity and animals. Rather, they dignify animal life also as possessing breath by the creative act of God, possibly even implying a degree of sentience alongside humanity.

To summarize: the second feature of the creation of Adam in Genesis 2:7

involves God's breathing into Adam the "breath of life." Although this expression certainly can be taken to imply the impartation of sentience by a divine act, the breath of life is also found in conjunction with animals. It does not denote the creation of an immaterial entity within human nature, which sets humans apart over against animals. In fact, it might point to a degree of divinely donated sentience in the latter.

A Living Soul

The real burden of Genesis 2:7 for thinking about human nature comes in the final clause, which declares that, after Yahweh breathed into the dust-formed Adam the "breath of life," Adam, according to the Authorized Version, "became a living soul." The English versions reflect divergent assumptions about this passage. First, the AV translates "soul," reflecting the ancient equivalent in the Greek Old Testament (LXX), *psychē* ("soul"). Most modern versions render "became a living being," but the NLT counters with "and the man became a living *person*," deferring to traditional interpretation of *nefesh*. Precisely what does this passage say? Does this text assert the unique quality of human existence, namely personhood, classically expressed by the term "soul," or does it declare the animation of the inspired dust as it comes to life?

Resisting the temptation to launch into a massive review of the over 700 occurrences of *nefesh* in the Old Testament,[9] we note that its etymological meaning "throat" makes itself felt strongly in passages where *nefesh* clearly refers to breath, desire, or appetite. Insight into the meaning of the expression in Genesis 2:7 arises first and best from its grammatical construction and the literary context in Genesis 1–3. First, the Hebrew idiom employed is well known. The expression *wayyehi ha'adam lenefesh hayyah*, "and the man became a living being," employs the grammatical construction known as the "lamed of product." That is, the subject of the verb "to be" is seen as becoming whatever is named in the predicate, which is noted with the prefixed preposition. So the idiom is not a reference to any reception of a soul, nor the acquisition of a segment of his nature called a soul. We are not to imagine Adam's reception of some intangible personal essence whose presence makes him human, distinct from the animals, and eligible for everlasting life. The *nefesh* here is not a possession, nor is it a component of Adam's nature, a "part." The pile of dust, upon being inspired by divine breath, actually became a living *nefesh*. The term "living *nefesh*" then denotes the totality of Adam's being. Adam does not "have" a *nefesh*; he *is* a "living *nefesh*."

But what is a "living *nefesh*"? The simplest answer arises from the immediate context. First, the term "living soul" (*nefesh hayyah*) appears four times in the preceding context and once shortly after. In Genesis 1:21, 24, 30 the term refers simply and clearly to animals.

> And God created the great sea monsters, and every *living creature* that moves, with which the waters swarmed after their kind, and every winged bird after its kind; and God saw that it was good. (Gen. 1:21)
> Then God said, "Let the earth bring forth *living creatures* after their kind: cattle and creeping things and beasts of the earth after their kind"; and it was so. (Gen. 1:24)
> [God said,] "And to every beast of the earth and to every bird of the sky and to every thing that moves on the earth *which has life*, I have given every green plant for food"; and it was so. (Gen. 1:30)

In these passages, the expression *nefesh hahayyah* can be rendered "living creature." After the creation of Adam in Genesis 2, God then begins seeking a partner for Adam, resulting in the creation of the animals. The process resembles the making of Adam. First, "*out of the ground the* LORD *God formed* every beast of the field and every bird of the sky, and brought them to the man to see what he would call them." But the verse then moves on to say, "and whatever the man called a *living creature*, that was its name" (Gen. 2:19). But "living creature" translates the same phrase that denoted Adam, *nefesh hayyah*, completing the literary similarity between Adam and the animals. Made from the dust of the ground, and possessed of the "breath of life," they are each a "living *nefesh*."

Of course, the reader should have expected this. After all, in Genesis 2 God scandalously declares his own creative work "not good" as long as Adam was alone. So God launches into an extended quest to create a partner for Adam. The relationship of the helper to Adam is captured in the Hebrew expression *'etser kenegdo*, "helper suitable to him." "Suitable" appears nowhere else in the Old Testament—only here, in connection with the creation of the woman.[10] Other than the pronominal suffix, it comprises the prepositions "like" and "opposite, across from." This helper is to be "like" Adam while also "opposite" him. The narrative frames the creation of the animals clearly, and even humorously, as an attempt to make another creature that is sufficiently like Adam to be compatible, but sufficiently unlike Adam to serve as a helper. Yahweh's bringing of the animals to Adam "to see what he would call them" suggests Yahweh's expectation of some declaration of approval. Alas, while Adam did comment on, or name, every animal, the helper suitable to him remained elusive. The failure underscores the intention of the creation of the animals as candidates for partnership with Adam, hence like him, in as many ways as possible. Thus each one, like him, is a "living *nefesh*," and this clearly underscores the conclusion that a "living *nefesh*" is not a being separate from the rest of creation because it possesses an intangible inner spiritual entity that determines its identity. Additionally, if *nefesh* denoted something distinctively and transcendently human about Adam, we would certainly expect the promiscuous failure, resulting in the creation of the entire animal kingdom to give way to a dramatic statement, once the woman is made, that she at last has a *nefesh* like Adam. Ironically, Adam's squeal of approval celebrates not the woman's *nefesh*, but her body: "At last! This is now bone of my bones, and flesh of my flesh." Apparently Adam had not been coached on the essential spirituality of his nature! The text clearly implies the culmination of creation to be the act of "one flesh," physical sexual union between the man and the woman. They might not be "soul mates," but they are definitely "flesh mates."

Even though the observations I have made are ancient, dualistic assumptions often prevented their implications from emerging. For example, the medieval Jewish exegete Rashi noted this equation, but argued that the human *nefesh* "is the most highly developed of all of them, because to him was granted understanding and speech." He was forced to this view because earlier he programmatically claimed that "there were two formations—a formation of man for this world, and a formation of man for the resurrection. . . . [God] made him of both, of earthly and of heavenly matter: the body of the earthly, and the soul of the heavenly."[11] Calvin also noted the linking of "living *nefesh*" to both humanity and animals, but countered that the reference in Genesis 2:7 is only to the "lower faculty of the soul."[12] Calvin is quite clear that he specifically repudiates "the frigid doctrine of Aristotle," who envisioned the functions of the soul intimately tied to physical existence. Ideology trumped the clear wording and sense of the text.[13]

The broader usage of *nefesh* in the Old Testament confirms and expands the analysis offered above. Many occurrences of *nefesh* do of course speak of human personality. These include desires, thoughts, speech, and virtually every other dimension of human personality. This does not imply the existence of a soul in the classical philosophical sense, however. Sufficient is the summary of Daniel C. Fredericks, who comments regarding the use of *nefesh* to speak of human nature, "Care should be taken not to import a Greek paradigm of psychology to *nephesh*; though at times it refers to the inner person, it seldom denotes a 'soul' in any full sense."[14] What interests me here is not the passages that speak of some aspect of human sentience by the term *nefesh*, but the passages in which *nefesh* is used in quite the opposite way. Several texts equate *nefesh* with blood, for example. In the denouement to the flood narrative, God defines the new order of life as one in which humans will be allowed to eat meat: "Only you shall not eat flesh with its life, that is, its blood" (Gen. 9:4). The term "life" translates *nefesh*. If *nefesh* denotes some transcendent spiritual entity of personhood, its equation here with the blood of slaughtered animals is jarring. The following verse also clearly equates *nefesh* with blood: "And surely I will require your lifeblood [literally "your blood for your *nefesh*"]; from every beast I will require it. And from every man, from every man's brother I will require the life [*nefesh*] of man" (Gen. 9:5). These references denote physical life itself, embodied in blood.

The link of *nefesh* to blood and death potentially illuminates Genesis 35:18:

"And it came about as her *nefesh* was departing (for she died), that she named him Ben-oni; but his father called him Benjamin." This text speaks of a woman's *nefesh* going out of her at death. The context is death during childbirth. In antiquity, such deaths often transpired as bleeding to death due to birth trauma. So this text probably does not allude to the departure of a transcendental spirit. So linked is *nefesh* to physical existence that a corpse is even referred to as a *nefesh* in Leviticus 21:11: "nor shall he approach any dead person [*nefesh*], nor defile himself even for his father or his mother." Perhaps here, too, the key is the linking of *nefesh* with blood. This passage might refer to a corpse that is very recently dead, possibly from violent causes, with freshly shed blood on it. The biblical sanction against blood might render this corpse particularly unclean. So tied is *nefesh* to the basic fact of living, physical existence, that in many passages *nefesh* substitutes for the pronoun, lending intensity to the sentence.[15]

The linking of *nefesh* to physical existence and not to a transcendent, immortal inward essence of personhood fits well with the Old Testament's overall disinterest in the afterlife. Despite efforts by scholars such as James Barr to portray the Old Testament as committed to a view of the immortality of the soul, the evidence remains pitifully thin. The best evidence here is a simple comparison with the evidence for belief in the afterlife among Israel's neighbors. No doubt exists at all that the Babylonians, Assyrians, Egyptians, and Canaanites (documented in Aramaic inscriptions and Ugaritic texts) had a vital belief in the afterlife. The "cult of the dead" was virtually the common denominator in all ancient Near Eastern religious traditions.[16] The Ugaritic texts refer to the departed spirits of the dead as *repha'im*, who are depicted eating and drinking with the gods.[17] Indeed, a parallel idiom referring to the departed feasting with the deity in the Panamua inscription refers to the *npsh* of the deceased king. Thus it appears that the Old Testament term was indeed used in the immediate cultural environment to speak of the immortal dead in their transcendent existence. What is striking is that, while the Old Testament duplicates every known usage of *nefesh* documented in the cultures of the ancient Near East, it *does not* duplicate the use of *nefesh* to refer to the personal existence of the dead in another realm. This omission probably results from the categorical rejection of the cult of the dead in any form in the Scriptures and its prohibition of any attempts at contacting the dead. The Old Testament demands that the faithful live their lives of obedience in the "here and now" and offers very little insight into the realm of the dead. When the hope of immortality is entertained, the form taken is typically that of resurrection, not immortality.

To summarize: the term *nefesh* in Genesis 2:7 refers not to a part of Adam's nature, nor to some possession such as a transcendent personal spiritual hypostasis termed a "soul" that lives forever and distinguishes humanity from the animals. Rather, *nefesh hayyah* denotes Adam as a living creature like the animals created in Genesis 1 and 2. It underscores Adam's linkage with the animal creation, not his difference from it.

So Where Did the Soul Come From?

If nothing in Genesis 2:7 supports the notion that humanity was endowed, by a special act of divine creation, with an intangible, immortal, and personal "soul," the question must be asked, *From where did such an interpretation of the Old Testament arise?* I will conclude by sketching one possible answer to this question, then illustrating the damaging impact such interpretive moves have on our reading of the Genesis narrative.

The existence of beliefs in the afterlife and the immortality of disembodied human personality in the ancient Near East explain why these notions eventually became part of Jewish and Christian thought. Eventually, the religious veneration of the dead that pervaded the cultures of antiquity found its way into the biblical communities. The transformation of *nefesh* into immortal, disembodied human consciousness probably began no later than the moment a Greek translator of the Old Testament decided to use *psychē* (often translated as "soul") as the equivalent for *nefesh*. That choice created the danger that a Hellenistic reader, ignorant of the biblical rejection of the cult of the divinized dead, would assume that *psychē* meant in the Old Testament the same thing that it meant in the surrounding culture. As far back as Homer, the body denoted simply the carcass, a corpse, stripped of the dynamism of human personality. Plato even understood the body as a tomb, and saw death as the final release of the soul. Of course these were not the only alternatives. Aristotle's views on the soul were not as distant from the Old Testament as Plato's, for example, yet the dominant view was more generally derived from Plato. Thus, the cultural setting provided the tools for transforming the Old Testament's "this worldly" sense of *nefesh* into an "otherworldly" concept. Other facets of Hellenistic thought, such as Stoicism, probably played a role as well, but by the turn of the era, a full-blown opposition of body and soul was often taken for granted. This dualism also permeates the deuterocanonical literature.

In the centuries just before the birth of Jesus, a dualism of one sort or another was the ideology *du jour* providing the controlling model for reading the Old Testament. So pervasive was the body-soul distinction that it shaped a sophisticated hermeneutical method. Origen and the so-called Alexandrian school of biblical interpretation sharply distinguished between the "body" of the text (its literal sense) and its "soul" (its exalted meaning). Among Christians, this exalted meaning, this "soul" of the text, was soon taken to be one and the same with church dogma. Thus it soon became common to move from the text of Genesis to the teaching and idiom of the New Testament, and back again, with virtually no conception of the terrain over which one was flying. The Old Testament was not translated into Christian doctrine, but rather transformed into it. The result was more than just an erroneous notion of *nefesh*. No, these strategies of reading, in their ingenious morphing of the text into church teaching, often suppressed important themes in the text. This move bears illustrating.

Traditional Christian exegesis identifies the serpent in Genesis 3 as Satan, taking the form of the serpent. Exegetes through the centuries have wrung their hands over when Satan had to have fallen, how he made his way into the garden, how anything evil could have entered the garden, how he got control of the serpent, and why he spoke first to the woman. The latter question typically received answers implying intellectual, spiritual, and social defects in the woman, despite the fact that God himself had said it was "not good" for the *man* to be alone, not the woman. This interpretation results from assuming that we must render Genesis 3 in terms of the spiritual universe depicted for us in church doctrine, a universe ruled by Satan and populated by demons. That is, the method is one of dualism: the Old Testament text's "real" meaning is not "serpent" but "Satan."

What happens if we drop the dualism? What happens if we analyze the serpent's role exclusively in terms of the context, just as we did *nefesh*? The key to the analysis is the transition between the garden narrative of Genesis 2 and the opening of the temptation narrative in Genesis 3. Genesis 3:1 tells the reader two things about the serpent. First, it asserts that the serpent "was more crafty than any beast of the field which the Lord God had made." The most important fact about this statement is that the term *arum* is actually the same word used in the immediately preceding verse for Adam and Eve. After the joyous cry of Adam that the woman is "bone of my bones, and flesh of my flesh," the etiological comment about marriage and "one flesh" climaxes with the narrator's comment: "And the man and his wife were both naked and were not ashamed." Apart from the plural form, the word "naked" (*arummim*) in Genesis 2:25 is the identical term used to describe the serpent. Thus the serpent possesses the identical quality that characterizes the man and the woman in the unashamed bliss of their nakedness, their "one flesh"-ness. What do we make of this striking similarity that characterizes the man and the woman, and also distinguishes the serpent from every other animal?

The significance of the similarity emerges from the second comment made about the serpent, namely, that he is the most *arum* "of any beast of the field which the LORD God had made." This expression points back to Genesis 2:18-20, where God creates "every beast of the field." The linkage identifies the serpent as one of those beasts. But these animals were all created as candidates for partnership with Adam. Every single animal was presented to Adam, including the serpent, and we are told that none was found suitable to be the companion. Not only was the serpent created as a potential partner for Adam, but he was also rejected from serving that function. As a result of the failure of any of the animals, including the serpent, to be Adam's companion, the story takes a sharp turn and God "builds" the woman, starting with a longitudinal section taken from Adam. The union of the man and the woman is summarized in the term translated "naked" in Genesis 2:25 and "clever" in Genesis 3:1.

The significance of the serpent being the "most *arum*" best lies in the fact that, as such, he would have been the most suitable of all the animals to serve as Adam's partner, since he possessed in the highest degree that quality that characterized the man and woman in their shame-free union. This explains in the narrative why he alone among the animals can speak, and even engage in rhetorical disputation. He would have been the most like Adam of all the beasts of the field, the most capable of providing the kind of companionship that is celebrated between the man and the woman. If the serpent's speech and reasoning with the woman indicate a degree of personality, then the serpent's hostility against the woman is immediately understood.

This reading answers every question generated by the narrative. Who was the serpent? He was the highest of all the animals, the one most like the man and woman in their communing bliss. Why did he choose to destroy the bliss of the garden? He resented his own rejection from serving as Adam's companion. Why did he approach the woman? He hated her most because she fulfilled exactly what Adam and God desired. The serpent initiates the well-known conversation of Genesis 3 in order to remove the competition or avenge his own rejection.

My point in this excursus is simply that the text itself will often provide all the answers we need for reading it. The only reason an interpreter would import the figure of Satan into Genesis 3 would be a kind of dualistic reading in which the text itself was not taken to communicate its own meaning, but served merely as a kind of vessel for a very different meaning, one drawn from some other source. But if we drop the dualistic approach, we find in the text a satisfactory account for the actions and motives of the main characters.

Conclusion

In the end, this essay is not about the soul as we know it, because Genesis 2:7 is not about the soul, as we have traditionally conceived it. The real concern is how one reads the Scriptures. Can the scriptural witness stand as a largely self-referencing body of literature? The exegesis of Genesis 2:7 clearly points to a situating of Adam in the midst of a range of creatures with whom he shares greater and lesser degrees of compatibility. He is made from dust, as they are. He has the breath of life, as they do. He is a living being, a *nefesh hayyah*, as they are. His interactions with them assume this commonality, as my comments on the serpent indicated. No exegetical justification exists for finding here the notion of abstract, immortal, disembodied personhood that we usually mean when we speak of the "soul," just as it is equally unnecessary to introduce "Satan" into the serpent narrative. These narratives get along just fine without that metaphysical assistance.

Although this text does not affirm an intangible, immortal "soul" in the classical sense, it does pressure us to make several strong affirmations about human personhood. First, the text, in describing the creation of humanity, points strongly to physical existence in continuity with the earth and animal life as a vital element in human existence. Indeed, the text's focus on physicality as the vital center of human personhood strongly suggests that we may not separate the physical from the "spiritual." So, for example, in cases of traumatic brain injury or coma, the tendency to speak of the injured person in the past tense is a serious breach of their human value as created persons. Likewise, we cannot justify causing the physical death of such a patient merely by asserting that "it is not really them anymore" as if some "soul" has already departed. This consideration does not easily answer the difficult end-of-life questions surrounding the traumatically injured, but Genesis 2:7 calls us at least to recognize that their physical existence is a vital facet of their value as human persons created by God. So if modern neuroscience seems to lead in a physicalist direction, perhaps it is simply following where Scripture has already led.

Second, the fate of all of creation hinges on the destiny of humanity. Genesis 2–3 stress that all creation turns on the role of humanity. In Genesis 2:5 the writer states that the world lacked any life, no plants or animals, precisely because "there was no man to till the ground." Somehow, the text risks the claim that the flourishing of all life on the planet is inextricably bound to the fate of humanity. We are somehow ready to believe Romans 8:18-30, which underscores the eschatological interrelatedness of humanity with the rest of the cosmos, after pondering such claims. Such a statement clearly binds human personhood inextricably with stewardship of the earth and its nonhuman occupants. We can perhaps understand why, in a letter penned around the turn of the second century, Barnabas wrote of a longing for the coming of Jesus, "For man is earth which suffers, for the creation of Adam was from the face of the earth."[18] Whatever human personhood is, it emerges from encounter with the physical universe, and its trajectory decisively affects the physical universe. We are "suffering earth" and the earth likewise suffers us.

Third, only of humans does God say "it is not good" in respect to aloneness. After reading seven times in Genesis 1 that "it is good," one almost smells the burning of literary rubber as Genesis 2 screeches to a halt and Yahweh utters his "not good" in repudiation of human aloneness. Whatever integrity we might affirm for the individual human person, human personhood can only finally emerge as God intended through creation in the framework of relationship, not out of some inner possession or part of human nature. Human personhood is socially emergent.

Fourth, Genesis 2 joins Genesis 1 in defining human existence principally in terms of standing under the divine word. Genesis 2 stresses this quality of responsibility to God's word as distinctively human, though Genesis 1 depicts the material world also responding to God's word. Even so, humans even in Genesis 1 receive more than simply an irresistible command "to bring forth." Humans receive commands that are clearly statements of *vocation*. In Genesis 1, it is the command to rule and subdue the creation. In Genesis 2, the command is to guard and tend the garden. The vocational dimension appears also in Adam's naming of the animals in a quest for partnership in tending the garden. In Genesis 1, the act of naming is a distinctively divine action; yet in Genesis 2, it is the action of Adam. This naming asserts Adam's godlike care and tending of the creation.

Fifth, and continuing the theme of humans standing under a distinctive divine word of vocation, Genesis 2, with its forbidden tree combined with the threat "you shall surely die," clearly marks out a distinctive zone of relatedness to God that includes the alternative of disobedience and alienation alongside obedience and partnership. Whatever else humanity shares with the animal world, humanity alone can look into the face of the Creator and say, "No, thanks." Whatever else human personhood means, in Genesis 2 it entails the ability to be tempted, and to turn from the divine word.

One final point: If the Bible does not in fact demand, nor even support, a classically dualistic read of human nature as "matter" and "spirit," perhaps this is a mercy. What if, for example, quantum physics is correct, and there is no final distinction between matter and energy? What if, in the end, materialism is just as naive and uninformed as idealism? What if our dichotomies, and our attempts to overcome them, all participate in a fundamentally flawed conception of the unity of existence in God's creation? In these cases, having hewed closely to the parameters of the biblical description, we would be much more inclined to relate matters of faith to matters of embodied historical existence. We would not be scandalized by discovering that depressed people can grow spiritually when they take medication. And we would not be at all shocked to discover that, when people pray and praise, sometimes cancer is healed. What if in fact we are beings who, though infinitely rich and complex, nevertheless exist as a complete unity that unfolds in a multitude of ways at a myriad of levels? What if the whole question of body, soul, spirit, mind, and brain simply boiled down to bandwidth?

CHAPTER 5

What Is a Human Being?

The Anthropology of Scripture

Patrick D. Miller

What is a human being?[1] That is the anthropological question in any context and by any mode of inquiry—theological, sociological, philosophical, biological, anthropological, and the like. It has been with us and always will be. At least part of the answer to the question is that human beings are *those who ask who they are* and try to answer that question. They may respond in very theoretical modes, as, for example, Descartes's claim to find the human in the rational (*cogito ergo sum*), or Rousseau and Kant's discovery of the essence of the human not in a physical nature but in the moral, or Karl Marx's economic answer. Or one may answer the human question in more personal terms, as in the anguished tones of Jean Valjean's famous "Who am I" soliloquy in the musical *Les Miserables*, where the answer has everything to do with his neighbor and whether he is defined by his own name and identity or by an oppressive force outside himself that has renamed him with the numbers of a convict: 24601.

In our own time, the question is sharply present, if not always so identified, in the psychological and physical sciences, especially the neurosciences. In the former instance, the issue of the human revolves around concepts of the self; in the latter, the focus of attention has been heavily on the mind and the brain. The two have been joined nicely in the title (and substance) of the book by the philosopher Karl Popper and the neuroscientist Sir John Eccles, *The Self and Its Brain*.[2] Clearly, these are avenues into the search for the particularity of being human, of knowing ourselves, avenues down which theology should be eager to go in its continuing efforts to account for what it means to be human—that is, to ask the anthropological question as a theological one.

In the conversation between theology and science, however, one must be aware of both the dangers and limits posed by these different routes to knowledge of the human. One danger is the assumption that notions of the self can serve fully to account for the reality of the human, thus producing a depiction that takes its orientation from a secular beginning point rather than from a theological one. That is immediately evident when one begins to explore the way in which language of the self has largely replaced language of the soul.[3] Fear of dualistic modes of analysis and a vague sense that soul language is archaic and uninformed by scientific ways of thinking have contributed to a handing over of the language of human individuality to a more secular vocabulary. Indeed, the decline of soul reference may itself reflect an unease with a definition of the human that seems from the very beginning to characterize human existence in terms of something outside itself. That is, soul language by definition suggests some connection to the reality of God, or, as Karl Barth put it, the one "who lives by the Spirit of God."[4] Neither Freudian notions of the ego nor contemporary psychological descriptions and investigations of the self can take one very far toward a more theological understanding of the human, though their analyses may provide significant insight into the nature of the human.

Neuroscience has opened the door to fathoming the mysteries of consciousness and the operation of the brain, so that the mind and its functioning are no longer a matter of purely philosophical or psychological inquiry. The profitable, even necessary, conjoining of the scientific and the philosophical in understanding the workings of the mind is signaled by the conversation between Eccles and Popper. Happily, that conversation reflects some resistance to a reductionistic understanding of the mind as something whose reality can be dealt with by a deeper examination of neurons or brain waves. Knowledge of the more technical aspects of the working of the brain should help us understand more fully the *mechanics* of human thinking in its mental and emotional dimensions. That is a part of who and what each person is, and the personality in its fullest sense is an outgrowth of those mechanics. So matters as central to human nature—and playing their part in theological interpretations of the human—as memory and the experience of beauty have their seat in the workings of the brain.[5] Here, again, however, the language of the soul is a reminder that there is something in the human reality that transcends the most complete analysis of the physiology and neurology of the human being.

Scripture and the Anthropological Question

The answer to the question, *What is a human being?*, however, is surely not a matter of adding something to the modes of analysis of the human that other fields of inquiry produce. Resistance to talk about the "soul" is appropriate if that is simply an addition to something else. I would suggest that another avenue of inquiry may be found in pursuing the anthropological question as it is asked rather directly within Scripture itself. The responses to that question one finds there can contribute to our thinking about what it means to be human.

The place in the Christian tradition where this question is most pointedly and directly raised is in the Psalms, most famously in Psalm 8. But the question does not arise only there. It is asked again in a royal prayer for help, Psalm 144, and one further time in one of Job's laments, which belong to the psalmic tradition of lament and complaint against God. All three of these biblical formulations of the question, *What is a human being?*, and the responses they give to the question are dimensions of Scripture's answer to the anthropological question.

I will look at each, but I need to begin with an observation of the most obvious feature that is characteristic of each formulation. I would describe this feature from three different angles: (1) The question is never simply, What is a human being? There is always more to the question. (2) Hence, the answer to the question that is offered in each instance is indirect in that it is in response to the more specific formulation of the question rather than to a generalized and abstracted request for a definition of human existence, of human being. (3) The very asking of the question makes the answer, that is, the effort to define the human in some way, by definition, a *theological* matter.

For in each instance, the question is "What is a human being *that you . . . ?*" "What is a human being that you regard/care for/think of/test/visit?" The question is never asked abstractly, never posed as a theoretical question. It is always asked in dialogue with God, and its formulation is a basic clue to the fact that the Psalms are not going to answer the anthropological question about who and what we are as human beings except in relation to God. One of the things to be noted about the way the psalmists take up this question is that their responses are largely assumptions about the nature of the human that are *not peculiar* to biblical or even religious thought but are common to human experience generally, whether perceived within a religious context or not. The critical difference is that the question of the human in the biblical context is also always a question about God's way with the human.

The Place of Human Life in the Cosmos (Psalm 8)

My assumption is that, if the psalmists ask the question, one should stick around to see what sort of answer they give, before going off to other sources one might expect to be productive of meaning and insight. The starting point, naturally enough, is Psalm 8. This psalm is best known for its speaking about the human, but that speaking is totally wrapped in a speaking about and to God. It begins and ends in the exclamation: "O Lord, our Lord, how majestic is your name in all the earth." The psalm intends only to express praise to God and never departs from that. All that it says about the human is part of its "Wow!" about the Lord. Indeed, it is only in awe before the created universe as the work of the fingers of God that the psalmist even thinks of man and woman, of human life.

But what this reflection on the universe as reflective of the glory of God does is precisely to raise a question about the place of human life in the cosmos. And at this point, the psalm uncovers what is surely a basic human anxiety, not a peculiarly Jewish or Christian one, but the fundamental human experience of feeling insignificant in the face of the vastness of the cosmos, whether it is perceived as God's creation or as a happenstance. The intrusion of the first person "I" in the psalm at this one point is, I think, not accidental: "When *I* look at your heavens. . . . " The rest of the song is a *corporate* expression, "Oh Lord, *our* Lord," and *generalizes* about human beings, but in this verse a single voice speaks out. I think that is a reflection of the fact that this human sense of insignificance in the universe is not a theoretical conclusion from scientific analysis, though it may be that also. It is a very personal recognition that, somewhere along the way, every one of us encounters. The "I" of this psalm is what makes us aware that the general question, *What is a human being?* is fundamentally a question, What am I? What possible meaning and significance can I or any other human being have in the midst of this cosmos that seems to have no end in time or space? (Whether that is a correct scientific perception does not matter. It is how I feel it, and so do you.) To be human is to experience a kind of fundamental anxiety in the face of the universe. That is something that distinguishes human beings from other sensate beings. The psalm reveals that this is not a modern phenomenon. It has always been thus. In our time, such anxiety before the cosmos has a new prominence as cosmologists talk about the fate of the universe, the death of the sun in five billion years, and the ultimate end of the universe in a fiery conflagration or in trillions of years of slow and unending evanescence into cold, dead silence. Our own experience so conforms to that of the psalmist that we know we are onto something about ourselves. As James Mays has put it, "To be human is to be afflicted with the capacity for this subliminal glimpse of the significance of our insignificance."[6]

As the question, What is a human being? is asked, a further claim is raised about the human reality: What is a human being *that you have been mindful of such a one, that you have taken note of or paid attention to him or her?* Insignificance before the universe has raised the question of the human, but the bigger issue than what is this speck of dust in the vast cosmos is what is this speck of dust before the one who created that vast cosmos. The claim that is being made here is not simply that we are created, like the rest of the universe, or even that we are, as human beings, dependent upon the Lord of the universe, though both of those things are true. It is rather the implicit claim that being human means to be the *recipient of God's attention*, to be noticed and regarded by the Creator of the universe. To be human is to be regarded, attended to by some other, and not to be ignored and disregarded. In Arthur Miller's great drama, *Death of a Salesman*, Willy Loman's wife says to her sons these words about her husband, an ineffective, failure of a father and a salesman who has lost the touch: "He's not the finest character who ever lived. But he's a human being, and a terrible thing is happening to him. So attention must be paid. He's not to be allowed to fall into his grave like an old dog. Attention, attention must be finally paid to such a person." That is Miller's fundamental anthropological claim in his play: This human being, however ineffectual and problematic he or she may be, is one to whom, by virtue of his or her humanity, attention must be paid. In Miller's play, it is a plea on the part of one of these human beings on behalf of another. Psalm 8 makes the daring claim that it is our very nature to be attended to by the Almighty, that we are remembered and regarded simply and precisely because we are human beings.

This is not a casual claim. It becomes the ground on which the outcry of the troubled sufferer appeals to God. The reader of Psalm 8 goes on to hear in the next psalm that:

> [The Lord] does not ignore the cry of the afflicted;
> He who requites bloodshed *is mindful of/remembers* them. (9:13)

And Jeremiah, when he cries for help in one of his laments, expresses his plea in exactly the words of the psalmist's query: "O LORD, you know; *remember* me and visit me" (15:15).

Even as science sets sharply before us an awareness of our insignificance as human beings in the vastness of the universe, so science has its own form of this second insight. It is found in the anthropic principle, an indication in the nature of the universe that it has been fine-tuned for life. That is, the universe is so formed that if it were even slightly different, younger or older, hotter or colder, more or less dense than it is—that is, if any of the chemical and physical properties of matter were changed even slightly—life and intelligence would not exist in the universe, at least not life and intelligence as we know it. This is anything but a theological claim, but it is a nontheological way of suggesting that somehow the creation was made for us. In its theological expression, as we find it in Psalm 8 and the Christian tradition more broadly, it is the assumption that to be human is to be known and attended to by the Creator.

There are complex ways through election and covenant that God's special attention to the descendants of Abraham and Sarah is claimed, but that is a different matter. What the psalmist speaks about is a kind of divine attention and regard that belongs to being human, not to being a child of Abraham. The forms of that attention merit further exploration, for it seems that there is a corollary to this definition of the human as the creature attended by God. That is, it seems to belong to *the nature of God* to care about the human. The biblical narratives and the psalms join in expressing this attention by telling us that the ears of God are "fine-tuned" to hear the cries of the human in pain.[7]

The third claim of this psalm about human existence is as astonishing as the second one. Indeed, it is the psalmist's recognition of what the divine attention means for human nature. What it means is a place in the world we inhabit that can only be described in royal and divine terms: crowned with glory and honor and only a little less than divine. Over against the awareness of human insignificance in the universe is a claim that human life is given a role to govern the world of which we are a part, that part of being human is the responsibility to organize, control, care for, and govern the world in which we live out our lives: "You have given them dominion over the works of your hands, you have put all things under their feet." Human beings may and do muck it up, but it is a part of the human identity "to create its own world of culture out of the world that is there."[8] Psalm 115 makes the same point in a slightly different way: "The heavens are the LORD's heavens, but the earth he has given to human beings" (v. 16). It is a religious and theological claim that "you" have given human beings dominion over the works of "your hands," that human rule of the natural order is a divinely given vocation. It is also a part of general human experience that being human means turning nature into culture, seeking to tend to control, and use the natural order. So the psalmist once again answers the anthropological question in a way that connects with common human experience.

There is a critical difference, however, precisely because the question has been asked as a theological question and in relation to thinking about the glory of God. The awareness of insignificance before the vastness of the cosmos does not finally lead to a despairing nihilism because that cosmos is "your heavens . . . the moon and stars that you have established." We do not contemplate a meaningless void that just happened, but a creation that was made good by the God who has also created us and called us into being. So also the human rule over culture is not destined to be an anarchic self-interested exploitation of the natural world around us but a divine vocation symbolized by the righteous and just rule of a king whose responsibility is the well-being of his subjects. To place the anthropological question entirely in the context of the praise of God is to perceive the human reality in a way that makes it neither ultimately despairing nor ultimately chaotic.

Before leaving Psalm 8 and indeed as the taking-off point for going elsewhere, we should observe the literary context in which this psalm is placed and its somewhat abrasive fit among the psalms of which it is a part. Psalm 8 belongs with a group of psalms that begins with Psalm 3—after the introduction to the Psalter in Psalms 1 and 2—and concludes with Psalm 14. All of these psalms are prayers for help, commonly called laments, with the exception of Psalm 8 and the first part of Psalm 9. Psalm 8, as a more hymnic poem thus stands somewhat apart from its context. The reason for its inclusion here is not difficult to see. At the end of Psalm 7, a fairly typical cry for help, we hear the vow to give thanks to God when deliverance comes, a typical element of the lament. The last line is: "I will . . . sing praise to the name of the LORD, the Most High." Psalm 8 is offered, then, as the mode of expression of such praise, as it begins with exaltation of the name of the Lord: "O LORD, our Sovereign, how majestic is your name in all the earth." The repeat of that expression of praise at the end of Psalm 8 then leads us into the beginning of Psalm 9, with its line in verse 2, "I will sing praise to your name, O Most High," and takes us into the praise and thanksgiving of the first part of that psalm before we are plunged again into the cries for help of the suffering and afflicted ones (9:13-20) whose voices have dominated this first part of the Psalter.

The Transiency of Humanity (Psalm 144)

Psalm 8 thus makes its claim about the royal nature of the human, the godlike character of human existence, in the midst of other voices who cry out in the face of oppression, sickness, and suffering. These other voices also ask the anthropological question. One hears it again in Psalm 144, in a voice that may be that of the king. Just before a strong petition for the Lord's help, the psalmist as king addresses God and asks again, *What is a human being?* The question is similarly formulated: What is a human being that you regard such a one, or a mortal that you think of him or her? (Ps. 144:3). The answer this time, however, is different. It is not, "You have crowned him with glory and honor," but rather, "They are like a breath; their days are like a passing shadow" (v. 4). The psalm then goes on to call upon the Lord to come down and "set me free and rescue me from the mighty waters" (v. 7). So the answer to the human question this time is different. All that is said is a claim about our transiency. Like Psalm 8, there is an awareness of our insignificance, but here it is not so much finitude as the sense that we are really almost nothing, and especially that we are so briefly around that we are no more than a quick breath of air. The question about the human in relation to God brings forth once more a generalized statement about human life. But this time, it points to our limitation, our mortality, our transiency. And there is no other word in response to the question here, except again the assumption that in our mortality and transiency we are still regarded; we are known by God; we are attended to by another. The Creator pays attention to the creature; the infinite to the finite; the eternal to the transient. And the psalm that so thoroughly underscores the human condition as fleeting and transient, Psalm 90, makes a *claim* and a *prayer* that belong to what the Psalter teaches us about who we are. The *claim* is simply this: "Lord, you have been our dwelling place in all generations." And the prayer is this: "Teach us to count our days" and "establish thou the work of our hands." Help us to know our limits and make our time count for something.

To Be Known by God (Job)

The claim that God pays attention to human beings is the point of continuity with the final asking of the question, What is a human being? in Scripture, this time in the mouth of Job. Indeed, Job rings the changes on the question and underscores this fact of human existence as the reality of being visited and paid attention to:

> What are human beings, that you make so much of them,
>   that you set your mind [fix your attention] on them,
> visit them every morning,
>   *test them every moment?* (7:17-18)

Job shares with Psalm 144 the answer implicit in the question, that human existence is marked by divine attention. But Job's experience identifies that aspect of human reality as a *problem*, so much so that he does not answer the question. The only answer to the question is in the question itself. The human *reality*, which is to be regarded by the divine, to be known by God, is the human problem. The "visiting" of God in Scripture is always an ambiguous matter. It may be for good or ill. God's attention is a constant searching and testing of human life. Better no attention at all. So Job says, "Will you not look away from me for a while" (v. 19). If this is who we are, and Job once more testifies that it is so, then human life, human existence, is not worth a bucket of warm spit, as Job says, in effect, in the next line:

> Will you not look away from me for a while,
>   let me alone until I swallow my spittle. (v. 19)

James Wharton has characterized Job's view on this essential feature of human existence as follows:

> In his desolate suffering . . . Job has experienced God's "inordinate attention" as a nightmarish terror that makes death preferable to such a "life." God's unaccountable claim on Job has become a burden he would gladly be spared for the last, brief days of his life (7:13-16). The glad hymn of Psalm 8:4 is here transformed into a cry of lamentation. . . . The Hebrew word translated "visit" here and "care for" in Psalm 8:4 has nothing to do with "dropping by." Rather it

indicates what God "metes out" to human beings whether for good (Psalm 8:4) or for ill (Job 7:17).[9]

Even as we listen to Job's words, we realize that we have not left the Psalter and the answer to the question that is to be found in its pages. For they are filled with the laments and cries for help of Job and his human confreres. In that same Psalm 90, the people declare:

> For we are consumed by your anger;
>   by your wrath we are overwhelmed.
> You have set our iniquities before you,
>   our secret sins in the light of your countenance.
> For all our days pass away under your wrath;
>   our years come to an end like a sigh. (vv. 7-9)

There is no more constant voice in the Psalter than the one that cries out in torment and suffering to God. We know it at its most radical in Job. But one hears this voice again and again in the Psalter. Sometimes, as in the Psalms around Psalm 8, that is about all one does hear, whether it is the voice of a king or simply one who has been afflicted, faint and pleading before the Lord, as the superscript of Psalm 102 says. The experience of suffering looms large over the Psalter and seems to be the primary human experience. The one who is crowned with glory in Psalm 8 is also a creature of suffering; the one who is *astonished* by God's attention as making us kings and queens is also one who is *undone* by God's attention, an attention experienced as testing and undoing. Or, in other psalms, the human creature is undone by God's inattention that means no help in the face of the destructive forces of life that take away one's humanity. It is not necessary to try to create a theological consistency between the experiences of God's *disturbing and destructive attention* and God's *abandoning inattention*. In both instances, the human reality is finitude, transiency, and suffering; and in both instances the anthropological significance once again depends upon God. If one cannot make claims about the royal place of the human in the creation without that being seen in relation to the mystery of God, one also cannot deal with the reality of pain and suffering without that also being seen in relation to the mystery of God. Neither the psalmist nor Job knows how to speak about the human apart from the reality of God.

Humanity in the Face of Jesus (Hebrews 2)

One could legitimately stop at this point in our probe of the Psalms' answer to the question, What is a human being? There are some things we know now, and they fit with our experience; they connect with things that others outside the community of faith claim about human life.

But the anthropological question is asked one more time in Scripture, and perhaps our reflection on its meaning would be incomplete without attention to the final instance, which is in fact a quotation of Psalm 8. It is to be found in Hebrews 2:6-9.

Three things are immediately noticeable about the appropriation of Psalm 8 in this New Testament passage.

(1) The presence of the expression *ben 'adam*, traditionally translated as "son of man" but in the NRSV as "mortal," has led inexorably to a hearing of this text as not simply about humanity in general but about the one who was known as the "son of man." It is important, however, to recognize that the NRSV translation is not misleading at this point, that the term "son of man" means and is best translated as "a human one." This title is the most anthropological of all the christological titles. It is a way of speaking in titular terms of the incarnational reality that this one was truly human and representatively human.

(2) The Greek translates the Hebrew *elohim* as *anggeloi*, as "angels" rather than "god(s)."

(3) The term "a little lower" has been read through the Greek as "for a little while," a legitimate interpretation of the Greek at this point. So the expression refers not to the status of the human being described in these verses but to the *temporality* of "his" status—that is, to a brief period of time in which this representative human being was lower than the angels.

All of this leads to an important christological understanding of the answer to the question, *What is a human being?* That is, there is an *incarnational* answer to the anthropological question also. The human being under whom all things have been made subject (so Psalm 8) is the one who emptied himself, being born in human likeness (so Hebrews 2). The writer to the Hebrews hears in the Psalms the word that whatever we say about the human reality must take into account the face of Jesus Christ.

The New Testament underscores this in spades when it makes Psalm 22, the model lament, the interpretive key to understanding the passion and death and resurrection of Jesus Christ. For as it constantly interprets what is going on by means of the verses of Psalm 22, it makes clear that the one on the cross identifies with all those who cry out in the words of Psalm 22 or in laments like that. If suffering is a part of the *human* reality, it is also necessarily at the heart of the *incarnational* reality. Hebrews 2 recognizes how fully that is the case when it notes that we do not yet see everything in subjection to him. There are still powers and forces at work in the human creature. That is true, whether the human being in view is humanity in general or the incarnate one. But then the Hebrews writer says the critical words: *"But we do see Jesus."* "We do see Jesus, who for a little while was made lower than the angels, crowned with glory and honor *because of the suffering of his death,* so that by the grace of God he might taste death for everyone" (Heb. 2:9). The suffering and death that belong to our humanity is not the last word. Nor is it a trumping of the glory and honor, turning them into dust and ashes. Hebrews says that it was precisely in the suffering and death of Jesus that he was crowned with glory and honor. What therefore is to be said about the human cannot be confined to general statements about humanity apart from God. It cannot be said apart from the discovery that in Jesus Christ we see who we are and we also see God for us. And what is said about the human cannot be said as a general statement that assumes that what we see now is all there is to see. The answer to the question about who we are is finally eschatological, where tears are no longer part of the human reality, where joy is the order of eternity, and where our transience disappears in the disappearance of death. We cannot see that yet. But we do see Jesus. That will have to do. I think it is enough.

CHAPTER 6

Soul-Searching Questions About 1 Samuel 28

Samuel's Appearance at Endor and Christian Anthropology

Bill T. Arnold

The main title of this chapter contains, of course, a *double entendre*. The questions I explore here involve a degree of "soul-searching," first, because a *prima facie* reading of 1 Samuel 28:3-19 may result in the conviction that Samuel's "soul" was present at Endor, and that this text therefore has troubling implications for the monist anthropology under consideration in recent discussion. So the first intended meaning of my search explores whether we must identify Samuel's appearance here as his "soul," or whether there are alternative explanations. This is also, second, a "soul-searching" quest because the phrase denotes a vigorous and sometimes painful examination of one's beliefs, especially when such examination raises doubts about or challenges heretofore held convictions. I offer this chapter as a modest attempt to join other Christians who are currently reevaluating long-held and cherished assumptions about Christian anthropology and the nature of human life.

This chapter begins with a summary of the history of interpretation of 1 Samuel 28:3-19 as a means of opening the discussion of the significance of this text for the contemporary debate in Christian anthropology. This is followed by an examination of the exegetical issues of the text, exploring specifically its textual contours in light of its canonical placement, and the historical context in light of gains made in recent research. I will close with general reflections on the data from Israel's Scriptures and their implications for our understanding of human personhood as informed by recent innovations in the neurosciences.

So, my soul-searching questions are the following: How did believers in antiquity read this text? What information can we glean from the latest hermeneutical approaches and most recent historical investigation that may shed light on this reading? And, what are the implications of this text, and of the data from the Hebrew Scriptures generally, for the current debate?

History of Interpretation

This passage has presented challenges for readers through the ages. Israel's first king, Saul, is facing the greatest crisis of his reign. He has led the nation to the brink of another war with the Philistines and he rightly fears that the impending battle could be a moment of truth for him and the legitimacy of his reign. He has been unable to determine a divinely directed path through the crisis (28:6), and in desperation he seeks out and finds a necromancer, a "spiritist." In a turn of events unprecedented in biblical literature, King Saul consults the medium of Endor, who brings up the deceased prophet Samuel. Much to the surprise of readers through the ages (and of the medium herself, see 28:12), the venerable old prophet comes up out of the ground (v. 13) and reminds King Saul that he predicted these circumstances while he was still alive and that the doom about to befall him is unavoidable (vv. 16-19).

Christians of many traditions often explore the historical realities behind key events narrated in the Bible. So, for example, many have debated the precise understanding of the collapse of the walls of Jericho or Jesus walking on the water, while others focus on the central events of salvation history, such as the Exodus and the Sinai covenant, and the resurrection of Jesus. Although the account of Samuel's appearance through the medium of Endor raises similar questions, I have in mind more specifically the question of whether this text proves the existence of a disembodied, intermediate state, as some contemporary readers insist.[1] The neurosciences will no doubt continue to present further innovations in our understanding of human personhood, and as they do so, this text will likely require increased attention. Can it legitimately provide grist for the mill that shapes Christian anthropology? If so, does it portray a disembodied human soul? This portion of the paper summarizes the way the text has been interpreted in antiquity in order to gain a heuristic depth perception in our own interpretation. Obviously this brief paper cannot survey the entire history of interpretation on 1 Samuel 28:3-19. Instead this summary considers the various ways classical interpreters have attempted to explain or understand the precise nature of Samuel's appearance, leaving aside discussion of other features of this fascinating text.

Ancient readers of 1 Samuel 28:3-19 may be categorized into two groups.[2] The first group of early writers on 1 Samuel 28:3-19 assumed the figure at Endor was not Samuel at all, but only a delusional and deceptive apparition, having its origin in demonic forces and offering a forged prophecy. Tertullian, for example, argued that the appearance was demonic and he appealed to 2 Corinthians 11:14b-15a for evidence: "Even Satan disguises himself as an angel of light. So it is not strange if his ministers also disguise themselves as ministers of righteousness." Others who specifically quoted Paul's text in a similar vein were Pionius, Eustathius, Ambrosiaster, Augustine, and Pseudo-Augustine. Many more commentators from the first centuries of church history fall into this category, although they did not use the Pauline quote: Pseudo-Hippolytus, Eustathius of Antioch, Ephraem, Gregory of Nyssa, Evagrius Ponticus, Pseudo-Basil, Jerome, Philastrius, and Ambrosiaster.

Most of these authors assert that it is impossible for a holy prophet to be disturbed and raised from the dead by necromantic rituals. Saints may be able to exorcize evil spirits, but the reverse is not true—demons are not able to call up dead saints. Thus, these early Christian thinkers concluded that a demon or Satan himself deceived Saul (and the woman) by appearing as Samuel.[3] Most contemporary critical commentaries decline even to speculate about such possibilities, while others, in extreme attempts to square the text with one's theology, have resorted to such creative explanations as hallucinogenic narcotics or a "psychological" ecstatic trance without the benefit of mind-altering drugs.[4]

The second group of early writers on 1 Samuel 28:3-19 assumed the appearance of Samuel was real. These authors believed Samuel himself appeared at Endor, resurrected by God or by the woman through efficacious but illicit necromantic practices. So, for example, Justin Martyr argued for the existence and survival of the human soul based on this text.[5] Other authors who assumed Samuel actually appeared at Endor include the historian Josephus, as well as Origen, Dracontius, Zeno of Verona, Ambrose, Sulpicius Severus, and Anastasius Sinaita. Interestingly, Dracontius mentions necromancy and cites this episode, in which the woman is said to have conjured Samuel's soul by means of a Python.[6] Augustine expressed conflicting opinions at different stages of his life on whether Samuel himself appeared or a delusive demon appeared instead, but his mature conviction seems to favor the latter.[7] He further compared Samuel's appearance at Endor to that of Moses' appearance at the Mount of Transfiguration.[8]

Some of the interpreters in this category appear to have worked from a specifically dualist anthropology, but others apparently assumed a resuscitated physical body, perhaps not unlike the resurrection body of Jesus. Those ancient and classical authors who took Samuel's appearance at Endor in this way—that is, in a physical sense—were closer to the ancient Israelite perceptions, as we shall see, and so such interpretations do not require the existence of a disembodied, intermediate state for the deceased Samuel.

Before turning to the exegetical considerations of the text, we may pause to ask what relevance these traditional readings of 1 Samuel 28:3-19 have for the debate before us. In short, the first approach is irrelevant and the second is only tangentially relevant. If, as in the case of the first interpretation, the appearance of Samuel was only delusional and was not actually Samuel himself, then obviously the question of whether the Endor episode requires the presence of Samuel's disembodied soul becomes immaterial. On the other hand, if the second interpretation is granted, and it is accepted that Samuel himself appeared at Endor, we are left to evaluate the degree to which a later dualist anthropology was imposed on the text by those who used it to argue for the existence of the soul. As I have implied and as I hope to show below, those authors who assumed a resuscitated physical Samuel better understood the ancient Israelite context of this passage, and are less guilty of sleight-of-hand hermeneutics. Those authors in the second category who assumed a resuscitated physical body rather than a disembodied soul are, I believe, closer to the original aim of this passage, as we shall see. In other words, if ancient Israelites were faced with the question before us, I believe they would respond, "Of course there is no existence apart from the physical!" Therefore, Samuel's appearance at Endor, once accepted as real and not delusional, must also be accepted as in some sense physical.

Exegetical Considerations

I turn now to ask whether a contemporary reading in light of today's "new biblical hermeneutics,"[9] respecting the integrity of the final form of the text while at the same time considering the historical and sociological contexts, might shed light on the debate before us.

A casual reading of the text immediately raises questions of the ancient perceptions of death and the afterlife in Israel's Scriptures. On the basis of a straightforward reading of the text, it appears all the characters of the story—the medium, Saul, and his officers—as well as the narrator, assume the reality and effacacy of necromantic practices. More than any other passage in the Hebrew Scriptures, this text illustrates what some Israelites believed about ancestor worship and cults of the dead.[10] Materials from Ugarit and elsewhere in the ancient Near East have illumined the biblical evidence, and in recent decades scholarly investigations have come to new understandings of ancestor worship and related death rituals in popular religion during the Iron Age.[11] Against the wishes of the prophets and the leaders of normative religion in ancient Israel, some Israelites apparently persisted in the practice of necromancy and other death rituals. In such rituals, actions were directed to the deceased in an attempt to appease the dead or to secure favors from them. This text, then, represents a vestige of the customs and religious practices of Canaanites and some Israelites, despite the disapproval of normative Old Testament religion.[12]

The precise terminology and nomenclature used in 1 Samuel 28:3-19 are specific to necromancy, and leave no doubt of the practice in view here.[13] The narrator explains in verse 3 that Saul had previously expelled "mediums" (*'ovot*) and "spiritists" (*yidde'onim*) from Israel. Now, however, King Saul travels to the medium at Endor under cover of darkness and asks her to "consult" a spirit for him.[14] The recurring use of language for "bringing up" or "raising" also refers specifically to necromancy (28:8, 11, 13, 14, 15).

These specifics of terminology are pertinent because they reflect a sociohistorical context important for rightly interpreting the text. When the woman described the appearance of Samuel arising out of the ground (28:13), she reflected the concept of Sheol as a place for the dead beneath the earth's surface to which people descended at death, and this of course represents a cosmology quite unlike our contemporary Christian understanding.[15] This ancient cosmology, which the Israelites shared with their neighbors, included a flat, disk-shaped earth with mountains at its ends supporting a multilayered sky, or domed firmament (see figure 2).[16] The sun, moon, and stars crossed this firmament in regular and predictable patterns. The firmament had chambers through which the water above the firmament came down as rain, and there was also water under the earth, and water around the whole making up the cosmic seas. Below the visible flat earth existed a second level of earth, the netherworld, abode of the dead. Our passage's use of the expressions "bring up" and "rise up from the ground" reflects this cosmology, and they appear to be technical terms used specifically for necromancy, together with "medium," "spiritist," and "divine," all appearing in these verses.

In addition to these considerations of terminology and sociohistorical context, this passage contains interesting canonical links that are pertinent to our study. When the narrative opens this passage with a reference to King Saul's previous explusion of mediums and spiritists (28:3*a*, an action the narrator approves), we as readers are thereby prepared for a disconcerting tension created by the king's actions. By using the technical terms "mediums" and "spiritists," the narrative further critiques King Saul through literary echoes with the Pentateuchal proscriptions against these necromantic practices (Lev. 19:31; 20:27; Deut. 18:10-11, perhaps especially the Deuteronomy reference, see below).[17] Thus the text also raises interesting intertextual and canonical questions.

In fact, the Deuteronomistic historian responsible for 1 and 2 Samuel appears to have intentionally redacted an older narrative source about Saul, placing it

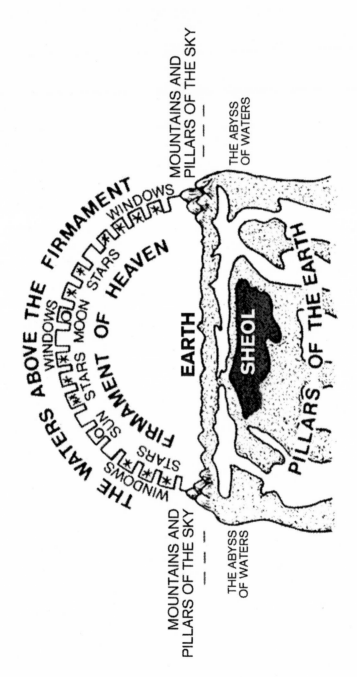

Figure 2

strategically in its canonical location in the Deuteronomistic history and using specific and precise terminology in order to characterize the ill-fated king further as part of a larger trajectory in the books of Samuel.[18] The reworking of the earlier source has highlighted the expulsion of mediums and spiritists (v. 3b), using the technical vocabulary of Deuteronomy 18:11 intentionally in order to draw out the implications of the intertext. The redactional reworking echoes the proscriptions against the very practice Saul was using. His actions themselves were condemnatory; his very words remind the reader of the illegality of his actions: "so that I may go to her and *inquire* of her" (28:7). The reader is not surprised to hear the resuscitated Samuel's condemnation; Saul has in effect sealed his own doom by inquiring of the dead.

This condemnatory portrait of Saul is part of a larger literary movement in 1 Samuel, which characterizes both Saul and David by contrasting them from the moment David is anointed (1 Sam. 16:13). I have argued elsewhere that the use of necromancy in 1 Samuel 28 was part of the editor's grand scheme in the books of Samuel for characterizing David vis-à-vis Saul. David, on the one hand, was the ideal anointed of the Lord, who consistently sought divine guidance by means of the sanctioned priestly ephod with its Urim and Thummim (i.e., through the casting of lots, see 1 Sam. 10:22; 14:37; 22:10, 13, 15; 23:2, 4; 28:6; 30:8; 2 Sam. 2:1; 5:19, 23; 16:23).[19] Saul, on the other hand, gradually drove away the prophetic word of Yahweh by becoming estranged from Samuel, and then by killing the priests of Nob (1 Sam. 22:6-23), who granted him access to the Urim and Thummim. Ultimately, Saul became the antithesis of David—that is, of the ideal anointed one—by turning to necromancy, the forbidden means of seeking divine guidance.

In sum, the author of the original account of Saul at Endor, as well as the later Deuteronomistic historian responsible for incorporating that account into our narrative, most likely assumed a resuscitated Samuel actually appeared at Endor. However, the text contains several linguistic and canonical indications that the purpose for using the older narrative source was to characterize King Saul and to highlight the contrast between Saul and David. This interpretation does not preclude a dualist reading of 1 Samuel 28:3-19, but circumvents the question to some degree by emphasizing the narrative's purpose. On the other hand, the sociohistorical background of the text makes it unlikely that a disembodied "soul" of Samuel could be involved. Like other data from the Hebrew Scriptures, this passage must ultimately remain inconclusive in matters of Christian anthropology, although the concept of physical resuscitation is suggestive.

Concluding Observations

I have asked my "soul-searching" questions and offered the following tentative answers. First, How did ancient believers read 1 Samuel 28? We have seen a wide variety of interpretations of this text from antiquity, none requiring dualism; in fact, the best interpretations assume a resuscitated physical Samuel. Second, What information can we glean from fresh literary approaches to this text and recent historical investigations? It appears an old pre-Deuteronomistic tradition of Samuel's resuscitation at Endor was used as a rhetorical device in the hands of the redactors of 1 Samuel in an attempt to condemn King Saul, characterizing him as the diametric opposite of David. Necromancy is viewed as a deplorable practice, the use of which made Saul illegitimate as king of Israel.

Now for a few brief comments to conclude this discussion. First, a warning—a superficial reading of 1 Samuel 28 may lead today's Christians to interpretations that appear to refute a monist anthropology. But as we have seen, believers from earliest times have disagreed about this difficult text, and no consensus can possibly emerge from 1 Samuel 28 defending a traditional dualism. Moreover, those interpretations of 1 Samuel 28:3-19 that assume a physicalist approach are closer to the ancient Israelite *Weltanschauung,* and the implications of this for the emerging Christian monism should be explored further.

Second, we should give closer attention to the Bible's phenomenological language with reference to the nature of human beings. We do so quite naturally and logically with regard to cosmology when reading the Bible. So for example, we know that the earth does not have "four corners" and we understand the "rising" and "setting" sun as a reflection of the ancient prescientific worldview rather than as a technical cosmological description for our times. Likewise we make the necessary intellectual adjustments when we read of earth's flat disk-shaped structure and the existence of Sheol below the surface of the earth. More examples of this adjustment may be instructive. In the priestly creation account, God calls forth "dry land" from the collected prehistoric waters under the firmament (Gen. 1:9). Surely this reflected the ancient Israelite perception of the earth as originally consisting of one major landmass, which perception they shared with most ancient, classical, and medieval philosophers.[20] Few of us would insist this text has in view a scientific *Pangaea,* the world-continent of all land masses that existed prior to the continental drift of the Triassic period (ca. 245-208 million years ago). Similarly, the movements of the celestial bodies, and even descriptions of weather, are all exactly as we would expect for ancient Near Eastern authors. In our reading of such phenomena, we naturally, even instinctively, filter these perceptions through our contemporary scientific cosmology. Yet tragically and famously, the church has not always done so.

Something similar has to be done when we read the phenomenological language of the Bible's anthropology. When the text makes reference to the process of human thought, there is a conspicuous absence of "brain" language, and perhaps it is instructive to point out that biblical Hebrew has no word for "brain."[21] It appears that none of the ancients understood how the brain functioned, or even anything about its use.[22] Yet biblical Hebrew has many terms for describing human personhood, including words conventionally rendered "spirit" and "soul" (*ruakh, nefesh*), and terms for internal organs as the seat of emotions, such as "heart," "liver," and "kidneys" (*lev/levav, kaved, kelayot,* etc.).[23] But all philological and literary contextual data from the Hebrew Scriptures related to Christian anthropology are notoriously difficult to interpret.[24] Recent studies have admitted the Hebrew Bible's purely physical perception of human personhood, acknowledging the impossibility of developing a Christian dualist anthropology on the basis of these data.[25]

Finally, a word about the last of my "soul-searching" questions raised at the beginning of this paper: What are the implications of the data from the Hebrew Scriptures for the current debate? Future work on Hebrew conceptions of human personhood must nuance the philological and literary evidence carefully. The Hebrew Scriptures distinguish between the spiritual and physical realities of this life. But such distinctions may prove to be *qualitative* rather than *quantitative*. The Bible refers not to two components or constituents of human life—as in body and soul—but to two dimensions, as in first and final, which also exist, however, simultaneously. Such a qualitative distinction between a person's "life" (*nefesh*) and "body" (*basar*) would also be closer to a proper eschatology, not simply of the individual, but of the world we inhabit now and *will* inhabit by God's grace (Rev. 21:1).

CHAPTER 7

Resurrection of the Body

New Testament Voices Concerning Personal Continuity and the Afterlife

Joel B. Green

ord, already there is a stench because he has been dead four days." Spoken by Martha, sister of the dead man Lazarus, in reply to Jesus' instruction to remove the stone from Lazarus's tomb (John 11:38-39), these words pinpoint the first of two central quandaries intrinsic to the historic confession of the Christian faith, "I believe in . . . the resurrection of the body." As Caroline Walker Bynum has demonstrated, Christian belief concerning the resurrection has stubbornly focused on the physicality of both resurrection and ultimate salvation.[1] As Martha recognizes, however, this belief flies in the face of the empirical observation that our physical bodies decay upon death; indeed, the warm climate and absence of embalming procedures in ancient Palestine necessitated both the use of spices to counter the repugnant odor of decomposition and the placement of the corpse on sand or salt to absorb the results of bodily disintegration.[2] The frailty of embodied existence seems to vacate the doctrine of (bodily) resurrection of all sensibility.

What is more, with the natural decay of the body, its constituent ingredients become so much a part of the fabric of the natural world, what fans of Walt

Disney's *Lion King* know as "the circle of life," that it would be impossible to reconstitute the body of one individual without violating the integrity of other bodies. This is because my body is made up of molecules that, in the long expanse of biological time, have belonged to other bodies, and are likely yet to be constitutive of still more bodies in the future. If resurrection requires the reassembly of our bodies at the end of the age, how will God adjudicate the inevitably competing claims to those basic elements?[3] This problem is only heightened by the practice of organ transplant and the prospect of organ cloning. Further, for many of us, extending our current bodies into eternity would be a prospect most unwelcome, given its infirmities, deformities, and other deficits. What, then, might "resurrection of the body" entail?

This line of thinking introduces a second issue. If not through persistence of this body, how might continuity of personal identity, from death to life-after-death, be guaranteed? How can I be sure that the *me* that enjoys eternal life is really me? Here we raise the question of personal identity in general, and the possibility of the survival of personal identity in particular—an issue that has suggested to some that the hope of resurrection turns on a dualist anthropology: mortal body, immortal soul. Given the self-evident finality of death for the physical body, without recourse to a separate entity or personal "essence" (that is, a soul, which constitutes the real me) that survives death, how can we maintain a reasonable doctrine of the afterlife? If, instead of possessing a body, I am a body, then when my body dies do I not likewise cease to exist?[4]

In this chapter, I propose to explore the contribution of the New Testament message of the resurrection to Christian anthropology by pursuing three lines of inquiry. First, I will sketch the development and significance of resurrection in the Scriptures of Israel. My aim here is twofold: to map something of the landscape within which we might locate resurrection texts in the New Testament, and to broaden our vision of the significance of resurrection in God's redemptive plan. Second, I will direct our attention to the account of Jesus' resurrection—or, better, postresurrection appearance—in Luke 24:36-49. This will press our thinking about the character of resurrection existence and the nature of personal identity (and, particularly, the persistence of personal identity beyond the grave). Third, I will turn to 1 Corinthians 15 as a way of focusing attention on Paul's understanding of a body suited for life-after-death. This will lead to some concluding, programatic remarks about the nature of the human person as this relates to identity in this life and the life to come.

I intend to show that, with reference to the texts we will examine, an anthropology that posits an ontologically distinct soul, which constitutes the "real person" and which guarantees survival of personal identity from this life to the next, is not only unnecessary but actually stands in tension with key aspects of the resurrection message of the Scriptures. Personal identity with regard to both present life and life-after-death is narratively and relationally shaped and embodied, the capacity for life-after-death is not intrinsic to humanity but is divine gift, and resurrection signifies not rescue from the cosmos but transformation with it.

The perspective I will sketch underscores the miraculous character of resurrection by locating its possibility solely in God's gracious initiative. It takes seriously and is congruent with what we are learning from the neurosciences regarding the neural correlates of the dispositions and behaviors by which we identify our humanity, as well as the reality that, throughout our lives, nature and nurture sculpt our brains and shape our bodily existence in ways that form and reform who we are.

Resurrection in Israel's Scriptures

In the world of the New Testament, how might people have understood proclamation of the resurrection? That we should approach this question with caution is suggested by two New Testament texts. According to the first, when coming down the mountain following his transfiguration, Jesus directed his disciples, Peter, James, and John, "to tell no one about what they had seen, until after the Son of Man had risen from the dead. So they kept the matter to themselves, questioning what this rising from the dead could mean" (Mark 9:9-10). Though recipients of Jesus' prediction of resurrection, his own inner circle of disciples are said to have found his words about "raising from the dead" incomprehensible. This may have been because Jesus apparently spoke of the resurrection of an individual (that is, his own resurrection), whereas resurrection belief in contemporary Judaism was corporate in its emphasis, as we shall see shortly. Alternatively, the puzzle experienced by Jesus' followers might have reflected simply the lack of standardization in resurrection-talk in Second Temple Judaism.[5]

Another text, this one found in the Acts of the Apostles, has it, first, that the people of Athens mistook Paul's proclamation of the resurrection of Jesus as a message about two new deities, Jesus and Resurrection (17:18); and, second, that when those gathered on the Areopagus heard Paul announce that God had raised someone from the dead, some scoffed while others were curious to hear more (17:30-32). Luke had already identified the presence of Epicureans and Stoics, representatives of two philosophical schools whose views on the afterlife contrasted. Epicureans held that the soul was a substance of fine particles or atoms that dissipated at death; no belief in an afterlife would be consistent with this view. Stoic views of the afterlife are more difficult to summarize, and many Stoics seem to have believed that human souls could survive for an indefinite period after death. In his analysis, Kevin Anderson observes that "it is impossible to tell precisely what any given Stoic would have made of Paul's preaching concerning the resurrection—although few if any would have found *bodily* resurrection acceptable—but Stoic views of the afterlife seem to have been open to Platonic influences. Thus, Luke plausibly represents them as being curious about this new doctrine of the resurrection, whereas the Epicureans would have nothing to do with it."[6]

Even if the language and idea of resurrection circulated widely in the world of early Christianity, diverse views concerning the resurrection pervaded that world.[7] Depending on the context, for example, talk of "resurrection" and "afterlife" might trigger thoughts related to the resuscitation of a corpse, revivification of the soul, flight of the immortal soul at the moment of death, transformation of the body for afterlife, and more. What might resurrection signify for God's people in the first-century Roman Mediterranean?

Life and Death

The idea of resurrection from the dead belongs to the later horizons of Israel's faith, as this is witnessed in Israel's Scriptures. Numerous texts record the burial of the dead (for example, Gen. 50:13; Josh. 24:32) without mentioning the fate of the dead. In fact, when death is mentioned, it is generally treated with little more profundity than as a reference to the cessation of life. As a whole, the Scriptures of Israel are largely uninterested in the fate of the dead.[8]

In Israel's Scriptures, *Sheol* does appear as "the place of the dead," but only rarely as the common location of the dead. Rather, in most instances the term refers to that human fate to which the wicked are consigned and to which the godly declare their aversion; it is the antithesis of heaven. That is, the subterranean world of the dead is associated especially with the ungodly, and this underscores the biblical distinction between life (lived in this world, before and in relation to Yahweh) and death (consigned to the underworld, separate from Yahweh).[9] This is interesting as a reminder to us that, for Israel's Scriptures, death is never a question merely of biological cessation. In fact, three affirmations regarding death pervade these writings: human existence is marked by finitude, death is absolute, and death is regarded as the sphere within which fellowship with Yahweh is lost.[10] Death is the cessation of life in all of its aspects, and especially the severance of all relationships—relationships with God and with every person and with everything in the cosmos. This perspective on death is grounded in the reality that the Hebrew Bible as a whole defines the human person in relational rather than essentialist terms. Human beings are assessed as genuinely human and alive only within the family of humans brought into being by Yahweh and in relation to the God who gives life-giving breath.[11] Those who worshiped Yahweh, then, could hardly venerate the dead or ascribe ancestral powers to the dead, since they were cut off from him (cf. Pss. 30:9; 115:17). Indeed, corpse impurity was a major contagion within the socioreligious economy of the people of God.[12] Accordingly, life beyond death would refer above all to restoration to Yahweh, and, then, to the reach of Yahweh's sovereignty even beyond that most potent of barriers to life, death itself.

Images of Resurrection

Hints of resurrection faith occur in a handful of prophetic texts. For example, in Hosea 6:1-3 we read of the prospect of the revival of God's people:

> "Come, let us return to the LORD;
>> for it is he who has torn, and he will heal us;
>> he has struck down, and he will bind us up.
> After two days he will revive us;
>> on the third day he will raise us up,
>> that we might live before him.
> Let us know, let us press on to know the LORD;
>> his appearing is as sure as the dawn;
>> he will come to us like the showers,
>> like the spring rains that water the earth."

This text attracted the attention of the church fathers, who read in it a prophecy of Jesus' resurrection on the third day, and early Jewish interpretation found here a reference to the end-time resurrection of Israel. In its own eighth-century context, this reading may not have been so clear, however. "Raising up" is more likely to have been heard as a metaphor for the restoration of the nation than as a reference to the literal raising up of persons whose life on this earth had ended.

Ezekiel 37:1-14, with its dramatic image of the valley of dry bones brought to life, also envisions Israel's restoration. This did not keep later Jewish interpretation from finding here a graphic depiction of the resurrection, however. Note especially verses 12-13: "I am going to bring you up from your graves . . . !" In both of these texts—one from Hosea, the other from Ezekiel—we find the interweaving of the promise of Israel's restoration with the re-creative work of the Lord.

Many scholars find a more direct reference to resurrection in Isaiah 26:19:

> Your dead shall live, their corpses shall rise.
> O dwellers in the dust, awake and sing for joy!
> For your dew is a radiant dew,
>> and the earth will give birth to those long dead.

Like the vision in Ezekiel 37, Isaiah's words appear in a context that proposes Israel's restoration and, indeed, exaltation among the nations. With regard to the meaning of this text in particular, debate centers on whether a literal raising up of corpses is envisioned. At the very least, however, we have here in Isaiah a further text that relates the notion of resurrection to the activity of God by which he restores and exalts his people, and by which he pours upon them the totality of his covenant blessings.

The first unambiguous reference to the physical resurrection of the dead appears in Daniel 12:1-3:

> "At that time Michael, the great prince, the protector of your people, shall arise. There shall be a time of anguish, such as has never occurred since nations first came into existence. But at that time your people shall be delivered, everyone who is found written in the book. Many of those who sleep in the dust of the earth shall awake, some to everlasting life, and some to shame and everlasting contempt. Those who are wise shall shine like the brightness of the sky, and those who lead many to righteousness, like the stars forever and ever."

This passage forms the climax of the revelation that began in Daniel 11:2, and marks the decisive triumph of God's people over the enemies of Israel. At last, Israel will experience salvation in its fullest sense. Not all will experience this deliverance, however, but only those found in "the book" (that is, the book of life—see Isa. 4:3; Mal. 3:16-18). Others will experience the resurrection as judgment. It is in this way that Daniel's concern with the vindication of God's righteous servants comes into clearest focus.

Even those texts that did not refer explicitly to resurrection of the dead would provide the raw material for a view of God that would blossom in the period of Second Temple Judaism. This view identified God as the source and sovereign over life, and this provided the ground for the affirmation of God's capacity to give back the life of the faithful tragically lost at the hands of Israel's enemies. Resurrection theology was profoundly theocentric, focused as it was on Israel's covenantal relationship with God; recognition on the part of the people of Israel of their own unfaithfulness to the covenant and, therefore, their experience of exile and foreign domination; and the hope of Israel that God's people might be "raised up"—that is, restored and established in a position of regency in the renewed cosmos. Resurrection-belief was thus cultivated in Israel's experience of exile, and in its radical understanding of God's justice. "The Old Testament God—the Creator, the Source of life, and the Lord of life—undoubtedly *could* raise the dead. That he *would* do so only became clear once death was perceived as contradicting God's righteousness and God's love."[13]

It is true, of course, that some Jews in the Second Temple period would not have shared hope in the resurrection. Luke, for example, distinguishes the Sadducees as persons who did not believe in the resurrection (Acts 23:8), and this characterization is echoed by the Jewish historian Josephus.[14] Nevertheless, we are able to identify the primary contours of resurrection belief among the Jewish people, and these help us to know what categories of interpretation might have been available to those who first heard the Christian proclamation of resurrection.

First, resurrection signals the end-time restoration of Israel and triumph over its enemies. Resurrection marks God's vindication of the righteous who have suffered unjustly; having been condemned and made to suffer by a human court, the righteous will in the resurrection be vindicated in the divine court. That is, proclamation of "the resurrection" is synecdoche for the eschatological restoration of Israel and, then, the advent of the messianic age, with its implications for cosmic renewal, the "new heaven and new earth." Second, and closely related, resurrection marks the decisive establishment of divine justice, where rewards and punishments are meted out in relation to the character of one's life before death. Injustice and wickedness will not have the final word, but in the resurrection will be decisively repudiated. Third, although space must be carved out for a certain pluralism at this point, generally speaking, Jewish perspectives on life-after-death continued to embrace a view of the human person as a psychosomatic unity, so that belief in resurrection typically did not entail the expectation of the liberation of the immortal soul from the mortal body.[15]

The Disciples and the Resurrected Jesus (Luke 24:36-49)

Our concerns with the nature of life beyond the grave and continuity of personal identity from life to life-after-death are not of recent vintage, even if they now receive heightened attention on account of recent work in neurobiology and the philosophy of mind. These closely related issues are woven into the fabric of Luke's account of the postresurrection appearances; this is signaled, first, in the priority given the (in)ability of people to recognize Jesus (see Luke 24:16, 31, 35); and, second, by Jesus' emphatic claim, "It is I myself," or "It is really me!" (my translation, 24:39).

Luke's presentation of the resurrected Jesus takes two routes at once, so as to demonstrate his corporeality without allowing his physicality to determine exhaustively the form of his existence.[16] On one side of the ledger is evidence that Jesus' postresurrection, bodily existence was out of the ordinary. He disappears and appears suddenly (24:31, 36), in the same way that an angel appears to Cornelius (Acts 10:30) and reminiscent of angels in Israel's Bible (e.g., Gen. 18:2; Dan. 8:15; 12:5).[17] His appearance is elusive, both to the two disciples on the Emmaus road (24:15-16) and to his followers gathered in Jerusalem (24:36-37). Indeed, the latter regard him as a "spirit," a "ghostly apparition," the disembodied residue of a dead person. It is difficult not to see in the disciples' responses a dualist anthropology; accordingly, in their imaginative categories, they were encountering a disembodied spirit, a phantasm. This analysis of things is flatly contradicted by Jesus, who immediately demonstrates that he is no ghost.

On the other side of the ledger, Jesus goes to great lengths to establish his physicality. As Luke will later observe, here Jesus begins to present himself "alive to them by many convincing proofs" (Acts 1:3)—an observation that urges our contemplation of the essential physicality of "life." Importantly, then, Jesus grounds the continuity of his identity ("It is really me!"), first, in his materiality, his physicality—in the constitution of flesh and density of bones: "Look at my hands and my feet; see that it is I myself. Touch me and see; for a ghost does not have flesh and bones as you see that I have" (24:39). Here is no phantom, no vision, no spirit-being. Jesus presses further, requesting something to eat, then consuming broiled fish in the presence of his disciples (24:41-43). Do angels eat? David Goodman asks this question,[18] noting that, from the second century BCE, it was axiomatic that angels did not eat ordinary, earthly food. Thus, for example, speaking to Tobit and Tobias, "Raphael, one of the seven angels who stand ready and enter before the glory of the Lord," observes, "Although you were watching me, I really did not eat or drink anything—but what you saw was a vision" (Tob. 12:15, 19). In Luke's report of Jesus' postresurrection existence, we find no witness to resurrection as escape from bodily existence (as one would expect if a Platonic dualism were presumed here), nor is it possible to confuse Jesus' postmortem existence with that of an angel; his, rather, is a transformed materiality, a full bodily resurrection.

The meal scene Luke briefly recounts serves a further purpose, however. It bears witness to Jesus' physicality, then serves to guarantee the postmortem persistence of Jesus' personal identity in yet another way—namely, by re-establishing within the Lukan narrative Jesus' fellowship with his disciples at the table. Within the third Gospel, meal scenes often provided Jesus with opportunity for disclosure of his mission (e.g., Luke 5:27-32; 14:15; 19:1-10) and, in the Emmaus episode, of his identity (24:30-31, 35). The eating scene Luke mentions here (see also Acts 1:4; 10:41) invites multiple layers of significance: restored fellowship with Jesus, Jesus' self-disclosure, material evidence of his resurrected status, and opportunity for teaching and discussion.[19] He is not only capable of eating, but actually initiates a resumption of the table fellowship that had characterized Jesus' ministry in Galilee and en route to Jerusalem. Hence, the postresurrection persistence of Jesus' identity is established, first, with reference to his physicality and, second, with reference to relationality and mission.

Luke thus navigates between two of the most popular views for imaging the afterlife—the one more barbaric, the other more sophisticated. First, he shows that Jesus' disciples did not mistake him for a cadaver brought back to life, a reanimated corpse. Luke distinguishes Jesus' resurrected body from the resuscitated bodies of the widow's son in Nain (7:11-17), Jairus's daughter (8:40-42, 49-56), Tabitha (Acts 9:36-43), and Eutychus (20:7-12). Second, he certifies that neither is Jesus an "immortal soul" free from bodily existence. Jesus is present to his disciples, beyond the grave, as a fully embodied person. What is more, his affirmation concerning himself could not be more emphatic: "It is I myself!" "It is really me!"—intimating the profound continuity between these phases of his life: before crucifixion and after resurrection.

To Luke's readers, the evidence marshaled thus far may seem to be enough, but the narrator gives no indication that, to this point, the doubts of Jesus' disciples have been laid to rest. Instead, Jesus moves immediately to a third kind of evidence: "Then he said to them, 'These are my words that I spoke to you while I was still with you—that everything written about me in the law of Moses, the prophets, and the psalms must be fulfilled'" (Luke 24:44). Here is the move Jesus makes: He weaves a story; or, rather, he picks up the story that is already present, the one in the Scriptures, within which, throughout his ministry, he has sought to inscribe himself. In an essential sense, his identity is lodged there, in the grand story of God. What is more, he shows that the Scriptures themselves can be read aright only with reference to him, only insofar as they are actualized in the continuity of his person from life to crucifixion and afterlife, in resurrection.

This Lukan emphasis may seem strange to people of the West in the early twenty-first century, accustomed as we have become to notions of personhood that place a premium on self-actualization and self-legislation. As Jürgen Moltmann helpfully summarizes, our anthropology is "dominated by the will to give the conscious mind power over the instrument of the body," but this emphasis stands in stark contrast to concerns with embodiment, relationship, and narrative so at home in the world of Israel's Scriptures.[20] The Israelite has a sense of self above all in relation to the people of God, and this in relation to the covenant and promises of the God of Israel. Personal identity is found in the historical narrative within which people live, in relation to the divine vocation given that people.

As Luke presents it, Jesus' identity is not grounded simply in his existence as a human being, but in terms of his relationship to God, his vocation within the purpose of God, and his place within the community of God's people—past, present, and future. And all of this comes together in a grand convergence in his resurrection. This is not death leading to the flight of the soul, freed from the encumbrance of a physical body, but the means by which the people of God would experience end-time restoration as God's people. This is not resurrection understood as escape, but as embrace; in his career we find Jesus embracing the whole of God's work, from creation to exodus to exile and, now, New Exodus, as God's purpose working itself out in the world. Jesus' identity is lodged profoundly in the grand story of God—which, then, can only be grasped in reference to his crucifixion and resurrection. Resurrection is not soul-flight, but the exclamation point and essential affirmation that Jesus has placed on display for all to see a life of service, even the service of life-giving death, and that this life carries with it the divine imprimatur, actualizing as it does God's own redemptive project.

Excursus: From Death to Resurrection

Prior to moving on to Paul's notion of the "resurrection body," it may be useful to follow briefly one more path of inquiry. According to Luke's narrative, Jesus died about 3:00 P.M. on a Friday (23:44) and was buried just before sundown (23:54), but early on Sunday morning his tomb was found empty (24:1-3) and he was seen later that day on the road to Emmaus (24:13-16). What happened to Jesus between Friday afternoon and dawn on Sunday? Perhaps better, where was Jesus between his death and resurrection?

According to the longer version of the Apostles' Creed, "he was crucified and buried; he descended to the dead"—a tradition that made its way into the church as an article of faith as early as the *Fourth Creed of Sirmium* (359 CE). Related to this article is the notion that, between his death and resurrection, Jesus preached to those in hell.[21] In spite of the fact that I have framed our question with reference to Luke's account, his Gospel evidences no interest in a descent into hell, and the only biblical text that might be of direct assistance is 1 Peter 3:18-20:

> For Christ also suffered for sins once for all, the righteous for the unrighteous, in order to bring you to God. He was put to death in the flesh, but made alive in the Spirit, in which also he went and made a proclamation to the spirits in prison, who in former times did not obey, when God waited patiently in the days of Noah, during the building of the ark, in which a few, that is, eight persons, were saved through water.

This passage bristles with difficulties, the two most pressing being: To whom did Christ go? and, When did Christ go? Because "spirits" (*pneuma*, "spirit"), used in an absolute sense, does not typically refer to humans (and especially not to disembodied humans!),[22] and because of the close parallels this text shares with the Jewish book *1 Enoch*, most scholars regard Peter's "spirits" as the fallen angels of Genesis 6:1-4.[23] Note how this view coheres with the subjugation to Christ of "angels, authorities, and powers" in 1 Peter 3:22 and the more general motif in 1 Peter of the triumph of Christ over the powers of evil. According to the tradition associated with the Creed, Jesus' proclamation to the spirits would have taken place between his death and resurrection; this view finds no basis in 1 Peter, however. Instead, Peter has it that the resurrected Christ preached to "the spirits" after having been "made alive in the Spirit"—that is, after his resurrection. In short, 1 Peter does not take us very far toward answering our question.

Can anything more be said? If we take seriously the perspective on spacetime developed by Charles Gutenson,[24] we can appreciate how limited are the horizons within which we typically struggle to answer our question, Where was Jesus between his death and resurrection? "Where" Jesus was cannot be examined apart from the question of "when," and we cannot assume that "when" ought to be measured in identical ways from our earthbound perspective and from God's.

The most straightforward answer to our question is given within Luke's narra-tive: "Today," Jesus says to the criminal crucified alongside him, "you will be with me in paradise" (23:43). What—or, rather, "when" and "where"—is "paradise"? The term itself, *paradeisos*, originally referring to a "park" or "nobleman's estate," is used in the Greek versions of Genesis 2 for Eden (cf. Ezek. 28:13; 31:8 LXX); given the apocalyptic notion that the Beginning would be mirrored in the End, the term was used for the final, paradisal state enjoyed in the new creation. "Paradise" appears only three times in the New Testament (Luke 23:43; 2 Cor. 12:4; Rev. 2:7); though we cannot assume that its significance in Luke must be measured in relation to other New Testament usages, it is of interest that, in Revelation, the term connotes the end-time consummation of God's purpose with its image of the restoration of divine presence and provision: "To everyone who conquers, I will give permission to eat from the tree of life that is in the par-adise of God." Paul's description in 2 Corinthians 12 of being "caught up to the third heaven . . . caught up into paradise" associates paradise with the third heaven in a way that is reminiscent of several texts from Jewish apocalyptic, both in terms of the notion of a heavenly journey and with regard to the numbering of the heavens; this language is at home in a thought-world that presumes that the first Eden (i.e., "paradise") was kept sealed in anticipation of the End, and, again, signifies life in the presence of God.[25] In the literature of Second Temple Judaism, Paradise could be used with reference simply to heaven, the divine abode and place of bliss, without temporal indicators.[26] It might refer to an inter-mediate abode of the righteous,[27] though most often it refers to the end-time dwelling of the righteous with God.[28] Interestingly, in the text outside of Luke's Gospel that contains the only other known reference to the "bosom of Abraham" (see Luke 16:19-31), "Paradise" is also found, and is used with refer-ence to dwelling in heaven immediately upon death (*Testament of Abraham,* 20:14).

Given Gutenson's perspective on spacetime, read together with the testimony of Jesus in Luke 23, then, we recognize that Jesus could be taken up into God's presence immediately upon death even if, from the vantage point of earth-time, the period measured from late on that tragic Friday afternoon to early on that stunning Sunday morning elapses between death and resurrection. Where was Jesus? Jesus was with God.

The "Resurrection Body" at Corinth

The theological focus of Luke's message of salvation is the resurrection.[29] Hence, though it is impossible to survey all of the New Testament material relevant to our questions about the resurrection, so abundant is the evidence related to this central ingredient of early Christian belief that our decision to focus on a key text in Luke-Acts hardly needs justification. The pivotal role of Paul in New Testament theology is unassailable, and this alone provides reason enough to turn our attention, secondly, to his epistolary witness to the resurrection. As it happens, resurrection-belief constitutes an important battleground in the Paul-Corinth correspondence, and this controversy comes into focus above all in 1 Corinthians 15. Here, then, is Paul's most sustained discussion of the resurrection.

Why Paul engages in an extended discourse on the resurrection at the end of his first letter to the Corinthians remains a matter of debate, though we should presume with most scholars today that Paul's theological concerns are motivated by issues intrinsic to the situation in Corinth and otherwise on display in his correspondence with them. Since Paul's primary stated objective in 1 Corinthians is to restore unity (1:10), the proposal made by Dale B. Martin concerning the nature of the Corinthian situation is especially attractive.[30] Following customary practice in the Roman world, persons of high status in Corinth, Martin suggests, would have extended hospitality to itinerant philosophers and thus have been exposed to more sophisticated notions about the afterlife. For them, Paul's talk of the raising of the dead would have been reminiscent of fables about the resuscitation of corpses, the stuff of popular myths. Taught to degrade the body, they would have found Paul's teaching about the resurrection incomprehensible, even ridiculous. Indeed, for them, salvation would have constituted escape from the physical world, not an eschatological affirmation of bodily existence. Those of lower status, to whom Paul can refer as "those who have nothing" (11:22), on the other hand, would have been incapable of welcoming itinerant philosophers into their homes and, thus, would have lived apart from their influence. They would have had closer contact with superstitions and popular myths, including those relating the resuscitation of corpses and the endowment of those corpses with immortality. Remembering the aim of this letter to catalyze unity, Paul's challenge is to represent the resurrection belief of early Christianity with enough sophistication to communicate effectively with those of high status while not alienating those of lower status. Even if Martin's position might deserve further nuance, it nevertheless makes good sense that Paul is struggling with a Corinthian Christian community within which something of the diversity of Greco-Roman views surrounding the afterlife was present and that this lack of agreement was playing havoc both with the integrity of the church and with this central claim of the Christian gospel.

In 1 Corinthians 15, Paul defended belief in the future resurrection by (1) appealing to what had already become Christian tradition (vv. 1-11), (2) observing that a denial of the future resurrection was tantamount to denying the resurrection of Christ, and moving on to an affirmation of Christ's resurrection as "first fruits" of the future resurrection (vv. 12-34), and (3) sketching how one might plausibly conceive of the resurrection of the dead (vv. 35-58). Of particular importance to us is this last subsection, 15:35-58, where Paul turns from the "what" of the resurrection to the "how," and, among other things, affirms the following: (1) There is a profound continuity between present life in this world and life everlasting with God. For human beings, this continuity has to do with embodied existence. (2) Present human existence, however, is marked by frailty, deterioration, and weakness, and is therefore unsuited for eternal life. Therefore, in order for Christian believers to share in eternal life, their bodies must be transformed. Paul does not here think of "immortality of the soul." Neither does he proclaim a resuscitation of dead bodies that might serve as receptacles for souls that had escaped the body in death. Instead, he sets before his audience the promise of their transformation into glorified bodies (cf. Phil. 3:21). (3) Paul's ideas are, in part, rooted in images from the natural world and, in part, related to the resurrection of Jesus Christ. As it was with Christ's body, Paul insists, so it will be with ours: the same, yet not the same; transformed for the new conditions of life with God forever. (4) For Paul, this has important meaning for the nature of Christian life in the present. For example, this message underscores the significance of life in this world, which many Christians at Corinth had not taken seriously. We should not imagine that our bodies are unimportant, then, or that what we do to our bodies or with our bodies is somehow unrelated to eternal life (cf. Col. 1:24).

For our purposes, a key concern revolves around the nature of the resurrection body, to which the NRSV unfortunately refers as "a spiritual body" in contrast to "a physical body" (15:44). At the very least, Paul underscores an essential continuity grounded in the import of the body to human existence and identity in this life and in life-after-death. The distinction Paul draws is between the *sōma psychikon* and the *sōma pneumatikon*. The first expression is drawn from Genesis 2:7, which has it that Adam was created a living *psyché* ("life" or "vitality," often translated as "soul"); hence, the first Adam was a *psychikos* body. (Note: neither Paul nor Genesis communicates that Adam had such a body, but rather that he was one.)[31] However, as is manifestly evident, this body was subject to death and decay on account of sin and, therefore, was ill-suited to eternal life with God. What is needed, then, is a different form of existence, which is given us by the last Adam, Christ, who does not simply receive life (as in the first Adam), but actually gives it. "Thus it is written, 'The first man, Adam, became a living being' [*psychēn zōsan*; citing Gen. 2:7]; the last Adam [Christ] became a life-giving spirit" (15:45). As a consequence, whereas the *sōma psychikon* is a body provided by God and well-suited for this age, the *sōma pneumatikon*, also provided by God, is well-suited for the age to come.

Characterizing the resurrection body in contrast to ordinary bodily existence in this world, Paul observes, "What is sown is perishable, what is raised is imperishable. It is sown in dishonor, it is raised in glory. It is sown in weakness, it is raised in power. It is sown a physical body, it is raised a spiritual body" (15:42-44). This helps further to distinguish the ordinary human body (perishable, inglorious, weak) from the resurrection body (imperishable, glorious, powerful) at the same time that it presses the question, What is the source of this new body? How is it constituted?

Paul insists that the first Adam was dusty, the second Adam heavenly, and in doing so makes use of the physical science of his world (15:47-49).[32] That is, *ek gēs choikos* ("[of] dust of the earth") and *ex ouranou* ("of heaven") refer to the nature of two kinds of body—the one made up of the stuff of the earth, dust, and thus well-suited to earthly life; the other made up of heavenly stuff, and thus well-suited to life in the heavens. This portrait of resurrection was not unique to Paul. Kevin Anderson has drawn attention to a belief in astral immortality which was widely held by the time of the Roman Empire. This is abundantly attested in such epitaphs as this one: "Mother, do not weep for me. What is the use? You ought rather to reverence me, for I have become an evening star, among the gods."[33] In the tradition of Israel, too, stars could be associated with heavenly beings or angels, so that eternal life might be cast as an angel-like existence. In Daniel 12:3, "those who are wise shall shine like the brightness of the sky, and those who lead many to righteousness, like the stars forever and ever." Star imagery was deployed to indicate royal position, so that we should hardly imagine that Daniel's expectation centers on an actual celestial transformation. Rather, the restoration of Israel is effected through resurrection, with astral imagery evoking enthronement.[34] Paul's language description of the resurrection body, "raised in glory" (15:43), easily finds a home among these ideas.

What is more, by referring to the resurrected body with the modifier *pneumatikon*, Paul clarifies that the form of embodied existence in the resurrection is given through Christ (himself a "life-giving spirit") and determined by the Spirit of God. As Anthony Thiselton translates it, God has provided for this age "an ordinary human body," "a body for the human realm," but, in the resurrection, God will provide "a body for the realm of the Spirit."[35]

In this way, Paul speaks to the nature of the resurrection body (i.e., one chosen by God, free from decay and weakness) and the agency through whom the body is transformed (it is God's doing), while holding in tension his vision of both a transformed body and an organic continuity between our present, mortal existence and our transformed existence. Even if, as Paul avers, "flesh and blood cannot inherit the kingdom of God" (15:50), it remains the case that the world-to-come will be inhabited by embodied persons. What is more, the transformation leading to a nonperishable existence is the consequence of (and not preparation for) resurrection. That is, nothing in the created human being is intrinsically immortal.[36] Resurrection and embodied afterlife are God's doing, divine gift.

If *continuity* is marked by embodied existence in this life and in the resurrection, the question remains how the "me" that is really "me" makes the transition into resurrected life. That is, if the question for the Corinthians must have focused above all on the nature of the *body* ("But someone will ask, 'How are the dead raised? With what kind of body do they come?'" [15:35]), we may nevertheless wonder, How does what "dies" "come to life"? (15:36). How can continuity of personal identity be sustained? We have seen that, in Luke 24, physicality, relationality, and narrativity comprise an answer to this question. What of Paul?

Importantly, when Paul's thought moves into this arena, he does not use the language we might expect, had we imagined that he had been decisively influenced by a dualist anthropology; words like "spirit" or "soul," which we might have anticipated from a dualist anthropology, are not found in these contexts.[37] Rather, he uses personal pronouns, together with the notable phrases *sun Christō* ("with Christ"; e.g., Phil. 1:23; cf. 2 Cor. 5:8) or *en Christō* ("in Christ"; e.g., 1 Thess. 4:16). These are not phrases descriptive of an essentialist ontology; they do not address issues of substance. Rather, they express "my" existence, the persistence of personal identity, in profoundly *relational* terms.

Epilogue: Resurrection and Identity

Finally, let me tease out some ways in which these exegetical and theological reflections bear on our portrait of the human person. In doing so, it will be useful to begin in conversation with a relevant consideration from the neurosciences. First, even for the nondualist, it is problematic to imagine that human identity is constructed or sustained solely in material terms. This is because, right up to the moment of death itself, the body is constantly remaking itself with cells being sloughed off and replaced at sometimes astonishing speeds. Even if the genesis of new brain cells, neurons, in adults is comparatively limited,[38] this does not mean that the brain is static throughout our lives. At a basic level, formative influences are encoded in the synapses of the central nervous system (those points of communication among our neurons); as those neural connections that are used are maintained and remodeled, those connections that fall into disuse are eliminated, and fresh connections are generated in response to our experiences. Drawing attention to the fundamental, neurobiological reality that human beings are always in the process of formation, Joseph LeDoux observes, "People don't come preassembled, but are glued together by life."[39] Even if our genes bias the way we think and behave, the systems responsible for much of what we do and how we do it are shaped by our experiences, our relationships, by learning. If this is true, then how can we speak of continuity of person identity?

Taking seriously the relevant considerations from our exegetical work, together with the evidence we have from the neurosciences, let me propose that our identity is formed and found in self-conscious *relationality* with its neural correlates and embodied *narrativity* or formative histories. By "formative histories," I do not mean "history" in an objective sense as "what really happened," but the stories within and by which we come to make sense of the events of our lives and world; hence, I prefer the term "narrative," which suggests a particular way of telling the story of our lives. What I want especially to underscore here, though, is that who we are, our personhood, is inextricably bound up in our physicality, and so is inextricably tied to the cosmos God has created, and in the sum of our life experiences and relationships. This perspective coheres well with Nancey Murphy's argument that personal identity focuses on human moral character and social relations, with their neural substrate; and with Charles Gutenson's perspective, which accords privilege to "my nested existence in a web of relationships as well as the profound impact those relationships have on my own identity."[40]

This means, second, that death must be understood not only in biological terms, as merely the cessation of one's body, but as the conclusion of embodied life, the severance of all relationships, and the fading of personal narrative. It means that, at death, the person *really* dies; from the perspective of our humanity and sans divine intervention, there is no part of us, no aspect of our personhood, that survives death.

Third, we have seen in the New Testament material we have examined that belief in life-after-death requires embodiment—that is, re-embodiment. And this provides the basis for relational and narrative continuity of the self. It also begs the question, How are we capable of traversing from life to life-after-death? Simply put, we are not. The capacity for resurrection, for transformed existence, is not a property intrinsic to the human person (nor to the created cosmos). This is, as Paul emphasizes, God's doing. Even if our transformed lives in Christ in this world anticipate, they do not constitute eschatological existence. The glorious, bodily transformation of which Paul speaks is the consequence of resurrection, not preparation for it. How, then, is personal identity sustained from this world to the world-to-come? On the one hand, Paul locates the answer to this problem under the category of "mystery" (1 Cor. 15:51-57). On the other, he hints at a relational ontology—that is, the preservation of our personhood, "you" and "me," in relational terms: *with Christ, in Christ*. This suggests that the relationality and narrativity that constitute who I am are able to exist apart from neural correlates and embodiment only insofar as they are preserved in God's own being, in anticipation of new creation.

This reminds us, again, that the capacity for "afterlife" is not a property of humanity, but is a divine gift, divinely enacted. It also underscores the reality that, in eschatological salvation, we are not rescued from the cosmos in resurrection, but transformed with it in new creation.

CHAPTER 8

Emergent Dualism

Challenge to a Materialist Consensus

William Hasker

These are heady times for all who are interested in the sciences of the mind and the brain. New imaging techniques such as magnetic resonance imaging enable us to map the living brain with a precision never before possible. Positron emission tomography provides a window into brain functioning by registering precisely the parts of the brain that are active in performing particular tasks. Careful study of cognitive deficits due to brain injury has led to greatly increased knowledge of the ways in which specific forms of cognitive processing depend on the integrity of particular regions of the brain. And increasing understanding of the brain's chemistry has led not only to a better appreciation of the role played, for instance, by neurotransmitters, but also to effective therapies for psychological illnesses that had formerly proved highly resistant to treatment.

Nor have things remained static on the psychological side. The long shadow of the Freudian mystique has finally lifted. Behaviorism no longer has a monopoly on the claim to be a "scientific" psychology. Cognitive psychology, less arbitrary than Freudianism and far more open to subjective, conscious experience than behaviorism, continues to flourish. New approaches to therapy are being devised, and to a greater extent than previously, objective studies are used as a check on their effectiveness.

To be sure, caution is still very much needed. Impressive successes in some directions can lend encouragement to claims that far outrun the available evidence. The interpretation of evidence can be biased by unexamined assumptions. And the temptation for the scientist to don the prophet's robes can be hard to resist. This is amusingly illustrated in the words of a leading brain researcher who writes, "I would be foolish to make predictions about what can and cannot be discovered or about when something might be discovered and the route of a discovery." Wisely said, one might think! But in the very next sentence he goes on, "Nevertheless, it is probably safe to say that by 2050 sufficient knowledge of biological phenomena will have wiped out the traditional dualistic separations of body/brain, body/mind and brain/mind."[1] Presumably the reader is not intended to draw the logical inference that the author is foolish!

All of us have strong reasons to be concerned with these developments. Psychologists will welcome the enhanced understanding of mental and cognitive processes, and those who are practitioners will desire to apply effective therapies and to abandon those that are less effective. Theologians need to assimilate well-confirmed scientific information about the person in order to develop a responsible theological account of personhood. And effective pastoral counseling needs to be guided in part (but only in part) by what is known scientifically about both the functioning and the malfunctioning of persons. An equally difficult task awaits philosophers, who need to bring together, to the extent humanly possible, the diverse insights and approaches of brain researchers, cognitive psychologists, theologians, and others into a coherent and comprehensive perspective. I must acknowledge that of late philosophers have not always been willing to undertake this task of synthesis, but it continues to be very much needed, and the present topic is a case in point.

This task in its entirety is not one that we can undertake here; indeed, we are still, in many ways, in the early stages of exploration that might eventually lead to such a synthesis. What we can and must do is focus on a few central issues on which consensus is, if not essential, then at least extremely desirable if anything like a common perspective among Christian psychologists, theologians, and philosophers is to emerge. Of course it may be that in even alluding to the possibility of a consensus I am being wildly optimistic. Certainly, in many respects we have needed to learn to live, and to function as professionals, without consensus—except, perhaps, a limited consensus on the most basic elements of our common faith, a consensus which is presupposed by our professional efforts rather than being their result. Yet if we believe that there is indeed a "way things are," and if our concern is in part to find out what way that is, then intractable disagreement about core assumptions is not something we can accept with equanimity as a permanent condition, however unavoidable it may be for the short run.

An important starting point for our mutual exploration is to ask the ontological question: *What is* this mind, this self, the "thing that thinks"? The more plausible kinds of answers to this question tend to fall into two broad groups, loosely designated as dualism and materialism. According to dualism, the human person is a compound of two elements. There is the physical part of a person, the body, and there is another component of a fundamentally different nature, called mind, or soul, or spirit. The body is the subject of the normal physical attributes of size, shape, mass, motion and rest, and so on, but not of attributes involving consciousness, such as thought, emotion, and sensation. The mind is the subject of mental attributes: it reasons, decides, feels emotion, and so on, but has no physical attributes whatsoever, not even location.[2] According to materialism, on the other hand, the person in some sense is the body; it is the single, unified self that walks along the street, poses for pictures, and devises novel theorems in mathematics. There is just one "thing," and that thing is the familiar body we see each day in the mirror.

While the ontological debate has been dominated by the antithesis between dualism and materialism, this antithesis has itself been the subject of much dissatisfaction. Attempts to transcend the antithesis are numerous, but any such attempt must be closely scrutinized in order to see whether it is resolving problems or simply hiding them under confusing terminology. In a way, this essay is itself such an attempt. It is my contention that both dualism as it has traditionally been understood, and materialism in all its current versions, are inadequate as accounts of the human person. In contrast with both of these I shall present, as my own entry in the competition, a theory that I term "emergent dualism." But in order to motivate the consideration of emergent dualism it will be necessary to spend some time pointing out the inadequacies of both materialism and traditional dualism.

This critical attention will not be equally distributed between materialism and dualism. For some audiences, long accustomed to think in dualistic terms, it would be essential to demonstrate at length the difficulties of such views in order to motivate an alternative. But I believe many of us are in a different situation. We philosophers, at least, have drunk deeply, as if with our mothers' milk, of the doctrine that mind-body dualism suffers from severe and intractable difficulties. (One might say, both the calcium from the milk and the aversion to dualism are by now "bone-deep.") Without doubt, the secular consensus regards some sort of materialist view as inescapable, even though there remain numerous differences over the details. And among Christian scientists, philosophers, and theologians there is a substantial movement to embrace some form of "Christian materialism," though here there is a distinct effort to safeguard in the process those aspects of human personality that are of special importance for Christian faith. In view of this, my procedure in the remainder of this essay will be as follows: First, I shall set out very briefly the main reasons I believe traditional dualist views are unsatisfactory. Then, we will consider at somewhat greater length the objections to materialist theories, including those now being promoted by Christian scientists and philosophers. Finally, I shall present emergent dualism as a view that satisfies many (but not all) of the desiderata prized by both dualists and materialists, and that avoids many (but again, not all) of the objections lodged against those two views.

Difficulties with Dualism

First, then, some brief remarks about mind-body dualism.[3] And I must begin by saying that some of the popular objections to this view are ill-conceived, or at best far from decisive. There is, first, the ancient, and by now extremely boring, objection that causal interaction between diverse substances, such as mind and body are alleged to be, is impossible. Once we have recognized that, as Hume long ago taught us, *all* causal relations are at bottom conceptually opaque, this hoary objection should be relegated to its appropriate place in the dustbin of history. Somewhat more plausible is the complaint that dualism leads to the denigration of the body, or to an undue alienation between the immaterial soul, conceived as the "true person," and the body in which that soul is temporarily domiciled. But while this may be a fair criticism of some historical versions of dualism, the feature objected to is by no means a necessary or inevitable ingredient in dualism as such. That it is not is clearly displayed in the "integrative dualism" developed by Charles Taliaferro.[4] Taliaferro's ontology is basically Cartesian, but he holds that in practical experience mind and body form an integral unit, so that I live through my body and my body's life is my own life.

Nevertheless, I come to bury Cartesian dualism, not to praise it! Even after the complaints mentioned have been set aside, there remain severe problems for the theory—problems which, in my experience, Cartesians are neither very willing nor well able to address. One of these is the Dependency Problem: Cartesian dualism would certainly not lead us to expect the detailed, fine-grained dependence of cognitive functioning on brain function that we find to be the case. Once this dependency is spelled out in some detail, it becomes more and more difficult to maintain the *independence* of mind from brain and body that is the hallmark of Cartesianism. The mind is "the thing that thinks"—perhaps so, but only, it seems, when supported in a very intricate and detailed fashion by cerebral processes, with specific sorts of information-processing depending on very specific portions of the brain. So far as I have been able to find out, Cartesians have no plausible explanation for this dependency, which goes far beyond anything their theory would lead us to expect.

The other leading problem for Cartesianism is the Continuity Problem. Biology shows us clearly that, in spite of the uniqueness of humans in certain respects, there is a great deal of similarity between us and other mammals in both structure and function. Furthermore, there is a fairly complete continuu stretching between humans, as the "highest" lifeform, and progressively lower forms such as fish, octopuses, insects, and bacteria. The challenge for the dualist is to say which, if any, of these other creatures possess immaterial souls. Unfortunately, it seems that any possible answer will be implausible, or embarrassing, or both at once. Descartes put the matter nicely, when he said that if animals "could think as we do, they would have an immortal soul as well as we, which is not likely, because there is no reason for believing it of some animals without believing it of all, and there are many of them too imperfect to make it possible to believe it of them, such as oysters, sponges, etc."[5] Descartes's own solution was to limit souls to humans and consider all other animals as mindless automata, incapable even of sensation. That solution has few defenders today, and for good reason. But to attribute souls only to "higher" animals—say, mammals and birds—still creates a strong impression of arbitrariness, not to say chauvinism. And on the other hand, the farther down the scale we go the harder it becomes to keep a straight face about the resulting picture. Remember that beings that have Cartesian souls—rather, that are Cartesian souls—are essentially immaterial and nonspatial, and are only contingently embodied. So we have the prospect of an earthworm that is akin to us in this regard—"brother Worm," as Charles Taliaferro once remarked! Furthermore, we shall have to say that God specially creates individual souls for worms, gnats, and even intestinal parasites! There is more that could be said about this, but for the present I propose to drop the curtain on this scene, so that we can go on to consider views with greater contemporary resonance.[6]

Materialism and Reduction

In this section I will not be considering the more blatantly reductionist views of the mind, such as eliminative materialism and logical behaviorism. Such views are seldom attractive to Christian scientists and scholars, and this is so precisely because they are so obviously hostile to Christian concerns about the human person. Christians who wish to be materialists or physicalists are usually keen to insist that they are *nonreductive* materialists or physicalists. Rather than conclude that humans are *nothing* but biological processes, they insist that we are that indeed, but also much, much more. Instead of buying into what D. M. MacKay called "nothing-buttery," they are firmly committed to "both-and-ism."

So far, then, so good. Both-and-ism is undeniably superior to nothing-buttery as a banner under which to march. Unfortunately, would-be nonreductionist views all too easily betray themselves by accepting assumptions that undermine the claim that human persons are "more than" mere biological processes. This is true of secular philosophical theories, as Jaegwon Kim pointed out in his American Philosophical Association presidential address, "The Myth of Nonreductive Materialism."[7] And it is equally true of the efforts of some of our "Christian materialists," as I shall attempt to demonstrate in this section.

105

As a way of focusing our discussion, the following remarks will be centered around the views expressed in the widely circulated book, *Whatever Happened to the Soul?*[8] Among the contributors to that volume, it is Nancey Murphy who most directly addresses the issues involved in reductionism.[9] In her discussion, Murphy provides a number of important clarifications, including definitions of various kinds of reductionism. She defines *ontological reductionism* (a position which she endorses) as the view that "as one goes up the hierarchy of levels, no new kinds of metaphysical 'ingredients' need to be added to produce higher-level entities from lower." Specifically, "no immaterial mind or soul is needed to get consciousness" (129). *Causal reductionism*, on the other hand, is defined as "the view that the behavior of the parts of a system (ultimately, the parts studied by subatomic physics) is determinative of the behavior of all higher-level entities" (128). With these definitions in mind she asks, "Is it possible to accept ontological reductionism without causal reductionism?" (131). To her credit, Murphy recognizes that the answer to this question is crucial for the viability of her entire enterprise. She writes, "If free will is an illusion and the highest of human intellectual and cultural achievements can *(per impossibile)* be counted as the mere outworking of the laws of physics, this is utterly devastating to our ordinary understanding of ourselves, and of course to theological accounts, as well, which depend not only on a concept of responsibility before God, but also on the justification (not merely the causation) of our theories about God and God's will" (131).

In addressing this question, it is important to realize Murphy is assuming that the standard laws of particle-interaction known to physics[10] govern all such interactions without exception. (For ease of reference, I shall designate this view as *microdeterminism*.)[11] But given this assumption, it is hard to see how causal reduction can be avoided. The larger entities, after all, are wholly composed of the particles of microphysics, and it would seem that the behavior of all such entities will be exhaustively determined by the behavior of the constituent particles. And this is the definition of causal reductionism.

Murphy previously thought she could escape this consequence through the use of the philosophical notion of the *supervenience* of mind on body (132-38). More recently, however, she has acknowledged that this defense against the charge of causal reductionism does not succeed.[12] And this means that she needs to look elsewhere, if she is to avoid causal reductionism.

Another notion used by nonreductive physicalists in order to stave off reductionism, one which is also endorsed by Murphy,[13] is what is known as "downward causation." To develop this notion, start with the idea of reality as organized hierarchically into a number of levels—say, inorganic, organic, mental or conscious, social, and perhaps others. What characterizes the higher levels is not new, additional elements that are added: there are no entelechies or immaterial souls. (Murphy's ontological reductionism is accepted.) Rather, we have novel forms of *structure and organization*, but these novel forms really do make a difference; there really is something new in the world as a result of their appearance.

Given this much, we can raise the question of causality: What is it, in this picture of the world, that exerts causal influence? In a great many cases, causality is "bottom-up": the behavior of higher-level entities is determined by what happens on the lower levels. The contention that *all* causality is of this sort is characteristic of causal reductionism. The thinkers we are now discussing, however, reject this: we must also consider "top-down" causality, in which wholes which exist at the higher levels exert a "downward" causal influence on the parts of which they are composed. In this way, then, causal reductionism is avoided. According to Roger Sperry,

> The principle of control from above downward, referred to as "downward causation," . . . says that we and the universe are more than just swarms of "hurrying" atoms, electrons, and protons, that the higher holistic properties and qualities of the world to which the brain responds, including all the macrosocial phenomena of modern civilization, are just as real and causal for science as are the atoms and molecules on which they depend.[14]

In order to complete the picture, we need to emphasize that, for typical advocates of this view, microdeterminism is strongly affirmed. Says Sperry:

> The expectation that downward macrodetermination should thus effect reconfigurations . . . in the neuron-to-neuron activity of subjective mental states—or in the micro components of any macro phenomenon—indicates a serious misunderstanding of what emergent interaction is. From the start I have stressed consistently that the higher-level phenomena in exerting downward control do *not disrupt* or *intervene* in the causal relations of the lower-level component activity. Instead they *supervene* in a way that leaves the micro interactions, per se, unaltered.[15]

It is easy to see why this notion of downward causation has seemed appealing. It seems to give everybody what they most want: the physicist keeps the uniformity and universal applicability of the fundamental laws of nature; the anti-dualist strain in modern thought is appeased through the banishment of souls and their ilk, and yet the psychologist, and perhaps the theologian, are allowed, by invoking upper-level causality, to go their own ways and carry on their business without the frustrating and futile attempt to consider everything in terms of fundamental physics. Unfortunately, downward causation so understood is a cheat and a fraud; it is a pernicious notion that can only be a source of confusion.

The idea of reality as organized into hierarchical levels, to be sure, is plausible and appealing, and there is no need to reject it. But the terminology of levels can mislead one into thinking of the different levels as concrete and as capable of exerting, on their own, distinct kinds of causal influence. It is as though one were thinking of a multistoried building, in which almost everything that reaches the upper stories comes in through the ground floor, but occasionally something comes down from the upper stories—say, a telephone call containing orders or instructions—that makes things on the ground floor go differently than they would otherwise have done. Such a picture is seriously misleading. The higher levels are levels of *organization*, not concrete entities. The only concrete existents involved are the ultimate constituents and combinations thereof, and the only causal influences are those of the ultimate constituents in their interactions with each other. If the higher-level organization is to make a difference, it can only do this by *affecting the interactions of the constituents at the base level*—but this it is forbidden to do by the thesis of microdeterminism. Causal reduction has in no way been avoided. This diagnosis of the situation is borne out by the examples we are given. Sperry again:

> A molecule within the rolling wheel, for example, though retaining its usual inter-molecular relations within the wheel, is at the same time, from the standpoint of an outside observer, being carried through particular patterns in space and time determined by the over-all properties of the wheel as a whole. There need be no "reconfiguring" of molecules relative to each other *within the wheel itself*. However, *relative to the rest of the world* the result is a major "reconfiguring" of the space-time trajectories of all components in the wheel's infrastructure.[16]

It is true, of course, that the wheel's component molecules move differently in relation to the rest of the world because they are part of a rolling wheel than they might otherwise—if, for example, they were part of a fragment of metal lying on the ground. But the macroscopic movements of the wheel as a whole are themselves quite thoroughly explicable in the reductionist style, in accordance with "bottom-up" microdeterminism. The example entirely fails to illustrate the point for which it was invoked. Downward causation, defined as Sperry, Murphy, and others have defined it, fails entirely to defeat causal reductionism. And this failure creates a serious situation for Murphy and other advocates of nonreductive physicalism. Unless some new strategy can be devised, the dire consequences of causal reductionism which Murphy previously acknowledged are now staring them in the face.

In fairness I must acknowledge that there is a way in which the notion of downward causation can be made coherent. In order to do this, it is necessary to acknowledge, as was suggested above, that the higher-level organizational properties *affect the interactions of the constituents*—that the protons, electrons, and other micro-objects, when placed in these complex configurations, behave differently, and follow different laws, emergent laws, rather than the laws that govern their ordinary interactions apart from such higher-level organization. Or perhaps it is better to say that, given the presence of the higher-level organization, *novel causal powers* emerge, powers which were not detectable in simpler configurations of the same elements.[17] The philosopher who has most clearly articulated such a view is Timothy O'Connor, and his work on this topic deserves careful consideration.[18] There is a price to be paid for this, of course; the thesis of microdeterminism must be abandoned, and the patronage of those who insist on the inviolability of the laws of physics may be lost. Nevertheless, I strongly recommend this view to nonreductive physicalists. So far as I can see, it is the only possible way in which they can honestly earn their claim to be nonreductive—though some may as a result challenge their right to be called physicalists.

Materialism and the Unity of Consciousness

The objections to materialism are not yet exhausted. Even a truly nonreductive materialism, one that recognizes the existence of emergent causal powers that affect the interactions of the ultimate particles, faces serious additional difficulties. One such difficulty concerns the unity of consciousness. Leibniz points out the problem as follows:

> In imagining that there is a machine whose construction would enable it to think, to sense, and to have perception, one could conceive it enlarged while retaining the same proportions, so that one could enter into it, just like into a windmill. Supposing this, one should, when visiting within it, find only parts pushing one another, and never anything by which to explain a perception. Thus it is in the simple substance, and not in the composite or in the machine, that one must look for perception.[19]

The difficulty here does not lie, as some have thought, in the fact that Leibniz's example was limited by seventeenth-century technology. If, instead of his "parts pushing one another," we fill the machine with vacuum tubes, transistors, or for that matter with neurons, exactly the same problem remains. The problem does not lie in the pushes and pulls but rather in the *complexity* of the machine, the fact that it is made up of many distinct parts, coupled with the fact that *a complex state of consciousness cannot exist distributed among the parts of a complex object.* The functioning of any complex object such as a machine, a television set, a computer, or a brain, consists of the coordinated functioning of its parts, which working together produce an effect of some kind. But where the effect to be explained is a *thought*, a state of consciousness, what function shall be assigned to the individual parts, be they transistors or neurons? Even a fairly simple experiential state—say, your visual experience as you look at the page upon which this argument is set down—contains far more information than can be encoded in a single transistor, or a single neuron. Suppose, then, that the state is broken up into bits in such a way that some small part of it is represented in each of the parts of the computer or the brain. Assuming this to be done, we have still the question: *Who or what is aware of the conscious state as a whole?* For it is a fact that *I am aware* of my conscious state, at any given moment, as a unitary whole. If I am told that this "I" *does not really exist,* and that my supposed unitary awareness of my present conscious state really consists of small bits of my brain each representing some small part of my visual field—if I am told this, I shall turn sadly away, realizing that either my interlocutor is deeply confused, or else he or she (or it, or they), which I have mistakenly taken to be a person with whom I have been conversing, is an entity fundamentally different from myself with regard to the matter under consideration.

So we have this question for the materialist: When I am aware of a complex conscious state, what physical entity is it that is aware of that state? This question, I am convinced, does not and cannot receive a plausible answer. In spite of this (or perhaps because of it), the question seems an elusive one; it slips away from us before we can fully appreciate its anti-materialist implications. The reason for this, I believe, is that we covertly supply a subject of awareness—a unified consciousness of some sort—that *brings together* the bits of information separately registered in different parts of the brain, and grasps them as a single, unified experience. Now, I have no doubt whatever that such a unified consciousness does in fact exist. But this consciousness is itself neither a brain, nor any part of a brain. *A person's being aware of a complex fact does not consist of parts of the person being aware of parts of the fact.*[20] Once we grasp this, materialism is seen to be in deep trouble.

Materialism and Resurrection

Yet another difficulty with materialism, for those of us who are Christians, is found in "the life of the world to come." The ordinary, naive believer naturally assumes that, if there is to be a future life, there must be a soul that survives after the body has perished. But it has become fashionable, in recent years, to make a sharp distinction, even an antithesis, between immortality of the soul and resurrection of the body, and to claim that it is resurrection rather than immortality that is crucial for Christian faith. This in turn is seen as favorable to materialism, which cannot affirm the immortality of a soul that does not exist, but has no difficulty with the resurrection—or so we are told.

Unfortunately, materialism does confront a severe problem in giving a plausible account of the resurrection.[21] This problem concerns the difficult topic of *personal identity:* In what sense is the resurrected person the *same individual* as the one who previously perished? In order to see the problem, let me rehearse a pair of truisms. First, my interest in a life to come hinges on those who enjoy that life being the *very same individuals* as those who previously lived in this world. "I myself will see him with my own eyes—I, and not another," said Job (19:27 NIV), and I hope and believe that this will indeed be the case. And when I hope, by God's grace, to be reunited with my parents and other departed loved ones, it is *those very individuals* that I expect to meet once again—not other persons extremely similar to them, however close the resemblance might be.

The other truism is slightly more philosophical in flavor, but still I think clear enough. Identity—in this case, personal identity over time—is a necessary relation, one that, if it holds at all, could not possibly fail to hold. I who am writing these words am the very same individual as one who, quite a number of years ago, entered into marriage with my wife. Assuming this to be true, I *could* not be distinct from that individual, for this would mean being distinct from myself, which is absurd. Furthermore, it is out of the question to suppose that anything true about some other individual—someone distinct from me here and now—could have any bearing on whether I am, in fact, identical with the person who took those marriage vows.

I hope you will agree with me that these two propositions—that identity of persons over time is crucial for the resurrection, and that identity is a necessary relation—are indeed truisms. Unfortunately, materialism is unable to honor them. Materialist views of the resurrection assert that, at some time after my death, God will *re-create* an assemblage of atoms (it probably does not matter whether they are the *very same* atoms or not) which is extremely similar (though probably not *exactly* similar) to me as I was before I died. And, the story goes on, this re-created individual will be I, myself. But suppose that, at the same instant, someone were to create *another* individual, either exactly like the re-created Hasker, or slightly *more* similar to the Hasker who perished?[22] In either of these cases, the re-created Hasker would not be identical with the one who had died. At best, we would have two presently existing individuals with an *equal claim* to be so identical—but since both cannot be identical with Hasker-who-died, neither is so. But this means that the identity of Hasker-re-created with Hasker-who-died depends on the nonexistence of another equal or superior claimant to that status, and this violates the necessity of identity. And this, in turn, means that the relation between Hasker-re-created and Hasker-who-died is *not* identity, but rather some kind of similarity relation. But if it is only *persons similar to us* who shall enjoy the blessings of heaven then we should wish them well, but we ourselves have no personal stake in the matter.[23]

I am well aware that the argument, thus briefly stated, may be difficult to follow for those not accustomed to these topics. Nevertheless, I believe it is both sound and, upon sufficient reflection, compelling. If I am right, then for Christians, at any rate, it can serve as the final nail in the coffin of materialism, which we can lay to rest with no hope or desire to see it resurrected.

Emergent Dualism

And now at last the time has come to unveil the view that, I hopefully assert, constitutes the best answer to the knotty problems that assail both materialism and traditional dualism.[24] A key notion for leading us beyond the impasse is that of *emergence*, an idea that has a natural appeal to those who have become mistrustful of both dualism and reductive materialism. The central idea is that when elements are organized into certain complex wholes, something genuinely new comes into being, something that is not reducible to nor explainable in terms of the elements. This general idea is capable of being developed and applied in a wide variety of ways and in many different contexts. In the early part of the twentieth century various sorts of emergentist views were widely held among philosophers and scientists, but subsequently they went into eclipse. In recent years, however, there has been a resurgence of interest, if not yet widespread acceptance.

For the particular development of emergentism that is of interest here, we start with the idea that human beings, and other animals, are entirely composed of ordinary physical stuff. To this extent, the view agrees with Murphy's ontological reductionism that "as one goes up the hierarchy of levels, no new kinds of metaphysical 'ingredients' need to be *added* to produce higher-level entities from lower." Still, the view is not really reductionist, as we shall see. One thing that prevents this is the step that has already been recommended to nonreductive materialists. We must acknowledge that "the higher-level organizational properties [e.g., in the brain] *affect the interactions of the constituents*—that the protons, electrons, and other micro-objects, when placed in these complex configurations, behave differently, and follow different laws, *emergent* laws, rather than the laws that govern their ordinary interactions apart from such higher-level organization." We can also say that "*novel causal powers* emerge, powers which were not detectable in simpler configurations of the same elements." These novel powers must, to be sure, be in some way already implicit in the physical "stuff," otherwise their emergence would be sheerly magical. But they do *not* follow from, and are not resultant from, any causal powers that are detectable in simpler configurations. Rather, they become evident when, and only when, the appropriate complex configuration of the base elements comes into existence. It is only because of such emergent powers that the mind, and with it the brain and body, can become genuinely responsive to rational and teleological considerations, so that we can act for a *purpose*, can think with the goal of *reaching the truth*, and can be guided by *rational principles* in so doing. Only in this way can we avoid the consequence pointed out by Murphy, that "the highest of human intellectual and cultural achievements can . . . be counted as the mere outworking of the laws of physics," a consequence which, as she rightly says, would be "utterly devastating to our ordinary understanding of ourselves" as well as to our theology. Such *property-emergence* is, I insist, an indispensable step that must be taken if we are to avoid a reductive materialism.

But property-emergence is not enough. It opens the way for the organism to behave in ways that are responsive to rational and teleological considerations. But it still does not address the problem pointed out by the unity-of-consciousness argument: It does not account for the *unitary conscious individual* that knows, and chooses, and acts. So in order to account for this, we must posit that, given the appropriate configurations of elements, a *new individual* emerges, a conscious self which has a unitary experience of the disparate items of information coded in various parts of the brain and which, given that awareness, *makes decisions* and *initiates actions* which the organism as a whole then carries out. Very briefly stated, then: the view is dualist, in that it posits a continuing, unitary, *psychic individual* that is distinct from the biological organism. But it is an *emergent* dualism, because the mental individual *emerges from* the organism and is sustained by it; it is not (as in traditional dualism) a separate element *added to* the organism from outside by divine fiat. An analogy I have often used to explain this is that of the "fields" known to physics, such as the magnetic field and the gravitational field, which are generated by physical objects yet distinct from them. And I believe this analogy can be helpful, but it needs to be kept in mind that it is only an analogy; it is not a literal description or an explanation and still less a proof that the theory is true.[25]

Given this much, it becomes possible to see how the view can respond to the objections leveled at both dualism and materialism. The chief difference from traditional dualism, of course, lies in the fact that the "conscious field" (as I have sometimes called it) is *generated and sustained* by the biological organism, not "added to" the organism from outside. And this means that the thorough, systematic dependency of mental processes upon brain processes comes as no surprise. The details of this dependency, to be sure, can only be spelled out by the brain researchers. Philosophers and theologians have no competence to strike out on our own in this area, but we need to be ready to assimilate the evidence as it continues to emerge, and emergent dualism leaves us fully able to do this. The key difference from Cartesian dualism on this point is that there is *no* presumption, for emergent dualism, that the conscious mind should be able to operate on its own independently of what goes on in the body and brain.

So the Dependency Problem is not a problem for emergent dualism, but neither is the Continuity Problem. Since the conscious field emerges from the appropriate configuration of the biological organism, we should naturally expect this emergence to take place in a wide variety of organisms. Less complex and sophisticated organisms will have less complex and sophisticated minds; that is what we should expect if the minds are generated by the organisms. We will not be embarrassed by the thought that termites and mosquitoes have souls, but neither will we be forced to burden God with creating those souls, and with disposing of them when they are no longer needed. To be sure, there remains the question of what sort of evidence we have that is relevant to the existence of awareness in the simpler creatures, and of what conclusions should be drawn from that evidence. But emergent dualists are free to follow the evidence wherever it leads them; their metaphysical views lead to no awkwardness whatever on this score.

Many of the advantages of emergent dualism over materialism are implicit in what has already been said. Causal reductionism is averted by the invocation of emergent causal powers—powers of the organism that are not reducible to, or deducible from, the powers exhibited by the elementary particles in isolation or in simpler configurations. The need for an experiencing self, as pointed out by the unity-of-consciousness argument, is met by the emergence of the conscious, experiencing individual. Furthermore, the emergence of the unitary conscious self enables us to make sense of free will in a way that is not otherwise possible. A meaningful act of free choice must, it seems, be an act of the person *as a whole*; it cannot be simply the "resultant" of forces and tendencies generated by fragmentary, subpersonal parts of the individual. A viable doctrine of libertarian free will must, in my opinion, make use of the notion of agent causation.[26] And emergent dualism, unlike materialism, enables us to give a coherent answer to the question, "*What is* this unitary self that decides?"

Finally, there is the question of emergent dualism and life after death. It should be said at once that emergent dualism does not lend itself to a doctrine of natural immortality. If anything, the tendency of the view is in the opposite direction: It recognizes the intimate dependence of mental functioning on brain function, and there is no particular reason to expect that the mental functions can be performed when the relevant parts of the brain have ceased to operate. The fact remains, however, that the conscious self is a *distinct individual*, not identical with the physical organism or any part of it. As such, it is capable of existing, if sustained by divine power, in the absence of the organism. For the mind to be able to function in such a state, God would need not merely to sustain its existence, but to supply in some way the kinds of support needed to replace the role normally played by the brain in generating and sustaining the field of consciousness. So emergent dualism, unlike Cartesian dualism creates no presumption that the souls of beasts should survive. Furthermore, the theory underscores the fact that eternal life is a gift of divine grace and not a natural endowment of the creature. It also recognizes the fact (which is also acknowledged by Thomistic dualism) that disembodied existence is a truncated and abnormal state of the person, one that cries out for the re-embodiment that takes place in the resurrection.

All this is not to say that emergent dualism is free from objections. Materialists will think it is too dualistic, while many dualists will object that it is too close to materialism. (A friend once compared me to a Civil War soldier who went into battle wearing a blue shirt and gray pants!) For myself, I am inclined to think that the greatest difficulties are found in the rather remarkable powers this theory attributes to ordinary matter. There is, to begin with, the power to generate consciousness itself—a power, to be sure, that all noneliminativist materialist theories must also ascribe to matter, though no one has any idea how the trick is done. Then there are the emergent causal powers attributed to matter both by my theory and by property emergence theories such as that of

O'Connor. These powers are essential if we are to avoid the pitfalls of causal reductionism. Yet most materialists will reject them, insisting on the universality and completeness of the laws of a completed physics. And finally, there is the power to generate the field of consciousness, the mind or self. Even O'Connor, who has gone with us most of the way, says that "the idea of a natural emergence of a whole substance is perhaps a lot to accept."[27] And I will admit that these are astonishing powers to attribute to mere ordinary, physical stuff. Yet there is something to be said on the other side, before writing all this off as impossible. It is fairly clear that, in spite of all we have learned about matter, our grasp on its fundamental nature remains tenuous in the extreme. The billiard-ball atoms of early modern science were readily graspable by the intellect, however remote they may have been from the truth about the world. Matter as conceived in quantum mechanics, on the other hand, can be represented in incredibly accurate mathematical formalisms, but we are very far indeed from grasping what it truly is. As Richard Feynman has said, "nobody understands . . . why nature behaves in this peculiar way."[28]

The other consideration to which I would point is found in our common faith that this "ordinary" matter is the creation of a God whose wisdom and power far exceed our comprehension. And this God has told us that he created us from the dust of the earth—so we have no choice, really, but to suppose that he endowed that dust with the powers required to enable the rich and various creation that he proposed to fashion from it. It may be that in the end only belief in the power of such a creative God can make emergent dualism a viable and credible hypothesis.

CHAPTER 9

Time, Eternity, and Personal Identity

The Implications of Trinitarian Theology

Charles E. Gutenson

The question of the constitution of human persons (Are we material, non-material, or some combination thereof?) presents a constellation of related questions. Further, matters as complex and involved as this one require consideration at a number of levels: scientific, theological, philosophical, exegetical, and so on. Any proposal will be satisfactory only to the extent that it can adequately address issues raised at any of these levels. In this chapter, although I shall exercise care to assure that proposals are coherent with the relevant scientific data, the focus will be primarily upon matters theological and philosophical. In particular, I intend to address a pair of questions that deal with the continuity of human existence: (1) Should we assume an intermediate state of human existence between death and the general resurrection? (2) What set of conditions or states of affairs assure that some person, who is present in resurrected life, is the continuation of the life of the same person in this life? The road to addressing these questions begins with examination of the nature of time and eternity.

Time and Eternity

We may grant that our analysis of the nature of time and eternity, as well as God's experience of them, will require us to engage in some speculation; this is because there is disagreement within the tradition on the matter, and because no definitive position can be developed from direct appeal to God's own revelation. However, if we might paraphrase Aristotle, one should not be concerned about this as long as one does not engage in more speculation than the subject allows. The literature on time and eternity generally presents only two viable options. As David Braine correctly notes, however, there are actually three.[1]

The first I will call the "commonsense" position. This view holds that God takes up a temporal location much as humans do. The past recedes from God, no longer to be present to him, though, by virtue of his omniscience, his "memory" of the past is infallible, and thus, to speak of the past "receding" from God is to say a very different thing than to say the past "recedes" from humans. Similarly on this view, God looks ahead in anticipation to what might happen in the future. Of course, God knows precisely what *he* intends to do at some future date, and God's ability to "guess" at what might happen in the future is far better than our own. According to this position, while God takes up a temporal position, he transcends time by virtue of his everlastingness—that is, his existence had no beginning, never comes to an end, and is never dependent upon anything outside himself. This view of time is most frequently held by process theologians, open theists, and some portion of "persons on the street."

The second position is generally called Augustinian timelessness, since the celebrated fourth-century bishop was the first to articulate it. According to this view, God exists outside of time in what is often called a "timeless realm." From there, God is able to observe all time in undivided wholeness.[2] There is no "past" or "future" to God's experiencing; rather, God experiences the totality of human experience so that all stand before him in undivided wholeness. Sometimes a spatial analogy is deployed. Accordingly, a human located at the earth's surface observes a relatively small portion of the surrounding landscape. However, lift the same person above the earth's surface, and that person will be able to observe a much larger portion of the surrounding landscape. Analogously, God, located outside of time, can observe all of human times together. The Augustinian position has a rich history within the tradition and is still widely held today.

The third position is often conflated with the preceding position, creating the illusion that there are only two theories. This third position is often called the "eternalist" position, and it can be traced back at least to Plotinus, the third-century father of neo-Platonism. It differs in one very important aspect from the Augustinian position. Whereas Augustinian timelessness relegates God to some "timeless realm" outside normal space-time, the eternalist position conceives of God as having all times in actual, undivided *presence*. God is not "outside" time, but rather is most preeminently "in time." Again a spatial analogy: So conceiving God's experience of time is to see him as "temporally omnipresent." Just as God is spatially omnipresent and, as such, has all *space* in actual presence,[3] so God is "temporally omnipresent" in that he has all times in actual presence. So, again, the primary difference between the eternalist position and the Augustinian is that, with the latter, a wedge is driven between God's actual presence and his creation, whereas in the former God is preeminently present to his creatures.

A reasonably thorough treatment of these matters would require a monograph-length work. Consequently, I shall summarily recount the reasons for finding the first two theories inadequate, and then present the "eternalist" perspective. Let me begin with Augustinian timelessness. Nelson Pike illuminates the difficulties with conceiving the interaction of a "timeless" God with the world of creatures.[4] What would it mean, for example, to say that an atemporal being engages in temporal actions? Further, conceiving God in some timeless realm seems to leave the world devoid of his actual presence. In fact, Pannenberg makes the same point when he argues that the Augustinian position leads to an overemphasis upon the transcendence of God and conceives eternity and time in opposition. Consequently, a person holding the Augustinian position is left with inadequate means to affirm the divine immanence. As regards the "commonsense" position, Stump and Kretzmann articulate one problem: "No life that is imperfect in its being possessed with the radical incompleteness entailed by temporal existence could be the mode of existence of an absolutely perfect being."[5] Furthermore, as one might expect, Pannenberg argues that the commonsense view overemphasizes the immanence of God. God is present to his creatures, but his transcendence of creation is merely his "everlastingness." Does this not make God, at every *actual* instance, another finite being?[6] Consequently, one holding the commonsense position is left without adequate grounds for affirming the divine transcendence.

Let us now turn to the third position. According to the eternalist, all times are actually present to God in complete and undivided wholeness. God knows things in their temporal sequence, but the divine life is not such that it experiences them in this way. More specifically, events do not fade from God's presence into the past as they do for humans, nor must God wait in anticipation of the future; rather, he holds all times in actual presence so that the divine life is not subject to the temporal fragmentedness experienced by creatures. Some have argued that this position is either incoherent or unintelligible. In light of contemporary theories about the nature of time and space, both claims are, I think, mistaken. Two claims from these theories are particularly relevant: first, that the speed of light is the limiting velocity of objects in space-time; and second, that, as objects approach that velocity, the passage of time slows. Many are familiar with the thought experiment based upon the age relationship between twins when one remains on earth while the other travels at relativistic speeds (i.e., speeds near that of light) to a nearby star and back. The twin who remains on earth ages along with the rest of us, while the traveler ages at a significantly reduced rate. In fact, if traveling at the speed of light, no time would pass for the second twin—though, of course, it would for everyone else.

How this refutes the claims of incoherency and unintelligibility is obvious. If God were traveling around the universe at the speed of light, absolutely no time would pass for him while the entirety of universal history would pass for the rest of the cosmos. In a very real sense, all history would stand before God "at once" due to the differing experiences of time in the differing referential frames. Although I do not argue that God is zipping around the universe at the speed of light, one can see that contemporary theories about the composition of, and laws governing, possible motion within the space-time universe obviate the claim that the eternalist conception of the divine experience of time is either incoherent or unintelligible.

For a general theist, there would be little else to say. I have made suggestions concerning God's experience of time; the next step would be to consider how these suggestions might guide our proposals aimed at resolving the questions raised at the outset. However, I am not a general theist; I am a Christian theist, and as such, one who embraces certain claims about the nature of God. For example, one of the central tenets of the Christian faith is that the one God exists, not merely as an individual subject, but as three persons. I believe this has bearing on the matter at hand.

In their sketch of *Twentieth-century Theology*, Grenz and Olson use the themes of transcendence and immanence for their study of the development of theology.[7] They consider properly balancing these two themes as one of the critical problems of modern theology, and we have already noted that Pannenberg thinks that both Augustinian timelessness and the "commonsense" view fail in this regard. In fact, Pannenberg has asserted that the problem of God's transcendence and immanence is not resolvable apart from conceiving God as a differentiated unity.[8] Bringing these matters together, the doctrine of the Trinity allows us to conceive the Father as the transcendent one; specifically, the Father holds all the times of the creatures in actual presence. However, by virtue of the fact that the three persons are but one God, we can say that "God" holds all times before him in undivided unity. The Son and the Spirit are sent into salvation history for the purpose of reconciling the world to God. Thus, they take up temporal location alongside the creatures, being immanent to them in all their places. Again, we can say that "God" is immanent to the creation. Consequently, the doctrine of the Trinity provides resources for moving beyond an abstract affirmation of the transcendence and immanence of God.

By now, the reader may suspect how these notions may be deployed to answer the query concerning an intermediate state. Let us, however, make this explicit.

The Necessity of an Intermediate State

There seem to be three reasons Christians affirm the existence of an intermediate state. First, a majority of Christians, I suspect, hold a dualistic anthropology that holds that humans are comprised of matter and spirit, generally expressed as a physical body and an immaterial soul (often assumed immortal). An immortal soul, once created, would continue to exist. Second, humans die at different times and, as best we can tell, the general resurrection has not yet occurred. It seems to follow that there is some intermediate state where the immortal soul "resides" during the period between death of the body and the general resurrection. Third, some Christians observe that Jesus seems to provide an account of persons present in such an intermediate place (Luke 16:19-31).[9] In short, we must affirm a state of existence for immortal souls after death, but before the general resurrection, because Jesus himself so believed. It should be noted that not all Christians have felt inclined to draw this conclusion; in fact, the Christian tradition on this matter is far more ambivalent than is commonly recognized.[10] For example, Anabaptists tended to embrace a position known as "soul sleep," according to which the first two points above are affirmed, but the third is not. They believed that there is an intermediate *state*, but not an intermediate *place*. The state is analogical to human sleep; so the soul continues, but does not exist consciously. Obviously, holders of this position have no problem concluding that, whatever points Jesus intended to convey, say, in Luke 16, they are not intended to answer questions about the period between a person's death and the general resurrection. Must we, however, affirm the existence of an intermediate state at all? I believe the answer to whether we must is clearly no; and in fact, there are good reasons to believe the answer to whether we *should* affirm the existence of such an intermediate state is also no.

One could simply deny the need for an intermediate state on the grounds that there is no existing reality that requires it—that is, one could reject dualistic conceptions of the human person on the grounds that there are no such things as immaterial souls that exist independently of one's physicality. There is adequate evidence to demonstrate that one need not be a crass materialist to embrace such a position. For example, one might affirm the existence of resurrected life, but simply deny the existence of an immaterial soul, and then hold that God re-creates persons at the time of the general resurrection, leaving persons nonexistent in the meantime. A variety of objections have been raised to this "re-creation" proposal, but none seem particularly persuasive.[11] However, there is another alternative.

I have argued for the superiority of the eternalist position regarding the divine eternity, and it is now appropriate to consider how the eternalist position would influence our speculation about the necessity of affirming an intermediate state.

Recall that the eternalist conceives God's experience of time such that the entire course of universal history stands before him in undivided wholeness. For God, the general resurrection is just as present to him as the moment of anyone's death, and thus from God's perspective there is no interim time period between one's death and the general resurrection. The eternalist does not assert that the passage of time as experienced by humans is an illusion any more than the physicist who notes that the experience of time is different for persons in different frames of reference. So, God's experience of time and eternity is real as is the human experience, though they are quite different.

For the Christian, to think of human existence in any frame of reference is to conceive life as sustained by the gracious relationship between the person and God as the giver of life. We are left, however, to speculate about what happens to that relationship when one's physical body dies. We have noted both the proposal that the dissolution of the body means the dissolution of the person as well as the proposal for an intermediate state; but what if we need to think about this in an entirely different way? What if we need to think of human existence after death not as continuing some*where* else, but rather more like some *when* else? Perhaps as one dies, the aspects of our created reality that cause us to "see through a glass darkly," those aspects that create epistemic distance between us and God, those aspects that prevent fully experiencing God's presence, begin to break down, so that in essence we are taken up into the divine eternity. What would that be like?

According to the eternalist, it would quite possibly mean experiencing time as God does through the dissolution of the fragmentariness of human existence and an awakening to an experience of life in undivided wholeness. When one dies, perhaps it is not merely the totality of that life, but the whole of history which appears to that person in undivided wholeness. Consequently, to those taken up into the divine eternity, the general resurrection would be just as present as the moment of their death. For them, there would be no interim period before the general resurrection; rather, to die is to be present to the general resurrection, and thus to be ready for participation in resurrected life. Accordingly there would be no need to posit an intermediate state.

Of course, the issue is not what God could or could not do, but rather what our best speculations allow us to conclude that God has actually done. Is it possible that God has created humans with ontologically distinct physical bodies and immaterial souls? Of course. Could God have also decided to create a cosmic holding tank for disembodied or quasi-embodied souls? Certainly. However, one wonders why he would have done so, and until we have better reasons to think he has, we should, with a nod to Ockham, embrace the simpler position made possible by the eternalist conception of the divine eternity and pare away the unnecessary metaphysical claim of an intermediate state.[12] We turn now to the question of personal identity, beginning with an assessment of the nature of personhood.

Human Personhood

To address the constitution of personal identity, we must first consider what it means to speak of humans as persons and what underlying concepts determine personhood. Generally speaking, attempts to define human personhood have tended to be rooted in one of two underlying ontologies: a substantialist (or essentialist) ontology or a relational one. According to the substantialist, the primary ontological category is that of "substance," and perhaps the oldest form is that conceptualized by the Greeks according to which all reality is composed of substance and accidents. All things were conceived as composed of an underlying substratum, or substance, and all physical manifestations were conceived as accidents of those prior substances. Accidents include weight, extension, color, and so on. As one might expect, attempts to speak of pure substance, which underlies physical matter, tend to get one entangled in confusion, as when Origen, in *First Principles*, spoke of pure substance as being intelligible (that is, nonmaterial) and imaginable merely as a point. What it means exactly to speak of a pointlike, nonmaterial substance that underlies the physical manifestation of objects is a puzzlement to me. It seems it would be difficult to distinguish "pure substance" so understood from nothingness. In a similar vein, Hegel would later respond to Kant's distinction between phenomena and noumena, saying that "things in themselves" (something akin to pure substance, prior to outward relations) are empty abstractions. For these reasons, it is evident that attempts to make sense of a thoroughly substantialist ontology are problematic at best, and as such, attempts to ground human personhood in a thoroughgoing substantialist ontology are likewise problematic.

An alternative is a relational ontology, for which the primary ontological category is relation. Here, talk of a substance existing antecedently to material objects would be, as Hegel noted, to engage in meaningless abstraction. In a relational ontology, the various objects of the world are constituted by their various relations. Weight, extension, location, and the like can all be conceived as relations between and among objects. Some theorists have taken relational ontologies to an extreme by making claims to the effect that a given object "just is its relations." However, one wonders precisely what this means—especially in light of the fact that the very term "relation" implies that some "things" stand in some sort of reciprocity with each other, "things" that are neither antecedent to nor independent of but which must be, in some sense, distinct from relations. In other words, although it is difficult to make sense of pointlike substances underlying material objects, it is equally difficult to see how the notion of substance can be allowed entirely to dissolve in favor of a purely "relational" ontology. Both "substance" and "relation" must be retained if an intelligible ontology is to be deployed. The question for us is how the notions of relation and substance are to be understood in a discussion of human personhood.

It is interesting that one of the more fertile periods in the historical development of the concept of person was the early church's attempt to articulate the doctrine of the Trinity. This deserves some serious reflection, for if the manner in which the Christian tradition understood the concept of person, as applied to humans, is to be derived from the development of the trinitarian doctrine, important implications for our discussion follow. The tradition was painfully aware that the developing doctrine of God had to avoid both tritheism and modalism. Consequently, it had to be able to answer the question about the unity of God without equivocation while yet affirming the reality of the distinctions of the persons. Further, it has become clear that the trinitarian persons must be understood in a way that precludes conceiving them as first three independent persons and then one God, for this would give the impression that three divine subjects, through an act of the will perhaps, voluntarily function as one God. At the same time, however, the doctrine of God cannot develop in a way that conceives the three persons as merely the manifold expressions of the self-same divine subject. This gives the impression that the persons are only figurative ways of speaking and that they do not have any real distinctiveness. Neither position could be an adequate expression of the Christian doctrine of God.

One way around this difficulty is to conceive the persons *themselves as relationally constituted,* so that one really ought not to speak of the Father as God or the Son as God or the Spirit as God without reference to each one's constitutive relations. Of course, this language is sometimes deployed, notwithstanding the fact that it opens the door to misunderstanding. To use the term Father is already to imply the Son, as Athanasius noted as early as the third century. Furthermore, in speaking of the inner-trinitarian life of God, relational concepts such as "begottenness," "procession," and "perichoresis" were deployed by the early church to express the relationality of the Trinity as revealed in salvation history. Consequently, we should say that the Father cannot be conceived as God except as the Father of the Son, and the One who sends the Son and the Spirit into the world; the Son cannot be conceived as God except as the Son of the Father and the One who is sent by the Father to do only what he sees the Father doing; the Spirit cannot be conceived as God except as the Spirit that binds the Father and the Son and who glorifies the Son and in him, the Father. In other words, the three persons are only personal in light of the constitutive relations they enjoy with each other, and they are only thereby the one God.

Unfortunately, the importance of this early insight into the relational composition of personhood has waxed and waned. For example, we have the definition given by Boethius in the sixth century: "a person is an individual substance of a rational nature." Here, the focus is away from the relational aspect of personhood in favor of individuality with rationality assuming primacy. This movement has been further exacerbated through the modern period, which has tended to overemphasize rational autonomy as the core of personhood. Is it the case that the individualistic and rationalistic aspects of personhood rise when the implications of the trinitarian doctrine drop out of sight? Do we inevitably fall into predominantly substantialist categories—even if more implicitly than explicitly—if we do not allow the doctrine of the Trinity to remind us of the profound relationality of the divine life? I suspect that a reasonably thorough examination would demonstrate a good deal of support for answering these questions in the affirmative. Nevertheless, we have seen a resurgence of trinitarian theology of late as well as a corresponding appreciation for a more communal and, hence, more relationally constituted concept of personhood.

How do these points inform our understanding of personhood? Obviously, if the very concept of personhood developed primarily along relational lines as part of the early Christian church's developing doctrine of God, we need to proceed by considering the extent to which relationality ought to inform our understanding of personhood. Gunton makes the connection explicit: "To be made in the image of God is to be endowed with a particular kind of personal reality. To be a person is to be made in the image of God: that is the heart of the matter. If God is a communion of persons inseparably related, then surely Barth is thus far correct in saying that it is in our relatedness to others that our being human consists."[13] In other words, to be made in the image of God is to exist as a person of a particular type—namely, one analogous to the personal existence of Father, Son, and Spirit. Since the personal being of the members of the Trinity is constituted by their inter-relations, the relational concept of personhood must, at least analogously, apply to human persons. If the trinitarian persons are constituted by their relations one with another, we must ask what sorts of relations are constitutive for human personhood.

Gunton argues that the constitution of human personhood unfolds along two lines: our relatedness to God and our relatedness to other creatures. Since all human existence is tainted by sin, Gunton rightly observes the manner in which this is addressed through our relationship with God:

> We are persons insofar as we are in right relationship to God. Under the conditions of sin, that means, of course, insofar as the image is reshaped, realised, in Christ. But since we are here enquiring about human createdness, we shall leave that in the background, a very real background, nevertheless. The relation to God takes shape through the Son and the Spirit. To be in the image of God is to be created through the Son, who is the archetypal bearer of the image. To be in the image of God therefore means to be conformed to the person of Christ. The agent of this conformity is God the Holy Spirit, the creator of community. The image of God is then that being human which takes shape by virtue of the creating and redeeming agency of the Triune God.[14]

This rich statement deserves some expansion.

First, I am inclined to agree with Gunton's assessment that we are persons only to the extent we are in right relationship to God; perhaps one could say that we are not fully personal otherwise. This might seem problematic, since I am concerned with a theory of personal identity that includes Christian and non-Christian alike. I do not think this the case, however, since to say that one is not *fully* personal apart from right relationship to God is not to say that one is not personal *at all* apart from that relationship. Second, Gunton does not appeal abstractly to God, but rather speaks of specific formative effects that follow from our relatedness to the appropriate trinitarian persons. In particular, the Son is both the original agent of creation, as reported in John 1, and, by virtue of the incarnation, represents the express image, as human, of the divine life. If we are to be formed by this image of the divine life, however, we must be shaped by the Spirit, for the Spirit is the agent empowering the formation of humans into the image of Christ. While Gunton mentions the Father only indirectly, it is the Father who sends the Son and the Spirit into human history and is, thus, the initiator of the divine rescue mission. Finally, Gunton connects the idea of human personhood with the formative work of the triune God. We are persons only as we become increasingly conformed to the image of Christ. It is only as these relations between humans and the triune God unfold that humans become what God has always intended—persons after the model of the divine life. The extent to which human personhood is mediated to humanity—or rather, is constituted *for* humanity through relationships with Father, Son, and Spirit—is profound. However, it is not only through these relationships that humans are constituted as persons.

Perichoresis is the term the early church fathers used to describe the self-giving of the inner life of the Trinity. The Father gives himself to Son and Spirit, holding nothing back; the Son gives himself to the Father and the Spirit, holding nothing back; and the Spirit, likewise, gives himself to the Father and the Son, holding nothing back. If human persons are to conform to the image of Christ, some aspect of human personhood must be constituted by relationships, not just between humans and God, but also between humans; that is, human personhood is partially constituted by mutually perichoretic relationships between humans. Gunton observes, "This means, first, that we are in the image of God when, like God but in dependence on his giving, we find our reality in what we give to and receive from others in human community. One way into the content of the image, its concrete realisation, is through the concept of love."[15] So, personhood is relationally constituted, both with regard to our relatedness to God and our relatedness to each other.

It is now time to draw together these various threads. To exist as a human person is to exist in a complex web of relationships: relationships with Father, Son, and Spirit, as well as with other personal and nonpersonal creatures. The personal development of each and every human is profoundly affected by the nature of these relationships. Who I am, the specificity of my own personal existence, is critically dependent upon the others with whom I have community. Although one must affirm the existence of an enduring "I" that serves as the subject of my actions and the relatively absolute aspect of personhood, we also need what has been called the "self"[16]—the aspect of "me" that is influenced by inner and outer relations. Consequently, while "I" endure over time, my "self" changes over time. There is a sense in which one might say that the enduring "I" is an abstraction apart from the relational consequences of one's "self." On the other hand, one's "self" would be an ephemeral reality apart from the enduring nature of the "I." We might connect the "I" with the aspect of "substance" noted earlier—that is, we cannot conceive persons "just as" relations, since the term "relation" implies mutuality of distinctive "things." Thus, we affirm an ontology which gives priority to relation as that which makes a given person *that particular* person, without denying some sense of "substance." Who we are as particular persons, then, is mediated to us through our relations with Father, Son, and Spirit, on the divine side, and with personal and nonpersonal realities on the creaturely side. What, then, constitutes personal identity? To this question, we now turn.

A Trinitarian Proposal for Personal Identity

As we put the question at the beginning of this chapter: What set of conditions or states of affairs assure that some person, who is present in resurrected life, is the continuation of the life of the same person in this life? From the nature of the unfolding argument, I suspect that the reader has anticipated at least the general contours of my proposal. Before making it explicit, however, let us briefly survey the primary contenders for a theory of personal identity, beginning with "physicalist" theories.

Clearly "physicalist" theories, which suggest that personal identity is secured by virtue of having the same physical makeup, are inadequate for any one of a number of reasons. First, at the micro-level, human physical makeup is in a constant state of flux, so that, even from moment to moment, we would be hard-pressed to locate enduring physical persons. Second, if we argue that physical makeup constitutes personal identity, we have the unfortunate consequence that for a person with a particular physical handicap or disease, we could only say that the same person existed in resurrected life if he or she had the same physical conditions. This would be rather a disappointment to all who are counting on being rid of these infirmities.

Another physicalist theory is presented by Frank Tipler in his essay, "The Omega Point as Eschaton."[17] Tipler observes that the physical remnants or artifacts of every physical activity in which we engage are never lost. Although the physical artifacts of our speech acts quickly fall to levels no longer accessible to current technologies, Tipler notes that they are present and, in theory, recoverable. If the artifacts are recoverable, the acts themselves can be reconstructed. Tipler raises the possibility of the development of technologies that would make possible the recapture of all the artifacts necessary to recreate the entire record of the lives of all persons. At this point, Tipler, attempting to construct a theory of resurrected life without appeal to divine agency, posits a supercomputer that would carry out the appropriate reconstructive tasks. Capturing all the physical artifacts of a person's life is what enables the recreation of particular persons as the same persons they were prior to their deaths. But, can personal identity be secured in this way? I do not think so.

Although it is true that physical manifestation is central to our acts, there are other aspects of acts that may not involve overt physical expression. For example, the motivations for our acts are essential to our being able to understand "who" we really are; yet, one wonders how motivations could be deduced from the artifacts of acts. Perhaps something about motivations could be inferred from the acts themselves, but surely this would not be adequate to get the requisite degree of specificity to determine things like mental states. Do the mental states and motivations that connect one's mental life with specific acts differ throughout the course of one's life? It seems clear that they do, and such differences likely occur because the person has changed in some way. So, one who engages in some act for some motivation would be a different person from one who engaged in the same act for a different motivation. Merely reconstructing the physical manifestations of these two persons' acts would not enable one to determine the data essential to personal identity. How can one ensure personal identity without access to a person's inner life? One cannot.

A second theory of personal identity depends upon memory. Accordingly, what makes a given person that particular person is precisely his or her memories; and what makes the life of some person in resurrected life the continuation of the same person's existence in this life is the very same set of memories. We must first recognize that memory is, at least partially, a physical trait (cf. the neural correlates of memory)—that is, memories are stored physically in our brains. Damage to certain parts of the brain results in the loss of certain memories, and stimulation of other parts causes certain memories to be called to consciousness. Must one appeal to more than a person's physicality, say to an ontologically distinct soul, to account adequately for memory? It is not clear that one must. As one can see, theories of personal identity grounded in the neural correlates of memory would also be a physicalist theory. Of course, appeals to memory would overcome the problems of access to one's inner state; hence, it would be a superior physicalist theory. There is, however, another difficulty.

Whatever their substantial makeup and origin, memories are, if anything, fallible. For example, I recall myself to have been quite a good basketball player in high school. However, I seldom run into teammates and high school chums who remember it that way, and this, of course, clearly indicates the fallibility of the memories of those with whom I have consulted on the matter (or, less likely, the fallibility of my own memory). How many of us have recalled an event in a particular way, only to discover that our memory was faulty? Not only is memory fallible in this way, it is also faulty in that there are many events that have occurred in our lives of which we have no memory. In fact, how many have a fairly complete memory of events from earliest childhood? I suspect none; yet, the events to which those memories correspond played a profound role in our formation. Some have argued for an infallible memory source, physical or not, and that the memories recorded there constitute personal identity. The problem, of course, is that there does not seem to be adequate evidence to support the claim that such an infallible memory source exists. Although memory has a role to play in personal identity, more is required.

A third theory of personal identity appeals to the "sum total of one's life experiences." Here the appeal is not to some particular faculty, but to a person's relatedness to everything encountered during one's life. What makes me who I am, on this account, is my internal and external historical existence. My relation to other persons, to God, to concepts and certain nonsubstantial realities such as emotions, arguments, and so forth, constitutes personal identity. Such a theory takes with full seriousness my nested existence in a web of relationships as well as the profound influence those relationships have on my own identity. In short, this theory allows for both the relative and absolute senses of person. First, our formation as particular persons is worked out in the myriad of circumstances that attend existence as physical persons in a physical cosmos. At the same time, appropriate allowance is made for factors, such as motivations and emotions, that cannot be reduced to some physical manifestation. Accordingly, this theory constitutes a significant improvement over what has preceded.

However, a problem remains: *Where* is the repository of the sum total of one's life experiences? If such a repository is purely external, have we again lost access to a person's inner life? To suggest that one's memory constitutes that repository reopens the problems already noted. So, I am left in something of a quandary. I am sympathetic to the claim that one's existential, historical existence is what constitutes personal identity, but there is a problem locating the repository of that history. From issues addressed only in this chapter, the proposal of an ontologically distinct soul as this repository might be a plausible one. Yet, other speakers raise grounds for questioning this thesis. I am left with the question, Can one address these issues without assuming the existence of an ontologically distinct soul? Yes, one can.

My proposal has three claims: (1) personal identity is intimately connected with the totality of one's life experiences, (2) personhood is rooted in relationality, and therefore, personal identity must be similarly rooted, and (3) a specifically Christian concept of personal identity involves God's revelation of his own tri-personal nature and corresponding relations to the world of creatures.

Given previous discussions, I can treat the first two points together. The connection becomes apparent when one observes that to have a history of certain life experiences is to stand in and be formed by particular relations with God, other persons, and the rest of creation. I am who I am precisely because my own unique history of relations has formed me as a person. I take it, then, as self-evident that if personhood is a consequence of the relations within which one lives and is formed, then who one really is (i.e., one's personal identity) is likewise constituted. Thus, all of the arguments presented earlier for the relational constitution of personhood are also arguments for a relationally constituted personal identity. In *Exclusion and Embrace*, Miroslav Volf writes, "We are who we are not because we are separate from the others who are next to us, but because we are *both* separate *and* connected, *both* distinct *and* connected; the boundaries that mark our identities are both barriers and bridges. I, Miroslav Volf, am who I am *both* because I am distinct from Judy Gundry-Volf, and because over the past 15 years I have been shaped by a relationship with her."[18] Here Volf expresses the dialogical nature of personhood by maintaining the delicate balance between distinction and connection, both of which are necessary in order to speak of persons in relations. There must be something about "me" that is distinct from the "other" and something about the "other" which is distinct from "me" if we are to talk about relations *between* "the other" and "me."[19] However, what makes this "me" this particular "me" is the formative interaction with all the "others" with whom I come in contact. Volf makes the point powerfully when he notes that even my "enemies" are present in my own self-identity, since I exist in relation to them as well. Since I am what I am in relation, I conclude that for a given person to be that particular person, both in this life and in resurrected life, is just to have the same relationality—that is, both to exist in the same relations and to have been formed by these.

The primary relationship in which we exist is our relationship with Father, Son, and Holy Spirit. Consider two ways that our relatedness to the trinitarian God is primary with regard to personal identity. First, God, by his very nature as creator and all that implies, must be conceived as the primary Other over against whom our personal identities develop. Thomas Torrance articulates this well when he writes, "Within the sphere of divine revelation an *epistemological inversion* takes place in our knowing of God, for what is primary is his knowing of us, not our knowing of him."[20] Catherine LaCugna makes a similar point: "Human persons exist in the first place because God subsists as triune love. Further, according to Zizioulas's anthropology, the relationship of the human person to God—not to other human persons—is decisive."[21] The triune God knows me better than I know myself. My own self-knowledge is flawed; I think I have one set of motivations, when my real motives are often hidden. Self-interest inevitably corrupts my perception of myself, but God sees what I do not see and knows me for the person I really am. I am as one who beholds his image in a mirror that distorts; what I see is never quite what is truly there. If this is true regarding my self-knowledge, imagine how much less other human persons know me as I really am. I hide myself. I present an image I want others to believe. And, as Freud has shown, much of this I do unawares. Consequently, my true nature, who I really am, is known by God in a more thorough way than by anyone else, *including myself*.

This is not to ignore the role that other creatures play in our personal development, but only to recognize the correct priority. Torrance puts this in terms of God's being a "personalizing" agent. "We must think of God, rather, as *'personalizing Person,'* and ourselves as *'personalized persons,'* people who are personal primarily through onto-relations to him as the creative Source of our personal being, and secondarily through onto-relations to one another within the subject-subject structures of our creaturely being as they have come from him."[22] And, we need to recognize that we cannot avoid this personalizing effect of our relationship with God, which Scotus recognized: "According to Duns, there are two ways in which a human being can be a person: in self-assertion against God or in devotion in openness to him."[23] God is the creator of all there is: our own potentiality as persons, the potentiality of other persons, the capacity for relatedness to God and others—everything that makes personal existence both possible and actual. Surely, no other could as profoundly influence human persons; we are who we are first over against the triune God and secondarily over against the rest of creation. It is through these relations that our personal identity exists.

Without my intending to be exhaustive, it is appropriate to comment upon the implications of the trinitarian nature of God for personal identity. First, the Father is the one who holds the totality of our lives in actual presence by virtue of the divine eternity. There is no need to appeal to God's or anyone else's *memory* to secure personal identity, for the Father ever beholds the actuality of every situation in which we exist. And, of course, the Father's love, as expressed in his sending of the Son and Spirit, plays the major role in our personal development. Second, the relation between human persons and the eternal Son is determinative in at least two ways. On the one hand, Jesus makes clear that our relationship to God is first and foremost a function of our relation to him—thus Paul's claim that God was in Christ reconciling the world to himself. On the other hand, the incarnate Son, as the culmination of the Israel story and the one in whom deity and humanity dwell, is the ultimate revelation of God's intentions for humanity. In Christ we have not only the perfect revelation of God, but also the perfect model for humanity, a model which ought to form who we are. Finally, the Holy Spirit as the giver of life and agent of sanctification is related to us in the most intimate way. The Spirit relates to us inwardly—through prevenient grace, for example—as he seeks to woo us into deeper intimacy. Later, through sanctifying grace, the Spirit leads those willing to become instantiations of the likeness of Christ. We may resist the Spirit's grace, and in doing so have our persons formed more as a consequence of our self-assertion. Either way, the role of the Spirit is primary. Additionally, as the persons of the Trinity relate to humans in their own distinctive ways, there is no aspect of human life, neither inward nor outward, that is not evident to the one God. Hence, all that ever need be known about a person is known by the one God, and therefore all aspects of one's personal identity are to be found in God. What is it, then, that makes some person in resurrected life the very same person that existed in this life? It is to be (re?)created by Father, Son, and Spirit as one who exists in and has been formed by the very same relations. This knowledge is something that only God has exhaustively and without error. Therefore, personal identity cannot be secured apart from the active and intimate involvement of God: Father, Son, and Holy Spirit.

Conclusion

We can summarize briefly. First, there is no need to posit an intermediate state between death and the general resurrection. A proper understanding of the divine eternity obviates the need for such a state. Second, personal identity is secured relationally with the trinitarian God as the primary agent and as the source of the exhaustive knowledge of a person's unique relationality. I conclude that a proposal for an ontologically distinct, immaterial soul is necessary neither to secure the continuation of persons after death until the general resurrection nor to secure a basis for personal identity. There may be other reasons to affirm such a soul, but those reasons will need to be found elsewhere.

CHAPTER 10

What About the Dust?

Missiological Musings on Anthropology

Michael A. Rynkiewich

W hat affect might recent research in the neurosciences have on Christian mission, mission theology, and missionary practice? The popular image of the modern (but not postmodern) missionary is someone who is carrying out the Great Commission as found in Matthew 28:18-20: "Go therefore and make disciples of all nations." For many, this is reduced to "preaching the gospel" and "saving souls." A strong dualist ontology in Western culture has contributed to the view held by many Western Christians that it is possible to save souls without bothering about the bodies, to speak words that convince without doing deeds that change, and to isolate individuals without considering their interrelatedness with community, land, and environment.

We are told that neuroscientists are identifying and tracing the component parts of the mental processes that are involved in perception, cognition, memory, emotion, and behavior.[1] The mind-brain links are mind-bogglingly complex, multilayered from atomic through multicellular networks and neural pathways. In this cybernetic system, cause and effect, so loved by positivists, are replaced by feedback relationships. Development, diet, and damage, among other factors, affect the neural networks that produce what we call personality, emotions, and morality. At the same time, when human challenges are met by focused cognition, the repeated use of pathways affects the neural architecture, expanding this part of the brain and contracting another.

Neuroscientists are moving toward a unified theory of mind-brain that implies a monist view of the human person. In short, no longer will we be able to isolate a separate ethereal mind or soul. A divided dualism with a mindless body and a disembodied soul will not square with science, nor, we are told, does it square with a careful reading of the Bible.[2]

How will we do mission without souls to save? What are the implications of a monist, or at the very least a fully integrated and indivisible dualist, view of the human person? Has mission been made a problem or has mission been corrected? What kind of theology of mission might a monist view of persons suggest? I am going to argue here that the monist-dualist debate in the neurosciences and biblical studies informs a theology of mission in three ways. It contributes to a more holistic theology of mission, it contributes to a more incarnational theology of mission, and it contributes to a more naturalistic theology of mission.

A Holistic Theology of Mission

Dualism in Western thought, particularly in Christian circles, has contributed to a theology of mission that has a dualistic individual as the object of conversion. This dualist construction of persons has led to a severe division between evangelism and social justice. This debate is real and current, and it affects mission strategy as well as mission support.

A recent exchange in *Evangelical Missions Quarterly* provides one example of the debate. This is no small issue, for indeed, "the future of the world (not just of world mission!) hinges on what we make of this word 'mission'."[3] Hesselgrave begins, not very helpfully, by casting the argument in terms of conservatives versus liberals. That is just a modernist way of dismissing the other side.[4] He traces the rise of a holistic paradigm of mission to John Stott's book *Christian Mission in the Modern World* and the wording of the Lausanne Covenant (1974).[5] After noting that "the new *Mission Handbook* (1998–2000) identifies that 'emerging paradigm' as the 'centrality of holism—life, deed, word and sign'," Hesselgrave charges that "this broad understanding of mission should be abandoned for two primary reasons." He claims that this paradigm is based on "a very questionable interpretation of the biblical text" and that "it is counterproductive from a practical point of view."[6] His textual criticism deals only with John 17 and 20, and not with Luke 4 or the rest of the story. His practical concern is that humanitarian aid (his definition of holism?) is fraught with technical and political difficulties. His solution is to privilege Matthew 28:16-20 over the rest of Scripture, and to read Scripture from the perspective of "completed revelation and . . . salvation history."[7] The conclusion follows: "We can feed some of the hungry, but we cannot feed the whole world. We can help heal some of the sick, but we cannot heal the whole world. We can support the rights of some disenfranchised people, but we cannot enfranchise the whole world. But we can evangelize the whole world, and no one else will do it if we do not."[8]

The journal includes several responses to Hesselgrave's critique of holistic mission. For example, Myers suggests shifting "from a set of propositions to a narrative framework based on the biblical story as a whole" because "a genuinely holistic approach to mission begins with a strong creation theology and then builds on the holistic framework that is consistently present in the whole of Scripture."[9] He calls for "holistic Christians who are healed from the dichotomies of the modern West . . . and who refuse a truncated view of mission that suggests that God is only interested in saving souls and the life hereafter."[10]

The debate between evangelism and social justice has divided mission circles since well before the Lausanne Congress on World Evangelism. It is typical of those who propose a more holistic theology of mission to cite the problem of a dualist Western worldview—to begin with creation, to insist on the relevance of the whole Bible, and to focus on the kingdom as the goal of mission.[11] Rarely in mission practice are evangelism and social justice given equal priority, and when a mission agency attempts both, rarely are they well integrated.

Creation theology is not the right place to begin. Rethinking a theology of mission in light of a monistic construction of persons pushes us back beyond creation to the triune God to get our view of personhood and mission. This road carries us around Western Catholic thought and through Eastern Orthodox theology.

John Zizioulas reminds us that the Western Greek fathers' concern with substance is a different starting point from the Eastern Greek fathers' concern with relationship in their theology of the Trinity.[12] Zizioulas argues that "the biblical doctrine of creation *ex nihilo* obliged the Fathers to introduce a radical difference into ontology, to trace the world back to an ontology outside the world, that is, to God."[13] The Eastern Greek fathers resisted defining God in terms of substance, and insisted that it is relationship that defines God's being. The personhood of the Trinity is understood first as a communion, as relationships, and it is these relationships that then define the persons.

As Stanley Grenz has claimed, " 'God is love' is the foundational ontological statement we can declare concerning the divine essence. God is foundationally the mutuality of the love relationship between Father and Son, and this personal love is the Holy Spirit."[14] Love is equally foundational to human personhood. Our bodies know God in personal relationship, or we do not know God at all. This is the driving force of mission; to invite bodies to enter into a life-giving relationship with God.

> Love is not an emanation or "property" of the substance of God . . . but is *constitutive* of his substance, i.e., it is that which makes God what He is, the one

God. Thus love ceases to be a qualifying *ontological predicate.* Love as God's mode of existence "hypostasizes" God, *constitutes* his being. Therefore, as a result of love, the ontology of God is not subject to the necessity of substance. Love is identified with ontological freedom. All this means that personhood creates for human existence the following dilemma: either freedom as love, or freedom as negation.[15]

The nature of human personhood follows. The human person is not a body (substance) but a body-in-relationship. If God exists by love, then there is hope for the survival of human persons when God loves them and they enter into relationship with God. "The goal of salvation is that the personal life which is realized in God should also be realized on the level of human existence."[16] Eternal salvation comes because humankind has come into a powerful relationship with "an ontological reality which does not suffer from createdness,"[17] that is, when a person is born from above.

God's mission through the church then is this: "The first and most important characteristic of the Church is that she brings man into a kind of relationship with the world which is not determined by the laws of biology."[18] Whether "determined" is the right word remains to be seen. However, we can agree that before the beginning, before creation, the triune God was intrinsically in mission: reaching out in loving relationship. The *missio Dei* is eternal because it is intrinsic to the triune God. God's mission now is an extension of God's mission then, not just a crash recovery program initiated at the Fall.

What is intrinsic to the triune God, then, is self-giving, other-embracing, relationship-building love. What is contingent is sovereignty, a characteristic that depends on the creation for its expression. Before that, there was nothing to be sovereign over. Thus, loving relationship is prior to sovereignty.[19] The objective of mission is not to explain how a sovereign God loves, but to show to the world how a God of perfect love expresses his sovereignty.[20]

Human personhood then follows through the *imago Dei* and is likewise relationally defined, contrary to one stream of tradition that prefers essentialist definitions.

> Humankind has been made in the image and likeness of God; because of that central fact our humanity can have neither true existence nor true relationships without communion with him. For that reason we have been given the double command, to love God and to love our neighbor. Another Orthodox theologian, Kallistos Ware, maintains that it is by meditation, rather than by subordination, that we are called to "unify ourselves and the world around us" holding the spiritual and the material "as an undivided whole." This is the essence of current environmental issues in which the interpenetration of the material and the spiritual is seen as a global issue for humanity in the wellbeing of the planet.[21]

The Fall shattered the unity of the monistic living being and damaged (not totally and not irreparably) the relationship between the living being and the tri-une God, on the one hand, and persons, on the other. This extended the *missio Dei* to the healing of the shattered unity, the salvation of the person, and the reconciliation of the person with God and other persons. These are not three separate processes, but different ways of saying the same thing. God is savior, healer, and reconciler. Redemption means reconciliation for the living being with God, and restoration of the body to relationship with God, because a body out of relationship is an individual, lost, lonely, and incomplete. Redemption and reconciliation are steps in the *missio Dei*, paths to God's ultimate goals.

Neuroscience research here is significant. The body would appear to have certain pathways for perception, emotion, cognition, and response. Some of these are multilayered. Joseph LeDoux's recent studies of our fear response, for example, show that perceptions of danger travel through two paths[22]—one to the amygdala through the thalamus and another to the amygdala through the visual cortex.[23] Synapses through the second route include more information but take twice as long to get to the amygdala as through the first network. The first route has little information but stimulates a response within a few thousandths of a second. The second route permits cognition and choice of response. The first route triggers an all-systems alarm to which the body reacts without any training. Both pathways store memories of the threat, but emotion heightens the first memory, and may distort it until the body responds in unreasonable ways. Posttraumatic stress syndrome is a category for veterans who dive for cover when surprised by a loud sound. The problem is that "the brain seems to be wired to prevent the deliberate overriding of fear responses."[24] Thus, what has been adaptive for ancient environments now makes New Yorkers wince at any stimulus that could signal a terrorist attack. "We are not slaves to our emotions, but they are hardly at our beck and call either. They propel us in directions that our rational minds don't always understand—fear most of all. The amygdala, like the heart in Pascal's famous phrase, has reasons of which reason knows nothing."[25]

Neurons and synapses appear to be working with sensory impressions from the now, but also with short-term and long-term memory. They are working with responses, but also with emotion. They are in connection, and this connection leads to causation, that is, agency in action.[26] Following Fuster,[27] Reyna argues that a "neurohermeneutic system works through an interpretative hierarchy utilizing cultural memories of past realities to represent present realities in ways that form desires about future realities."[28] Not just the connection between cortical areas and certain sense, emotion, or cognitive processes is in mind here, but rather that whole neural networks are connected to layers of interpretation that link up (note the links both ways) to cultural schema that form our worldview. Emmanuel Kant taught us that we cannot think without categories, but he was short of content for the categories. Franz Boas taught us that culture provides the content for the categories because the stuff of culture is concepts.[29]

How these connections work is yet fruit for discovery. The links can be personal as well as cultural, clear as well as mystifying. The studies show that emotions and memories link in the amygdala, and the associations that connect there are not always rational.

I still cannot help but tear up and drift home when I hear Neil Diamond's "Sweet Caroline". In December 1970 I was leaving Arno Atoll in the Marshall Islands after a year and a half of anthropological fieldwork. My father had died in July, and it was nearly a month before I found out. My wife left in September to attend the fall semester at the University of Minnesota. I had a plane wreck and a boat mishap trying to get from Arno to Majuro Atoll, the capital. Either could have taken my life. I stayed over one night in Honolulu with an old Pacific hand, Leonard Mason. At 8:00 P.M. I took off from the Honolulu airport in a near empty Boeing 707 on the "redeye" flight nonstop to St. Louis. My research had gone well, there were gains and losses, I would soon greet my wife with joy, but I would also greet my family with grief. As the lights of Honolulu floated by, "Sweet Caroline" came on the earphones loud and clear. The beat seemed to build toward a future, yet the words spoke of memories as well. All this, and more, forms its own network, a sweet spot somewhere in my brain.

The Wesleys, likewise, resisted a dualistic reading of the self. Their great concern was to unite the head and the heart, as in the famous verse:

> Unite the pair so long disjoined,
> Knowledge and vital piety:
> Learning and holiness combined,
> And truth and love let all men see.[30]

John Wesley's view of the place of reason and the senses is not foreign to our concerns. Miles suggests that Wesley does "insist that reason is not separated from the body or disembodied. Reason is, instead, fully embodied. It works with and through the bodily experience of the senses."[31]

If there is only body-mind, and within it neural networks that link to personal and cultural hermeneutic systems, then it is impossible to be in mission to the mind-soul without being in mission to the body. If our pathways are affected by development, diet, and damage, and they clearly are, then how can we expect people to change their minds (repent and believe) unless we also work toward repairing damage and building healthy bodies/brains so that there are no unnecessary stumbling blocks to the gospel?

This view of mission requires us to rethink the priority of the Great Commission, Matthew 28, and join it with Luke 4 and the rest of the story. In light of the whole story of God's personhood (the economy of the Trinity) and God's mission (creation, redemption, kingdom), we need continually to rethink our theology of mission. A dualism that allows missionaries to separate evangelism and social justice is contrary to the *missio Dei*.

An Incarnational Theology of Mission

Care for the neurons, the point of the previous section, is essential to mission. Paying attention to the synapses is no less important. If synapses represent and re-present perception and cognition, emotion and response, then are practiced pathways and imagined content the same for every culture? Clearly, cultures differ and cultures change. At the top of the interpretative hierarchy, there are schema made up of metaphors, concepts, propositions, and stories that form a network called worldview. No two individual worldviews are exactly the same, though where there is overlap and sharing, we tend to call that grouping a culture.

In a sense, the hierarchy begins with observation, though some of this is subtle and subconscious, as when we perceive a rustle in the grass while walking through the woods at night. Observation can lead to an automatic response, as when we freeze without being told to, by our brain or anyone else. Observation can also lead to analysis, where we take the sensations and sort them out in a reasonable manner. From this we form an interpretation of the current world around us, as when we decide that it might indeed be a snake. Finally, we make an application, initiating a plan of action based on our interpretation, as when we run away. All of this sensing, reasoning, evaluating, and planning involves complex systems with feedback circuits between "the prefrontal cortex, the limbic system and the various modules of reasoning in different areas throughout the cerebral cortex."[32] Though the overall process may be similar, the content and context differs. Over time, with repeated use of certain pathways, the process also begins to differ from culture to culture.

What we have learned recently from the neurosciences and biblical studies shows us that Europeans have used a peculiar theology of the construction of persons for the last several hundred years. The Enlightenment changed everything, but did not always bring light.

> Thus, the fundamental doctrine of the person changed from dependence on God to independence from any higher authority. It also changed from being relational to being avowedly individual. Because the dependent relationship with God had been severed, there was now no ontological basis for community. Autonomous human individuals do not readily give up their self-sufficiency to care for others in society. The contest between the twin giants of rational individualism and imposed collectivism began, fought out on the platform of the world stage.[33]

The gospel spoke to that theology, but now a new theology is emerging, and the gospel will speak to it as well. This new theology opens up the possibility that there are as many schemas of the construction of persons as there are cultures in the world. The gospel always speaks to the person who is there, not the person who is imagined. That is part of the meaning of the Incarnation. Jesus came "just as we are" so that we could respond with "just as I am."

The monism-dualism debate prompts us to ask, With whom are we in mission? Shenk asks, "How can the missionary maintain independence of the socio-political ideology of the West?"[34] An implicit premise of Western ideology is that persons are ontologically prior to relationships (or, to put it another way, individuals are prior to society). So we spend a great deal of time in Western social sciences asking how a person relates to various groups: to the family (psychology), to others (sociology), as leaders and followers (political science), and as producers and consumers (economics). Western missionaries share these assumptions about personhood and sociality, and they tend to concern themselves with conversion and growth of the individual while disregarding local constructions of personhood.

Other cultures have other assumptions. Thus, for example, we have had to move to other languages (*missio Dei, imago Dei, hypostasis*) and to other cultures (Greek Orthodox) and to other times (early church fathers) to get a handle on a biblical construction of persons that differs from the Western view that has coalesced in the last two hundred years.

As an example of other possibilities, Marilyn Strathern argues that, for Melanesian cultures, "we must stop thinking that at the heart of these cultures is an antinomy between 'society' and 'the individual'."[35] Such is not the case in Melanesia, where persons, as imagined in the West, do not exist. Anthropologists engage in discovery procedures to uncover conceptions of personhood that do exist.

Strathern and others have argued that personhood is conceptualized differently in Melanesia, with variations among the cultures. A baby is born into existing relations and forms a sociocentric self as it grows up. It builds relationships and loses relationships, endures teaching and disciplining, and develops responses and defenses. Yet, what I have written does not convey the notion of how much of the self is tied up in relationships. Melanesians conceive of a dividual, a divisible person who, in exchange, gives away parts of himself or herself. Thus, the composition and decomposition of relationships entails the composition and decomposition of the self. The Western dichotomy of persons and things, or subjects and objects, leads to the conception of a relationship as a version of commodity exchange. The Melanesian worldview includes no strong distinction between persons and things, so much so that what is exchanged is conceived as parts of persons. The agency of the self decides what to detach in order to elicit reciprocal detachment in order to attach it to the self. Thus, a person is a gift, an ongoing composition of given parts of persons.

When there is such a conception of personhood, to whom is the missionary addressing an altar call? In the context of a self that is constructed of bits and pieces of other selfs, what does conversion mean? Is there an autonomous individual out there who can make the decision, raise his or her hand, and walk down the aisle alone? Or must conversion be differently conceived? Might conversion involve the detachment of some persons and attachment of other persons by an agent who is constantly reconstructing himself or herself? How would Paul's metaphor that we "put on Christ" be received there?

Would conversion be giving of oneself to receive from God in order to establish a new relationship, or just the acquisition of some new knowledge?[36] Hiebert points out that one of the problems with the Western conception of self and conversion is that missionaries assume that knowledge is the measure of a convert. Hiebert argues convincingly that orientation toward God is a more helpful metaphor for conversion. The issue is relationship, not scholarship.

Monistic and dualist models for the construction of persons are just two of many such models, and not the most complex. Many questions can be raised. For example, in Western models, from Freud through Jung and down to today, Western models of personhood emphasize the degree and success of integration of the different parts of a person.[37] What if it is not integration, but facility in operating in different social settings that is important?

Evangelistic listening will be required if the missionary is "to avoid both simply *neutralizing* the binary oppositions of metaphysics and simply *residing* within the closed field of these oppositions, thereby confirming it."[38] People have a narrative, a way of making connections. Different groups of people have a different cultural neurohermeneutic. Our mission is not to convince the world that we have the truth with regard to the construction of personhood, but to introduce Christ as a person seeking relationship, to invite people to receive God's grace, and to encourage people to enter into a new community through the Holy Spirit.

A Naturalistic Theology of Mission

If we move in the direction of thinking about the soul as the relationship between our body and God, and the mind as the relationship between our synapses and our culture, then even with this monistic view, we are still missing some pieces to the puzzle. What about the dust, of which our bodies are made? Is the dust an integral part of our personhood? Where does the "new earth" come from? Scherer reminds us that our mission is penultimate. "Does the goal of mission remain making converts and planting churches wherever they do not exist, or does the expectation of the kingdom shift the church's priorities to activities which somehow anticipate a 'new heaven and a new earth'?"[39]

Most theologies of holistic mission still focus on people, especially individual persons, to the exclusion of the community, the land, and the environment. Missionaries with a dualistic view of the material and the spiritual have found it difficult to imagine the connections between these three and individual persons. Third World theologians now have to make up what is missing in mission theology, a conception of self that includes more than the individual.

It should not have been so. The biblical relationship between persons, land, and environment is clear. Right after the beginning, Adam and Eve heard, "Cursed is the ground because of you; in toil you shall eat of it all the days of your life; . . . until you return to the ground, for out of it you were taken; you are dust, and to dust you shall return" (Gen. 3:17-19). The Law reinforces the relationship, for the land is defiled if the people sin (e.g., Lev. 19:29; 35:33, 34; Deut. 21:23; Jer. 3:1, 2, 9; 4:20), and the land will "vomit out her inhabitants" if the people persist in sin (Lev. 18:25). The land, and by extension, the environment, need rest and renewal (e.g., Lev. 25:2; 2 Chron. 7:14; 36:21; Ezek. 39:16). In fact, the hope of the exile is epitomized in Jeremiah's purchase of a piece of land (Jer. 32:15), as the hope for the restoration of community is linked to the restoration of the land.[40] This hope is carried over into the New Testament. In Peter's second sermon we find this enigmatic phrase: "Repent therefore, and turn to God so that your sins may be wiped out, so that times of refreshing may come from the presence of the Lord, and that he may send the Messiah appointed for you, that is, Jesus, who must remain in heaven until *the time of universal restoration that God announced long ago through his holy prophets*" (Acts 3:19-21). Peter speaks as if his listeners will understand the connectedness of bodies and communities and land; but his latter-day hearers are mystified. Paul too speaks as if it is a common notion that "creation itself will be set free from its bondage to decay and will obtain the freedom of the glory of the children of God" (Rom. 8:20). This is linked to "the redemption of our bodies" (Rom. 8:23), not the escape of our souls from our bodies (Col. 1:19-21).

The dust is in the person. Theologies of place are being developed in the Pacific and elsewhere that show more than just relationships between person, community, and land. The link is symbolic and more than symbolic (like the Eucharist) of the inclusion of community, land, and environment. It is as earthy as birth, marriage, and death, where we commingle blood and dirt, pain and joy. Tuwere argues that the construction of personhood in Fiji cannot be understood outside the context of *vanua* (land/community), *lotu* (liturgy/church), and *matanitu* (government/social order).[41] Unfortunately, nineteenth- and twentieth-century missionaries were in the forefront of a theology of commoditizing the land, and are implicated in the practice of acquiring exclusive rights in the land.[42]

In the context of ethnic rivalry, political coups, and economic recession, Tuwere asks, "What does it mean to be a Christian community in Fiji today? What difference should it make to be a Christian church in light of the reality of the context (dust of the *vanua*) on the one hand and the reality of revelation on the other?"[43] In this theology, dust, community, and person are inseparable. Each person lives, or refuses to live, as the incarnated Christ would have lived in that place and time. Dust, person, community, and relationship with God are inseparable.

It would seem then that even the dust is in relationship with God. Presumably, a monistic view of the person is not an individualistic view, for a monistic view demands relationships in order to complete the person. Storkey critiques both the discipline of anthropology and the subdivision of theology called anthropology: "Of course, Boethius was wrong, or wrongly angled. To locate our human identity in some essential distinctiveness rather than in our relationality (especially our relationship to God) got anthropology off to a very bad start."[44] If our relationality in action and narrative (or narrative action) is the stuff that is traveling along the synapses, then our persons consist of our bodies and our relationships with God and others.

The dust rises and falls with the person. While the Old Testament reminds us that, in one sense, our bodies return to dust, the New Testament holds out the hope for the resurrected body. The dust is redeemed through Christ's resurrection from which comes the promise of our resurrection. "Finally, while recognizing the importance of the intellectual dimension, surely the most powerful apologetic is a community of believers who have been radically transformed by the grace and love of Christ and who consistently manifest in their lives the qualities exemplified in Christ's life. Jesus stated the basic principle to his disciples 2000 years ago: 'By this all men will know that you are my disciples, if you love one another' (John 13:35)."[45] The dust taken up into the Trinity (that is, the ascension of Jesus) completes our hermeneutic circle from creation to the restoration of all things. It is this mystery of communion with the triune God and with God's community (other people) that we lost when the Protestant Reformers decentered the Eucharist.

What does this mean for mission? I have been asking myself, after five years of observing missionaries in the Pacific Islands, whether God wants to give us a message or give us an embrace. Many Protestant missionaries seem to think that the job is to impart words, knowledge, and creed. This is a pale reflection of "the Word became flesh and lived among us" (John 1:14). The incarnation involved God coming to humans in a recognizable form so that those who embrace the message may "have fellowship with us; and truly our fellowship is with the Father and with his Son Jesus Christ" (1 John 1:3). It is an embrace that God wants to give us, so that we may embrace each other and complete the circle. The limits of reason as a method are found in relationship. We do not reason relationship; we are not dealing with an "it" but with "I AM WHO I AM."

Conclusion

In some ways, neuroscience is a different culture from theology. As with C. P. Snow's observations of the two cultures (science and humanities), the presuppositions, assumptions, and worldview of science and theology take us in different directions.[46] But, we intersect when we begin to talk about the nature of human beings and the nature of the world. Just as one response of some Christian groups has been to deny the reality of modern science, so a related response is to deny the reality of other cultures. In the process, our own culture is reified and deified.

For over a hundred years the Western cultural juggernaut has overcome other cultures with a theology founded, among other presuppositions, on a dualistic construction of persons. Now, as neuroscience brings into question this foundational presupposition, we find that we have been "wrongly angled" in our proclamation of the gospel. And this is not the only questionable presupposition of Western culture. "And so might evangelicals move from decontextualized propositions to traditional, storied truths; from absolute certainty to humble confidence; from mathematical purity to the rich, if less predictable, world of relational trust; from detached objectivist epistemology to engaged participative epistemology; from control of the data to respect of the other in all its created variety; from individualist knowing to communal knowing; and from once-for-all rational justification to the ongoing pilgrimage of testimony."[47]

To make this move in mission theology and practice means listening to different cultural streams within the Western tradition, but also to other theologies of other cultures in other places. Here is a summary of mission concerns from "alternate centers" in the world, similar to the challenge to evangelicals to rethink their worldview: "Possibly one underlying theme (of non-Western theologies) is holism: between the natural and the supernatural; between mind and body, theology and economy; between the individual and the group; between proposition and symbol; and between system and uncertainty."[48] There is a cry from below for the recovery of a lost wholeness, stolen by the Western advance, whose propagandists included missionaries. The call to Christ is not a call to individualism, but a call to see what Christ does for the whole of society—indeed, the whole of creation. The call is from a relational triune God to be redeemed and reconciled in relationship through the person and work of Jesus Christ, empowered by the previous, present, and continual work of the Holy Spirit. The call relates Christ to the person, however constituted. The call offers hope not for some ethereal soul, but for the material, the social, the economic, the political, the spiritual, the intellectual, the dispossessed, the oppressed, and the lost; the whole person, community, land, and creation. The ultimate purpose of God is the redemption and reconciliation of all things in Christ; the purpose of humans is to use everything good that has come from God to play our part in redemption and reconciliation of all things in Christ.[49]

CHAPTER 11

The Neuroscience of Christian Counseling?

Virginia T. Holeman

I magine the following counseling scenarios. In which situation is the counselor dealing with matters of the soul? Which situation is an example of Christian counseling?

Scenario 1
Gwen, an experienced licensed counselor, greets her new client, Dianna. Dianna complains that she has felt depressed and anxious for the past few months. She has no idea why she should be so down as all aspects of her life appear to be in good working order. As Dianna unfolds her story, Gwen's responses indicate that she is "with" Dianna emotionally. When Dianna begins to sob, Gwen observes Dianna's inability to manage her own emotionality. Once Dianna completes her story, Gwen and Dianna collaborate to develop specific counseling goals. Before the session ends, Gwen checks with Dianna to see if there is anything else that Dianna believes Gwen needs to know at this time. With Dianna's permission, Gwen closes the session in prayer.

Scenario 2
Fernando, a licensed psychologist, uses a solution-focused approach with clients. Fernando works hard to establish a caring and strong therapeutic relationship. After setting specific

goals, he and his clients work together to determine what has worked rather than focusing on what has failed and to identify exceptions to the problem rather than focusing on interactions that reinforce the problem. Fernando believes that active client participation is crucial for successful therapy. He makes it a policy to refer clients with whom he has not "clicked" by the second session. Fernando looks for the strengths that clients bring to their work, with a special focus on the client's network of relationships. Fernando regularly considers where God already may be at work in his clients' lives.

Scenario 3
Elizabeth is a licensed clinical social worker at the Maranatha Counseling Center. Her clients, James and Corrina, want to improve their marriage. Their arguments follow an escalating pattern of increasingly hostile and hurtful exchanges that seem to come out of the blue so that simple discussions explode into vicious fights. Elizabeth uses healing prayer as a major part of her work with couples. After explaining the process of healing prayer and gaining their assent to this form of counseling, Elizabeth leads James and Corrina in several healing prayer sessions.

Scenario 4
Dr. Joseph is a psychiatrist. His patient, Kathy, experiences extreme anxiety that culminates in panic attacks. Dr. Joseph listens to Kathy's story and he determines that her symptoms warrant psychopharmacological intervention in addition to regular counseling. He sees her involvement in her local church as one of her greatest strengths. Kathy leaves Dr. Joseph's office with a sense that he understands her condition and her larger concerns.

Counseling and Soul: A Match Made in Heaven?

The relationship between soul care and psychological care is at the heart of the two questions that precede these vignettes: In which situation is the counselor dealing with matters of the soul? One's response to the first question reflects one's understanding of "soul" and may even suggest one's beliefs about who has jurisdiction over "soul-work" (clinician or clergy). This in turn influences one's answer to the second question: Which vignette demonstrates Christian counseling? Recent discoveries in the neurosciences have made the answers to these questions far from straightforward, especially for clinicians who work within a Christian worldview. Discoveries about the brain have challenged classic understandings of soul and counseling psychology[1] so that theological and clinical assumptions about personhood (a concept strongly associated with soul if not considered a synonym for soul) are being reexamined in light of neuroscientific findings.[2] In this essay I explore these reformulations from the perspective of professional counseling[3] in general and Christian counseling in particular.

Before diving into the heart and soul of the matter, a brief review of the "on and off again" relationship between matters of the soul and counseling will provide some historical background for the discussion that follows.[4] While the people of God have been offering formal and informal guidance to one another for centuries, the professionalization of this support, Christian counseling, is a phenomenon of the twentieth century.[5] For most of church history, the spiritual leader of a community functioned as theologian and therapist, clergy and counselor. In the late 1800s and early 1900s things changed. As modernism became a predominant worldview of scholars and scientists, and as psychoanalysis emerged as a scientific, nonsupernatural treatment of the soul, a rupture gradually developed in the formerly seamless relationship between soul care and psychological care. This schism was particularly acute in the United States when behaviorism became psychology and counseling's sweetheart. From a purely behaviorist perspective, which dominated American psychology for much of the twentieth century, the treatment of psychological distress often boiled down to the manipulation of positive and negative reinforcers. Behaviorists such as John Watson and later B. F. Skinner considered unobservable phenomena (thinking, feeling, imagining, valuing) irrelevant to psychological inquiry. This particular therapeutic orientation had no place for soul care. And even though cognitive and humanistic psychologists reasserted the value of unseen phenomena in the mind, most soul matters were still barred at the therapy door.

While psychology ignored soul care during the 1950s, evangelicals, on the other hand, began to take a serious look at psychology.[6] For example, psychology courses emerged in evangelical undergraduate curriculum in places like Taylor University. In 1956 a group of psychologists created the Christian Association for Psychological Studies to provide a forum for discussions about psychology, counseling, and Christian faith.

Although the relationship between psychology and soul care was "on" for evangelical counselors and psychologists during the 1960s and 1980s, it was "off" for their secular counterparts. Secular mental health workers, whose expertise was in "personal" or "relational" counseling, were restricted by an implicit professional ethic from engaging in conversations related to religious topics, including the soul. At best, this avoidance was considered to be professionally responsible behavior because mental health professionals only practiced within their scope of competence and their secular training usually did not include courses on the care of soul. At worst, this reflected secular psychology's belief that soul issues were irrelevant to treatment issues. Conversely, counseling professionals who embraced a Christian faith continued talking about how they could combine care of soul and psyche even as their secular colleagues shunned it. Consequently, faith-based institutions of higher education began to offer masters and doctoral-level programs in counseling and psychology, respectively.[7] Degree plans from these institutions mirrored those from secular schools so that graduates could become licensed as counselors or psychologists.

As the secular mental health field entered the 1990s, a renewed interest in (broadly defined) spirituality emerged. This resulted in a flurry of scholarly publications that explored relationships between treatment and religious behavior/spirituality.[8] Today, it would be difficult to find a national professional conference sponsored by an organization such as the American Association of Marriage and Family Therapists, the American Psychological Association, or the American Counseling Association that did not include at least one workshop or even an entire track on spirituality. The relationship between soul care and psychology is "on," and continues robustly into the twenty-first century.

It might appear that approaches, secular and sacred, interested in the integration of the cure of psyche and soul now have much in common, but important differences exist even among Christian counseling professionals. Though most Christian counselors agree that their work seeks to remove barriers that separate clients from God, others, and self, no universal consensus exists about *what* makes Christian counseling *Christian*.[9] The crux of the matter seems to revolve around the sources of knowledge upon which a professional Christian counselor draws (empirical psychological research, Scripture, theology) and the priority given to each discipline. Put bluntly, when does too much psychology take the "Christian" out of Christian counseling? Available opinions range from "no psychology allowed,"[10] through systematized approaches that use specific "Christian" techniques with some psychological foundations,[11] to counseling professionals whose Christian worldview acts as a lens for evaluating and integrating secular psychological approaches within a Christian counseling setting.[12]

Recent discoveries in the neurosciences, however, suggest that another issue may explain differences in Christian counseling.[13] Rather than asking, How much psychology is too much? perhaps the question should be, What view of personhood (soul) is espoused by these various approaches to Christian counseling? I propose that different approaches to Christian counseling are based significantly on different conceptualizations of personhood, and that this in turn shapes treatment. It is to this concern that I now turn.

Views of the Personhood and Counseling

First, I discuss how different views of personhood affect approaches to Christian counseling. Second, I explore in more detail how current understanding of personhood, informed by the neurosciences, may shape Christian counseling.

Some Common Assumptions

Throughout much of Christian tradition, the soul has been perceived as the locus of a person's relationship with God. More recently, the soul has been the focus of evangelistic efforts ("saving souls"); it is the part of us that will live eternally with God if evangelistic efforts succeed or will live eternally separated from God if they fail. Clergy are thought to be the experts on the soul and the care of the soul has traditionally been under their jurisdiction. It is probably safe to say that most people of orthodox Christian faith assume that they have a soul. If asked to locate their soul, it is likely that many people would point to their head (associating the soul with the mind and the mind with the brain) while others would point to their heart. No matter where an individual situates his or her "soul," the boundary is slim between experiences of personhood and experiences of soul.

I hinted in the previous section that neuroscientific findings have raised interesting questions that relate directly to beliefs about the nature of personhood. Among the views of persons that have emerged from these scientific discussions are the following: reductive materialism, radical dualism, holistic dualism, and a range of monistic perspectives. The axis around which these perspectives organize themselves is the degree to which personhood is identified with the brain and the mind. This section describes these four perspectives and begins preliminary discussions about the implications that these views hold for Christian counseling.

(1) Reductive Materialism proposes that the "person is a physical organism, whose emotional, moral, and religious experiences will all ultimately be explained by the physical sciences."[14] No soul is necessary because neuroscience will eventually be able to reduce everything (i.e., communion with God and others, sense of self, values and beliefs) to the firing of neurons and the release of neurotransmitters. In other words, "you," your "mind," and your "soul" are nothing but brain events. This view clearly presents a challenge to the theoretical and theological basis from which Christian counselors work. Theoretically, if this view holds sway, then counseling as we know it today will cease to exist. A good therapist becomes one who most effectively and efficiently matches perceived psychological pain with brain events. For example, if Dianna (from the first case study) seeks help for her depression from a reductive materialist, that counselor will propose that her symptoms are caused exclusively by an imbalance in her brain chemistry, and then will prescribe the appropriate medication to alleviate the problem.[15] On the surface, one might also accuse Dr. Joseph (fourth case study) of reductive materialism.

I know of no approach to Christian counseling that adopts a reductive materialist view of soul; indeed, reductive materialism runs so counter to classical Christian teaching about personhood that it would seem to present an untenable position for *Christian* counselors to adopt.[16] The biblical materials affirm that, although our corporeality is important, we are in fact more than our bodies. We are beings made in the image of God.

(2) Radical Dualism puts forward the view that "the soul (or mind) is separable from the body, and the person is identified with the former."[17] Traditional,

Cartesian dualism captures the essence of this position, for it sees "the soul as an entity of a completely different nature than the physical, an entity with no essential or internal relationship to the body, which must be added to the body *ab extra* by a special divine act of creation."[18] In other words, the soul is a separate entity, has a separate existence, and is of an entirely different nature than the physical world. If reductive materialism magnifies the importance of the body by reducing the soul to brain events, radical dualism magnifies the importance of the soul by reducing the body to a temporary holding tank for the soul. I agree with Nancey Murphy, who argues that this view, like reductive materialism, is incompatible with Christian teaching, which emphasizes the importance of both body and soul.[19]

If one should counsel from a radical dualist perspective, then experiences of the immortal self are easily disassociated from experiences of the mortal self. A radical dualist view could lead to one of two extremes. Because the body has no eternal relationship with the soul, it can either be indulged or ignored since neither action influences the soul. Either option, indulging or ignoring, can lead to irresponsible living in the here and now. Even if one avoids these extremes, counseling from this perspective can ignore the interdependence of the mind and body. For example, were James and Corrina (third case study) to seek help from a radical dualist, their counselor might endorse only spiritual interventions. Contemporary problems in living or physiological problems have no bearing on treatment. I know of no school of Christian counseling that advocates a radical dualist view.

(3) Holistic Dualism, like radical dualism, is a form of substance dualism, but is characterized by a key distinction. It proposes that "the person is a composite of separate 'parts' but is to be identified with the whole, whose normal functioning is as a unity."[20] Here the soul is viewed as a separate ontological entity, whose functions are intimately and causally linked with the body. According to Moreland, the soul is

> an immaterial substance. . . . The soul is a very complicated thing with an intricate internal structure. . . . The soul is a substantial, unified reality that informs its body. The soul is to the body like God is to space—it is fully present at each point within the body. Further, the soul and the body relate to each other in a cause-effect way. . . . The soul and the body are highly interactive, they enter into deep causal relations and functional dependencies with each other, the human person is a unity of both.[21]

Holistic dualism is the prevailing view among professional Christian counselors. Earlier, I described a range of opinions about the degree of integration of psychology in Christian counseling. "Bible only" perspectives may be said to anchor one end of a continuum while integrationists anchor the other. A holistic dualist view of soul unites these divergent perspectives, even though their views of integration divide them.

How might this view of the soul influence therapeutic endeavors? First, holistic dualists vary in their perspectives about the etiology of psychological and emotional disorders. For some, problems arise from one of two sources—physical or spiritual. For example, in their masters-level counseling text, *Christ-Centered Therapy: The Practical Integration of Theology and Psychology*, Anderson, Zuehlke, and Zuehlke write, "All psychological problems that are not organic malfunctions arise from humanity's basic sinful nature—from our rebellion against God."[22] For others, a wider range of etiological options exist on the diagnostic horizon, including perceived emotional distress that may be the result of experiences such as grief, trauma, or interpersonal tension, rather than sin.

Second, holistic dualism encourages the development of counseling strategies "for Christians."[23] Counseling approaches that are not based on the Bible are often considered less appropriate, or even inappropriate, for Christian clients.[24] For example, advocates of biblical counseling propose that psychology serves its purpose for understanding the physiological reactions of the brain and the subsequent development of habits, but that this comes as a very distant second to the Word of God as the final authority on the human condition.[25] These specialized approaches reduce the concern voiced by many Christian clients that their treatment may be antibiblical.

(4) Monistic Perspectives on personhood draw upon the tightening mind/brain link reported by neuroscience.[26] Although the exact nature of this link has yet to be fully explained, monism asserts that personhood includes "the inner core of the whole person, *including the body*; the personal and spiritual dimensions of the self."[27] Generally monists also assert that the phenomenological experiences that we label "soul" are not reducible to brain activity and instead represent essential *aspects* of the self, rather than a substantial, ontological entity ("the soul") related to the self.

Brown suggests that emergence accounts for this phenomenon.[28] Emergent properties are specific modes of functioning that depend upon lower-level capacities and the interactions among them, but are not reducible to the sum of these lower-level parts. Brown identifies the capacity for personal relatedness as an emergent property that is dependent upon specific cognitive abilities, such as language, a theory of mind, episodic memory, conscious top-down agency, future orientation, and emotional modulation. Brown explains, "It is experiences of relatedness to others, to the self, and most particularly to God that endow a person with the attributes that have been attached to the concept of 'soul'."[29]

How might monistic perspectives relate to counseling? First, they eliminate the dichotomy between body/soul and physical/spiritual. Because personhood cannot exist apart from the body, care and attention to the well-being of the body in general and the brain in particular increases in importance. An impaired brain can limit the degree to which one's personal relatedness may be experienced and expressed in this life.[30] The impact of major depression upon interpersonal relationships is a case in point. Persons with major depression typically experience intense interpersonal isolation. They feel abandoned by God, even when they have been constantly reading Scripture for guidance, sincerely confessing known and unknown sins, and fervently praying for relief. This sense of utter abandonment is not because of sin per se but because the brain is not functioning correctly.[31]

Second, monist views emphasize the importance of the self in relation to others. Individuals are whole beings who are also part of relationship webs. They are both a part (their relational web) and a *whole* (the experience of self). For example, relationships with primary care givers are critical for infants' brain development as well as their intrapersonal and interpersonal development. Siegel also suggests the same factors that form the core of the caregiver-child dynamic continue to exert influence on brain function into adulthood.[32] As a result, personal identity is formed through relationships with others. Individuality is not lost through absorption into the community. Instead, community is required for individuality to grow and thrive. Counselors working from monist perspectives *must* keep the client's relational networks in mind during the course of treatment. This includes the therapeutic relationship.

Monistic views of personhood are slowly finding their way into the Christian counseling literature.[33] Although no approach to Christian counseling has yet claimed monism as its own, monistic views of personhood are consistent with the biblical portrait of humanity[34] and echo the contemporary emphasis on the relational nature of the Trinity.[35]

Christian Counseling: What Does Neuroscience Have to Do with It?

So what does Christian counseling have to do with neuroscience? The brain and mind are linked through networks of emergent properties that grow increasingly complex. Each property is whole in and of itself, but it is also a part of larger networks, including relational networks, human and Divine.[36] Therefore, a view of personhood that takes the tightening mind-brain link seriously leads to a particular understanding of the metapurpose of Christian counseling with specific attention to the role of the Holy Spirit in general and the counseling relationship in particular. That is, because personal relatedness is the heart of the Triune God, is important for brain development, *and* belongs to the essence of personhood, Christian counseling must seek to increase clients' capacity for personal relatedness with God, others, and self by enhancing clients' ways-of-being that support and deepen their interpersonal life, and by challenging clients' ways-of-being that inhibit their relational capacity. From this perspective the triune God's relationship with counselor and client, mediated through the indwelling presence of the Holy Spirit, forms a significant relational system in which counselor and client participate. As such, it informs the counseling process by means of top-down influence mediated through the Holy Spirit, and the counseling relationship becomes an essential avenue for expanding a client's capacity for personal relatedness with others and with God.[37] Because the Spirit of God superintends the counseling process *in toto*, I argue that specifically *Christian* interventions are not *necessarily required* for "Christian counseling" to take place. Rather, counselors may select interventions in terms of their consistency with the ethos of participation in God's redeemed community and in terms of their contribution to increasing clients' relational capacity.

The notion of top-down agency proposes that higher levels may inform, direct, and influence the present and future functions of lower levels of brain function. In this case, interpersonal relationships can influence one's brain, thereby shaping one's capacity for personal relationship.[38] I suggest that counselors' and clients' relationships with the triune God function at the highest level and, through the Holy Spirit who indwells participants in God's community, exert top-down agency in three ways: (1) through God's grace-filled influence within clients' lives, (2) through a counselor's relationship with the triune God, and (3) through the therapeutic relationship.

Client's Relationship with God

The client's relationship with God provides an important avenue for the expression of God's agency through the Holy Spirit. Anecdotal evidence from clinical practice offers many stories of unexpected transformations in clients' lives that cannot be credited to the work of the counselor but may be most logically attributed to the hand of God. Theologically, we may speak about this as God's grace surrounding clients as they walk through their therapeutic dark night of the soul.[39] Therapeutically, we can refer to outcome research on common factors by psychologist Michael Lambert.[40]

According to Oden, "grace prepares the will and coworks with the prepared will. Insofar as grace precedes and prepares free will it is called prevenient."[41] Although the concept of prevenient grace is usually a feature of soteriological discussion, it can readily be applied to counseling contexts as well. In this case, prevenient grace is that which goes before clients' therapeutic work, preparing the heart and will of clients to receive that which God has prepared for them in counseling. For example, clients may hear sermons or come across books that open their eyes to new personal and relational realities. In other instances, family members or friends may offer actions or words that "just fit" the direction of the therapeutic work. God works in clients' lives in ways that complement and even complete the work done through counseling. This is not within the control of the counselor, but I suggest is a manifestation of the agency of God's relationship with us.

This theological explanation is consistent with research conducted by Michael Lambert. Lambert identifies four common factors that contribute to therapeutic success *regardless* of the theoretical orientation of the therapist. His work indicates that the client and circumstances outside of the therapy setting, taken as a common factor, account for 40 percent of successful outcome variance.[42] Client/extratherapeutic factors refer to things that are not under the counselor's control. Clients bring these things with them into the therapy setting. Client strengths, personality characteristics, relationship with others *outside* of therapy, and unexpected circumstances of life are examples of this important common factor. Clients' faith and membership in a religious community are also included on this list.[43] Lambert, Shapiro, and Bergin provide additional empirical support for this, as they estimate that the rate of spontaneous recovery is about 40 percent.[44] Spontaneous recovery occurs in part because individuals access naturally occurring relational and environmental resources.

The shocking realization from these data is that therapeutic technique ranks far down the line of things that bring about change. If techniques (15 percent) matter so little in comparison to client factors (40 percent), might this not suggest that specifically "Christian" techniques may be nice, but not *absolutely* necessary for Christian counseling to occur? It appears as if clients may be well served by counselors who watch for ways in which God is already at work in clients' lives, and attend carefully to their own relationship with God and God's redeemed people.

Counselor's Relationship with God

Although the client's relationship with God provides one channel through which the divine agency may be expressed, the counselor's relationship with God provides a second. In the therapeutic system composed of counselors who have embraced the way of the cross of Christ and their clients, the kingdom of God is at work in counselors as they embody the ethical comportment and characteristics of participants in God's family within the therapeutic setting. One place this may be seen is in counselors' therapeutic stance in relation to clients. Counselors are respectful of clients, value them as children of God, and propose strategies that are consistent with a biblical worldview, which may or may not include specialized Christian strategies. This respectful stance finds support from Tallman and Bohart's research into the way in which the counseling relationship influences therapeutic outcome. They observe that

> therapists should be much more willing to listen to clients, respect their frame of reference, and genuinely collaborate with them. Collaboration means more than client participation and compliance. It means that therapy must be thought of as the meeting of two minds, each processing its own expertise and

competence, with goals and solutions co-created through mutual dialogue, instead of being chosen and applied to the client by the therapist.[45]

Divine agency may also direct a counselor's words and actions. Clinical lore is replete with stories about out-of-the-blue clinical hunches that open therapeutic doors or interactions that counselors could not recall, but which clients report as being a turning point in therapy. Christian counselors are acutely aware that therapy presents multiple moments through which God's grace manifests itself. Many will rightfully argue that it is only by the grace of God that their work with hurting people is effective. According to Nancey Murphy, "There is no special faculty needed in order to experience religious realities. What makes the experience religious is a meaningful combination of ordinary experiences, under circumstances that make it apparent that God is involved in the event in a special way."[46] In this setting, this means that no special technique is mandated in order to make counseling Christian. What is mandated is the presence of God, experienced by counselor and client as God's grace. Counseling therefore can unfold within the parameters of what counselors know about cognitive, affective, and interpersonal development without the need for specifically Christianized techniques. It is not the external strategies that define Christian counseling, but the agency of the kingdom of God in the lives of counselors who seek to bring this healing reality to bear upon the lives of clients. The person of the therapist-in-relation-to-God brings the Christian into Christian counseling.

The Therapeutic Relationship

Scripture affirms that God's relationship with the world is also expressed through the community of believers as the Body of Christ (e.g., Acts 2:42-47; 1 Cor. 12:12-25). I propose that the concept of top-down agency may be applied to describe this level of human-human interaction and suggest that the counselor-client relationship is a particular example of this. According to Grenz and Franke, "the overarching focus of the biblical narrative is the person-in-relationship or the individual-in-community."[47] Piehl further argues that "although individual bodies have identifiable physical boundaries, like individual substances, there exists an essential interconnectedness that flourishes due to the differences and which can be known only by reference to the social body."[48] This notion moves the accent from "Jesus and me" to who I am in relationship with the community of believers. The message of the cross is lived out through the lives of believers in relationship to one another.

While counseling is not discipleship, we can view the counseling relationship as a special example of "individual-in-community." If a rather particularized understanding of community is permitted—that is, at least two people in relationship—then the counseling relationship indeed fits this notion. Many clients experience a taste of agape love through their relationship with a counselor. This form of unconditional positive regard affirms clients as "children of God and persons of worth."[49] Just as in the Body of Christ we may learn what it means to "be" Christians, so within the counseling relationship may a person learn what it means to "be" a person-in-relationship. To that extent the therapeutic alliance expands clients' relational capacities. Tallman and Bohart (above) emphasize specific qualities of therapeutic relationships and anticipate the importance of the counseling relationship. Although specialized techniques may not be mandatory for Christian counseling, a good therapeutic relationship is *essential*.

Therapeutically, Lambert's discussion of common factors supports this. Lambert proposes that counseling relationship factors contribute 30 percent to successful outcome variance in counseling. Relationship factors describe a variety of relationship-mediated variables (such as counselor empathy, caring, warmth, and support) that are true *regardless* of a counselor's theoretical orientation. Bachelor and Horvath suggest that the "intrinsic quality [of the therapeutic relationship] is an active factor, contributing to the success of therapy over and above concurrent therapeutic gains. . . . Thus, the *relationship can produce change*."[50]

How may this happen? Relationship factors illustrate ways in which counselors *and* clients create an interpersonal environment that invites clients to explore their concerns with counselors. As previously noted, counselors extend empathy and warmth to clients. This creates safety and security within the counseling setting. In addition, counselors tailor their therapeutic stance to clients. Some people prefer a cognitive type of therapeutic response whereas others value overtly Christianized techniques. Good counseling is not a "one size fits all" relationship.

More specifically, Bachelor and Horvath describe three elements that are most characteristic of supportive therapeutic relationships. First, collaboration between counselor and client is a crucial ingredient. Counselors do not set themselves up as "experts" who treat clients like a scientist might treat interesting specimens. Instead, counselors listen to clients' stories to discern those treatment goals that are most important *to the client*, elicit clients' strength and resources, and *together with their clients* agree upon strategies that will help clients achieve their therapeutic goals. Counselors and clients work together to discover which approach to counseling is the "best" for this person with this particular dilemma at this particular moment in time. Second, empathic resonance fosters mutual understanding between counselor and client. In this form of therapeutic attunement, counselors reflect or resonate clients' emotional experience and assist clients in clients' management of overwhelming emotional arousal. Therapists also carefully monitor clients' levels of comfort and satisfaction with the therapeutic relationship. This allows them to address ruptures and misunderstandings promptly. Finally, mutual affirmation denotes respect and an appropriate level of emotional attachment between client and counselor. This unique interpersonal connection supports clients as they risk the expression of thoughts and feelings, heretofore forbidden or out of their conscious awareness.

Notice how these three key elements—collaboration, empathic resonance, and mutual affirmation—underscore the relational capacity of the counselor. Some clients' interactions can prove to be countertherapeutic and counselors will give "more" to maintain a strong therapeutic relationship. Therapist attributes such as self-integration, anxiety management, empathy, and self-insight help them to deal with negative client reactions. Bachelor and Horvath go so far as to suggest that "the personality organization of the therapist may be more relevant than therapist skills or focus on others" for managing these countertherapeutic behaviors.[51] Brown calls this "asymmetric relatedness"—that is, one person with greater relational capacity upholding and sustaining the relationalness or soulishness of another.[52] In this case the counselor sustains the therapeutic relationship that supports the developing relational capacities of a client.

Conclusion

Let us return to the counseling vignettes that opened this essay. We may now consider responses to our two questions: In which situation is the counselor dealing with matters of the soul? Which situation is an example of Christian counseling? On the basis of the perspective developed in this chapter, I suggest that all four counselors provided "soul care" in a clinical counseling setting from a Christian counseling perspective.

How can this be so when these counseling snapshots are so different? By taking the neuroscientific tightening of the mind/brain connection to heart, one can emphasize the enhancement of clients' relational capacities within a therapeutic setting, superintended and enabled by the agency of the triune God, and embodied in counselors' and clients' relationship with God and through the therapeutic relationship itself. We should observe that the counselors in all of these vignettes focused on their relationship with their clients, collaborated with clients in ways consistent with Lambert's common factors, and sought the guidance of God as they worked with their clients. Elizabeth's (scenario 3) Christian orientation is most overt in this case, while Dr. Joseph's (scenario 4) is the most oblique.

In effect, Christian counseling is less about technique and more about relationality. Attention to technique may be necessary because of clients' preferences or because the epistemological basis of a particular technique renders it incompatible for counselors and clients who participate in God's redeemed community. Unfortunately, however, much of the controversy over what is or is not Christian counseling revolves around what techniques are (or are not) used. If we take Lambert's work seriously—that is, if we take seriously Lambert's report that technique and theoretical orientation account for only 15 percent of successful outcome variance—then we might wonder what the fuss is all about. If relational capacities are indeed the essence of our personhood, then perhaps counselor education, training, and supervision should invest more energy in developing counselors with Christlike character who work with clients to create therapeutic relationships that may bring about hope and healing. Here one finds the heart and soul in Christian counseling.

Pastoral Care and Counseling Without the "Soul"

A Consideration of Emergent Monism

Stuart L. Palmer

Contemporary advances in the neurosciences have stimulated debate about the fundamental constitution of human beings. The age-old "mind-body" question is being revisited. Are human beings composed of a body and a distinct, nonmaterial soul? Or are human beings composed of a body without a distinct, nonmaterial soul? These questions have been on the minds of some neuroscientists, and the vast majority of them have asserted that the traditional body/soul dualism does not fit the growing evidence derived from scientific research.[1] Although Christian philosophers, theologians, and psychologists have recognized the profound implications these suggestions present and have begun to engage in dialogue and debate,[2] surprisingly there has been no significant response or consideration of these findings by major figures in the field of pastoral care and counseling. Given this situation, my present task is to explore what might be the practical results and possible benefits for the field if a pastor holds a view of human beings that excludes a distinct, nonmaterial entity called "soul." Of particular interest here is a view of the human person known as "emergent monism."[3] To accomplish this task I will discuss what is meant by "emergent monism," then turn to its implications for pastoral anthropology and its possible influence on pastoral care and counseling.

An Emergent Monistic View of Human Persons

In general, there has been consistent evidence that "specific mental processes or even component parts of those processes appear to be tightly linked to particular regions or systems in the brain. Within those regions, moreover, there often emerged a further specificity indicating that certain columns of cells were involved when a particular aspect of the task was being performed."[4] Along with these findings of localization and specificity has come a "timely counterbalance from work on neural networks within the brain. It emerged that many complex psychological processes are not necessarily localized to one part of the brain but often depend upon the intact working of networks of systems of cells located in widely separated parts of the brain."[5] Given this data, many leading researchers, when asking themselves what all this means for human nature in general, have suggested a variety of different interpretations. These interpretations range from one extreme to the other, from reductive materialism to strong dualism. Such extreme perspectives are incompatible with a Christian view of persons.[6]

In contrast, Philip Clayton has proposed a more satisfying intermediate interpretation, which takes the neuroscience data seriously without compromising essential affirmations congruent with a Christian view of personhood. He describes it as "emergent monism." Although the phrase is awkward and, like all "-isms," can be tainted by the limitations of a long history of interpretation, I have still opted to use Clayton's language; proposing a new vocabulary to describe the evidence arising from the neurosciences as it interfaces with Christian faith is beyond the scope of this chapter. Undoubtedly, though, the future of interdisciplinary dialogue between contemporary science and Christianity will require substantial advances in and enrichment of our terminology.

Clayton makes it clear that the human person must not be understood in solely dualistic or materialistic terms, but in terms of a "psychosomatic unity" made possible by an "emergent monism." How is this complex term defined? For Clayton "monism" involves two interrelated perspectives. First, humans can be viewed as one and only one substance—that is, by their physicality. Second, humans can be seen as participants in a distinct order, a finite created order in contrast to a Creator whose nature is essentially infinite. In comparison with the

Creator, all things in the universe share a common nature: finiteness. In this sense, all creation is monistic. Clayton thus defines "monism" from a physicalist and finite perspective, but then qualifies "monism" by associating it with another critical concept. The choice he makes is to associate monism not with "reductionism" or "determinism," but with "emergentism."

"Emergentism" as used by Clayton is a feature of what is broadly known as "Complexity Theory."[7] Emergentism, when applied to the question of the mind (i.e., consciousness and cognition/emotionality) and its relationship to the brain, makes three basic assertions. First, human consciousness and cognition/emotionality do not arise until physical systems reach a sufficiently high level of configurational complexity. The mind causally depends upon the dynamic complexity of the human brain. The interplay of many lower-level dynamics produces properties not existing at the lower levels. This complex, physiochemical system (i.e., the brain) generates unique properties having their own novel operational rules and causal influences (i.e., the mind). In other words, these properties are far more than the summation of the basic building blocks existing at a less complex level. Instead, something novel occurs: the mind, which at the same time is totally dependent on its neurological substrate. The influence of the brain on the mind is a dynamic reality that at times can be described as a "bottom-up" influence.

Second, "emergentism" avers that human consciousness and cognition/emotionality arise not in a closed system, but in an open system where malleable biology and neurology are influenced and shaped by environmental and relational factors. The human brain is not a static entity but a physiochemical system with enormous qualities of "plasticity."[8] Interpersonal and environmental conditions exert substantial, formative influence on brain circuitry and activation as well as on the subsequent unfolding of states of consciousness and the cognitive/emotional patterns of "self-organization."[9]

Finally, "emergentism" has it that the mind (i.e., consciousness and cognition/emotionality) is, in an important sense, irreducible. Consciousness and cognition/emotionality are novel features of the world and cannot be reduced to the neurobiological processes that cause it. Complex system interactions create their own rules of operation and their own forms of causal influence. The brain is a complex system whose processes organize its own functioning. The mind emanates from the activity of the brain, and thus it is fair to say that the mind itself is complex and has self-organizing properties. It is not reducible in the sense that a complete neurobiological account of these properties would ever appreciate the reality of the first-person, subjective, qualitative features characteristic of human personhood.[10] This irreducibility also suggests that, as these higher-level system operations emerge, they exert "top-down" (or whole-part) causal influences on the lower system levels as well.[11]

Thus, "emergent monism" is a way of making sense of the person who is a complexly patterned entity within the world. These diverse sets of emerging properties are nested within human physicality, which is further embedded in God's created finite order. Human persons are truly unique objects in God's world, with strange properties called "consciousness" and "cognition/emotionality" arising or emerging from the complex functioning of the physical organism's neurological substrate and profoundly influenced by interpersonal and environmental dynamics. It is no longer necessary to attribute "higher" human capacities and properties (i.e., spirituality, morality, relationality) to a nonmaterial "soul" because there is substantial evidence that highly complex system interactions within the human brain and body give rise to these phenomena both in society and in relation to God.

We should distinguish between "emergent monism" and the proposed "emergent dualism" of William Hasker.[12] He acknowledges the problems with Cartesian dualism and seriously considers the growing evidence from the neurosciences influencing the "philosophy of mind." His suggested "middle way" is a much more satisfying stance than some forms of "wholistic dualism" which assert humans function as a unity but are composed of separable "parts."[13] Hasker is not so brash as to speak of "parts" but does differentiate "emergent properties" from "emergent substances." Put simply, "properties" are capacities with no ontological difference while "substances" are not only capacities but are constitutive of a different ontology. A critical aspect of his argument is based on the apparent incongruity between holding an emergent "properties" position and reconciling that with a necessity to maintain "personal identity" in the "intermediate state" between death and final resurrection. This incongruity could be resolved in terms of a different view of eternity and perspective about identity.[14] In this context, emergent monism is still preferred.

Before considering the implications for pastoral anthropology and pastoral care and counseling, an important caveat is necessary. Cognitive psychology and human neuropsychology as fields of scientific endeavor are not complete. There is still much about human subjective and relational experience that has not yet been demonstrated to have neural correlates, nor have the neural systems involved in most complex human experiences been completely described. There remain many mysteries. However, neuroscientific evidence and explanations of attributes and experiences traditionally assigned to the "soul" comprise an accelerating trend. What is more, the neurosciences have strongly influenced the modern understanding of the person. Information from the study of human neurophysiology cannot be ignored. It must be considered in any Christian understanding of human nature.

A Different Pastoral Anthropology

Care and counseling offered by a pastor has often been linked to a long tradition expressed in the language of "soul care" or "soul cure."[15] To describe pastoral care as "soul care" suggests underlying assumptions about the basic makeup of human persons. In pastoral ministry it is essential that the pastor be aware of his or her anthropology—that is, how she or he views human nature and the possibility of human transformation and change. This anthropology is not simply derived from the Bible. Instead, it is forged in a dynamic blending of theology and biblical interpretation along with sociological, cultural, and scientific perspectives. A pastoral anthropology is always a work in process, which involves a creative synthesis demanding continuity, constraint, and flexibility. Two questions of critical concern requiring awareness of this creative synthesis are how a person's spirituality and cognition/emotionality relate to one another and how a person's material aspects (i.e., brain and body) and nonmaterial aspects (i.e., spirituality, morality, and psychology) relate to one another. Regarding these questions, pastoral anthropologies have often answered in ways influenced by either reductionistic or dualistic tendencies.

Reductionistic Tendencies

Two reductionistic patterns have been common in pastoral reflections on how spirituality relates to the psychological aspects of human beings. The first could be labeled "Psychological Reductionism,"[16] which is common among many mainline Protestant pastors. This position suggests that all expressions of spirituality in life are reducible to psychological phenomena. Spiritual explanations or vocabulary are at best unnecessary and at worst illusory. Communication tends to be framed in psychological terms such as "self" or "ego," with little or no mention of terms like "soul" or "spirituality." Life challenges are predominantly assessed as issues such as "anxiety," "depression," and "personality disorders," and not issues involving one's relationship to God. Guidance and support often involve procedures and processes derived primarily from contemporary therapeutic psychology. The long pastoral tradition with its rich and diverse insights concerning human spirituality and its influence on all aspects of human life are rarely considered or accessed.

The second is "Spiritual Reductionism," which is common for many conservative and/or evangelical Protestant pastors. This position suggests that psychological dynamics in life are reducible to spiritual explanations and vocabulary. Psychological perspectives are at best unnecessary and at worst a threat to the integrity of orthodox Christian faith. Communication tends to be framed in spiritual terms such as "soul" or "spirituality" and not in the language of psychology like "self" or "ego." Challenges in life are not related to psychological "self-esteem" or emotional "disorders" resulting from living in a broken world, but from personal sin, and/or lack of a thorough commitment to Jesus Christ. Guidance and support are most often given in terms of "repentance," "prayer," and renewal of one's spiritual life. This approach often draws very little from the historic Christian tradition and more often is dominated by contemporary Western culture's emphasis on individualism and private spirituality.

Dualistic Tendencies

Two dualistic patterns have also been common among Protestant pastors, one dealing with the relationship of spirituality to psychology and the other having to do with the mind-brain or soul-body question. The first could be termed, "Psychospiritual Dualism," which suggests that spirituality and psychological phenomena have very little relationship to one another. They are not identical or reducible one to the other, but are distinct and must be addressed differently. Communication involves a differentiation between "spiritual" realities and "psychological" realities. Psychological language is used for the "psychological" domain and spiritual language is used for the "spiritual" domain. There is very little overlap or influence between them. Life challenges are viewed as either a "spiritual problem" or a "psychological/emotional problem" but also could be seen as a combination of both. Assistance often involves either a pastor or mental health professional working from a single perspective or a team of specialists attempting to coordinate their work with little dialogue or integration of perspectives.

The second pattern of dualism could be given a variety of labels depending upon the degree of distinction between soul/body or mind/brain. It should be noted that this pattern is highly influential today. Whether the pastor tends to be reductionistic or dualistic in regards to spirituality and psychology, he or she is most often a dualist of one stripe or another when it comes to physical and nonphysical dimensions of human existence. So, depending on the position held, it could be labeled "Radical Dualism" or "Interactive Dualism."[17] These pastors acknowledge the physical dimension of human beings and will often agree that physicality does exert influence on psychological and spiritual functioning, but there is still a fundamental, ontological difference between the physical and the nonphysical aspect of human existence. The physical and the nonphysical are essentially different in nature. Communication influenced by such a perception suggests the real person is the "soul," the inner being, and the "body," the outer aspect, is not the true person. The inner world is emphasized and the bodily dimension is minimized and even trivialized. This dualistic perspective exerts influence on how the pastor understands and guides a parishioner with concerns such as the meaning of spirituality, salvation, ethical behavior, gender and sexuality, human pain, tragedy, and death.

A Pastoral Anthropology Informed by Emergent Monism

A pastoral anthropology informed by emergent monism is substantially different from those influenced by reductionistic and dualistic tendencies. First, consider the relationship of the "material" and "nonmaterial" aspects of personhood. Fundamentally, this anthropology is monistic, emphasizing as it does an embodied, physical anthropology. True personhood does not exist for the human being apart from its grounding in finite physicality. We do not possess a body or inhabit a body; we are a physical body. We exist as an embodied entity. As finite physical beings we are fundamentally tied to the created order. If we sidestep this fundamental, monistic assertion, we are in danger of minimizing or trivializing our essential physicality; if we step no further, however, we reduce human personhood to something less than personal, to simple biochemical phenomena and processes. Emergentism suggests a way of stepping further without negating our fundamentally physical nature. Inherent in our embodiment are signals of fragility and radical dependence as well as the need for adaptation and personal relatedness. "Higher" human capacities of consciousness, cognition/emotionality, morality, and spirituality are responses to these challenges. They arise from and are completely dependent on our physicality, which is embedded in and influenced by interactions with other persons and God. They are essential for surviving and also negotiating intimate personal relationships with other human beings and with the divine, infinite Creator.

A brief consideration of Christian spirituality illustrates the point. Spirituality defies easy definition, but, in general, many authors suggest that in its natural expression it involves a genuine quest for and experience of meaning as well as relatedness to the Divine.[18] Because of its abstract nature, spirituality can easily be viewed as separate and unrelated to concrete human existence and relatedness. But, given an emergent monistic perspective, natural spirituality is an emergent property conveyed through consciousness and cognition/emotionality tied to finite physicality. This natural spirituality can be more fully experienced and expressed through a religion, which is characterized by beliefs, rituals, social organization, and cumulative traditions. Obviously, religious spiritualities can be quite diverse, but we are concerned with a unique expression of religious spirituality termed "Christian spirituality." Christian spirituality is the fulfillment of the natural spiritual quest in terms of a deep and dynamic relationship with the triune God experienced in the context of Christian community. Christian spirituality is expressed relationally and physically, not just individualistically and privately. Finiteness signals fragility and dependence and thus is a catalyst for the expression of Christian spirituality in terms of community with others and with the triune God. Thus, Christian spirituality is not a loosely attached, nebulous phenomenon unrelated to physical existence; instead it is an "incarnate" spirituality that finds expression not only in our relationships with God and others but also in our embodied experience of gender, social location, socioeconomic class, racial/cultural identity, and moral/ethical perspectives.

Additionally, a pastoral anthropology shaped by emergent monism offers a more satisfying alternative to the previously noted approaches by suggesting how a person's spirituality relates to his or her psychology. Spirituality is an inherent capacity and quest for meaning and divine relatedness. It is an expression of complex dynamics emerging from human consciousness and cognition/emotionality. Spirituality does not exist independent of human psychology. It does not have its own unique processes and mechanisms, but is actually dependent on the dynamic workings of consciousness and cognition/emotionality. Spirituality and psychology are not synonymous, but neither are they easily divisible. This is illustrated by the bidirectional, nonlinear dynamic seen in the "bottom-up" and "top-down" influence noted in emergentism. These dynamics suggest that psychological states and conditions exert significant influence on the expression of spirituality, and spiritual orientation exerts significant influence on the processes and mechanisms of psychological existence. Numerous testimonies and documented research have in fact shown that shifts in a person's overall psychological state often exert influence on a person's reported spiritual life. For example, a person struggling with what psychology would term "clinical depression" experiences changes not only in their emotional state but also in their "spiritual" interests and perspectives. Moreover, there is evidence that a change in a person's spiritual life can exert influence over a person's psychological state.[19] Thus, persons experiencing a significant reordering of life based on an encounter with Jesus Christ in Christian community are likely to report changes in their emotional/psychological states as well.

Given the centrality of relatedness inherent in finite physicality, human psychology, and Christian spirituality, communication must be no longer in exclusively psychological or spiritual language but in the language of "relational personhood." Language of "personal relatedness" has an integrating influence. It melds together the perspectives of the physical, psychological, and spiritual, while avoiding reductionistic and dualistic tendencies. If terms like "self," "soul," and "spirituality" are used,[20] much attention must be given to redefine them in light of this different anthropological context. Challenges in life are not simply defined in the nomenclature of psychology (e.g., anxiety, depression) or Christian spirituality (e.g., personal sin, lack of faith) but in terms of capacities and deficits for engaging in authentic, genuine personal relatedness with others and God. If challenges are expressed in psychological and/or spiritual language, attention must be given to redefine their meaning in light of personal relatedness. Pastoral dialogue and guidance would be much more relationally sensitive and relation-minded. The pastor would think and formulate ministry in clearly relational terms and avoid highly individualistic and privatized conceptualizations.

Pastoral Care and Counseling Influenced by a Different Anthropology

Pastoral care refers to the broad range of pastoral activities meant to provide support and nurture for individual parishioners and/or the congregation as a whole. These include, but are not limited to, facilitating worship, administering the sacraments, visiting the sick, supporting the downtrodden, attending the dying, and comforting the bereaved. Pastoral counseling, on the other hand, is a more specialized and focused form of pastoral care. It is unique in that a parishioner seeks a pastor's assistance for a particular problem and the nature of the problem requires the pastor to engage in a more substantial and structured way of helping the troubled parishioner. How might "emergent monism" influence the practices of pastoral care and counseling?

Influence on Pastoral Care

An anthropology of emergent monism suggests three general needs requiring pastoral care. First, as finite physical beings, human persons are profoundly frail and vulnerable to the difficulties and calamities of life and are in need of relational presence and partnership. Second, human beings are in need of concrete personal relationships and a community of close physical proximity. Third, human persons are finite creatures needing a relationship with the divine, infinite Creator.

These needs are addressed most successfully in the context of a community of Christian faith. The pastor is in a unique role because he or she is commissioned to represent the values and grace of this community. Care for the frail and vulnerable is guided by relating in terms of initiating, attending, supporting, and comforting. The pastor seeks out opportunities to make contact with people who may be on the fringes of the community. She or he is sensitive to the needs of the powerless, homeless, poor, and forgotten. The heart of God is reflected in not forgetting or overlooking the marginalized. For those individuals and families struggling with distress, illness, death, and loss, the pastor is a partner in difficulty and calamity. Pastors recognize the importance of physical presence and a caring, comforting demeanor.

In providing care for dislocated and isolated people, a pastor is guided by relating in terms of introducing and incorporating. Each person is both a contributor to community and a receiver of community. From this perspective, the pastor is mindful of the person's level of participation in the Body of Christ and simultaneous involvement in the very life of the triune God. The pastor is oriented toward introducing individuals or families to others with similar interest or concerns. In addition, the pastor is sensitive to building concrete community through incorporating individuals and families into fellowship with others by encouraging the development of small group gatherings for study, training, support, and ministry.

In providing care for the whole congregation, a pastor is guided by relating as a leader who is involved in facilitating and administering. Worship provides both the content and the context for congregational care.[21] The pastor is uniquely set apart within the congregation to provide leadership that facilitates community worship. Worship orients the people of God toward their Creator and Redeemer and reminds each individual that life in Christ is a life of close community. Worship is expressed in preaching, teaching, and singing, but also in the administration of the sacraments—concrete and symbolic vehicles through which the transforming life in Christ is manifest in the local community.

Influence on Pastoral Counseling

Pastoral counseling as a focused expression of pastoral care recognizes the general needs of people, but provides the troubled parishioner a more intimate relationship designed for problem solving. Given a pastor's role and training, most pastoral counselors have suggested that pastoral counseling should be brief and time-limited, as well as structured and goal-oriented.[22] This is appropriate. But viewing pastoral counseling in this manner could give the impression that only a pastoral anthropology influenced by reductionistic or dualistic tendencies would be compatible. That is not the case. A counseling approach with these defining characteristics is fully compatible with a wholistic anthropology shaped by emergent monism, provided that some critical features are addressed. The four features needing redefinition and adjustment are problem definition, pastoral assessment, intervention(s), and referral coordination.

It is not necessary to classify a parishioner's problems in pastoral counseling as simply "spiritual" or "emotional" or "physical," although it may be presented that way by the troubled person. Instead, the parishioner's problem(s) need to be defined in terms of capacities and deficits in relationships. The presenting problem(s) will involve present, past, or future relationships, and how these are interacting with or have shaped the parishioners' subjective perceptions and interpretations of life. He or she is not just struggling with "guilt," "shame," or "depression," as if the concern is an isolated phenomenon located solely in the parishioner. Problems must be contextualized. Defining the problem as simply "guilt," "shame," or "depression" fails to do justice to each individual's irreducible engagement with other human beings and God. The pastor can focus attention on the presenting problem but must always define it in terms of the person's embodied existence (i.e., the wholeness of personhood—finite physicality, cognition/emotionality, spirituality—and how they are intimately tied together yet irreducible) and the person's relational context (i.e., with the Christian community and the triune God).

A pastoral assessment, sometimes called a "pastoral diagnosis,"[23] is related to the problem definition. In adjusting a pastoral assessment in light of an anthropology characterized by emergent monism, it is critical to recognize that the pastor is not engaged in a medical, psychiatric, or psychological diagnostic process. Neither is it an exclusively "biblical" or "spiritual" diagnostic process. Instead, it involves the pastor's identity and self-awareness combined with discernment and judgment as to the parishioner's capacity and deficits with respect to participation in community with others and God. Specifically, this wholistic assessment would include such items as (1) the degree of yearning or longing for intimate relatedness, (2) awareness of and response to embodied existence (e.g., physical ailments, physical limitations, gender, sexuality, social location, socioeconomic class, racial/cultural identity), (3) ability to receive grace from the triune God and others as well as to extend grace-oriented care and service, (4) willingness to live in an authentic manner within the local community of faith, (5) capacity to see and embrace the outsider and marginalized person(s), (6) recognition of personal gifts and their use in service, (7) growing realization of the moral/ethical character of living in community, and (8) demonstrated capacity to engage in ethical decision making.

As pastors orient themselves to assist the troubled parishioner, it is crucial that they not be dominated by what strategies or techniques to use but instead pay close attention to the person. Pastors need to give advice and direction as well as recommend the use of prayer, Bible reading, and devotional literature as part of their pastoral counseling, but most critical is the tone and nature of the ongoing interpersonal exchange with the parishioner.[24] The pastoral counseling relationship is the foundational intervention. All other techniques and strategies flow from it.

The pastoral counseling relationship is qualitatively different from a general pastoral care conversation. It is mutual but focuses primarily on the concern of the one seeking help. It is an encounter between two persons that offers the opportunity to experience for a short period of time genuine, authentic community. The pastor offers gracious acceptance and a loving embrace of the one who may be isolated, shamed, and marginalized. At the same time, the pastor recognizes distinctions between embodied persons expressed in such ethical boundaries as respectful interactions and maintenance of personal space. The intersubjective context in which this encounter is occurring is of critical importance. The pastor is mindful that what is unfolding and being illuminated in the exchange may profoundly transform the parishioner. The person's capacity for relatedness may be enriched and deepened by the exchange. This person-to-person experience may facilitate movement in resolving the problem or giving support, but on another level the pastor is aware that God the Spirit is uniquely present and influencing not only the pastor but also the parishioner. God the Spirit is permeating the intersubjective exchange and is uniquely working in and through it. The pastor is an incarnational witness of God's intimate involvement in this person's life.

The pastoral counselor does not just draw upon her or his own private knowledge or even on his or her own personal relationship with Christ, but also upon the rich resources of God's presence in community and the broader society. Pastors recognize their limits and are willing to work with others within and out-side the Christian community for the sake of the troubled parishioner. Other pro-fessionals (e.g., physicians, psychiatrists, mental health professionals) with expertise in one domain often do not think or conceptualize the person's prob-lems in a wholistic manner. The pastor with a comprehensive perspective is in a unique position. He or she can guide, tailor, and manage the referral(s) based upon a more complete picture of human personhood, which most professionals lack. Sometimes a pastor is reluctant to make and coordinate referrals because of a distorted view of the nature of human persons or because of the fear of losing a significant role with the parishioner. Making a referral does not cancel the pas-tor's role with the parishioner, but it may adjust it. The pastor continues to be involved with either counseling or care even when a parishioner is being assisted at the same time by a physician, psychiatrist, or mental health profession. The pastor offering counseling plays an ongoing, critical role in the care of parish-ioners no matter the counseling issue or concern.

Conclusion

Our task has been to consider what might be the practical results and possible benefits for the field of pastoral care and counseling if the pastor's anthropology were refashioned by a view of human beings that excludes a dualistic conception of "soul." The specific nondualistic view discussed and applied was Philip Clayton's "Emergent Monism." Other pastoral anthropologies were briefly dis-cussed and then compared with "emergent monistic" anthropology. The results suggest the superiority of the latter in that it provides a more satisfactory way of integrating physicality, consciousness, cognition/emotionality, and spirituality. When this different anthropology is applied to pastoral care it suggests a com-prehensive view of human beings that appreciates finite frailty and the need for involvement and community, and the necessity of personal relationship with God. When applied to pastoral counseling it results in modifications in certain dimensions of the counseling process and not a fundamental change in an appro-priately brief, goal-oriented model. Overall, this initial exploration suggests that a view of human nature excluding a dualistic "soul" would be highly beneficial for the pastor in providing care and counsel.

CHAPTER 13

Human Nature

An Integrated Picture

Malcolm Jeeves

Men go out and gaze in astonishment at high mountains, the huge waves of the sea, the broad reaches of rivers, the oceans that encircle the world, or the stars in their courses. But they pay no attention to themselves . . . the field of my labours is my own self. I'm not now investigating the tracts of the heavens or measuring the distance of the stars or trying to discover how the earth hangs in space. I am investigating myself, my memory, my mind. . . . What then am I, my God? What is my nature? (Augustine, Confessions 9)

We continue to ask Saint Augustine's question, but now in the light of vastly increased knowledge of how we are made. So what does it mean to be human? Was Thomas Metzinger, whom Joel Green cites in the opening chapter, correct to say that "contemporary science generates a radically new understanding of what it means to be human"?[1] Is it the case, as provocatively suggested by Francis Crick, that the full impact of contemporary neuroscientific views of humankind will result in a "head-on contradiction to the religious beliefs of billions of human beings alive today"? Was Crick correct to say that "the idea that man has a disembodied soul is as unnecessary as the old idea that there was a Life Force"?[2] So radical is the potential impact of advances in neuroscience that they have been likened to those of Copernicus and Galileo four centuries ago.

Seldom have questions such as What am I? or Who am I? been brought into sharper focus than in recent years with the public debates about reproductive and therapeutic cloning. These issues are very much in the public domain at the moment on account of unsubstantiated claims for the first cloning of human beings. All of these are a natural consequence from the high profile they were given when together an American president and a British prime minister made statements about the ethics and regulation of human cloning.

What about life after death if I no longer have an immortal soul to guarantee my survival after physical death? What does "after" mean as we ponder the meanings of time and eternity? And as those to whom Paul was writing at Corinth asked, in what form then shall they come (1 Cor. 15:35)? What about resurrection and immortality? Must we all pass through an intermediate state? If I no longer "have" a soul but "am" a soul—that is, a "living being"—what does that imply about "soul talk" in evangelism? Do our missionary strategies, traditionally thought of as "saving souls," need to be reexamined? How should the counselor or pastoral psychologist think about fellow Christians coming for guidance and advice if they no longer have souls but are souls?

Although the science with which we are primarily concerned in this volume is neuroscience, the issues cannot be restricted to this alone. As I indicated in chapter 2, some of the most exciting research is at the interface of neuroscience and evolutionary psychology. For example, the discovery of so-called mirror neurons has reopened with a fresh urgency, in some people's minds, issues concerning the uniqueness of human beings. This in turn links up with much that has been written in the past about locating the uniqueness of human beings in their possession of a "soul," which is then used to define the *imago Dei* possessed uniquely by human beings. As we have discovered in earlier chapters, it could be argued that public declarations such as those by Francis Crick illustrate how easy it is for those of us who are scientists to be guilty of not being up-to-date with what theologians and biblical scholars are saying. No doubt that occurs. It also happens that theologians can be found tilting at scientific windmills long since dismantled and, perhaps what is worse, some are found modifying their doctrines to fit the supposed contours of what they perceive to be the current scientific landscape while, unbeknown to them, it has changed yet again.

Does it matter then whether we pay any attention to what scientists are saying? We believe it does, since our claim is that all truth, whether revealed in Scripture or discovered using the talents we are given to study ourselves and the world in which we live, is an integrated whole. That does not mean that there will be neat solutions with no residual problems as we seek to do justice to truth from these different perspectives. At any one time there will certainly be points of tension and puzzlement that only time and more hard work will resolve. Where the evidence is yet to come we shall do our utmost to keep our minds open and our mouths shut.

Mind, Brain, Person: Contours of the Scientific Landscape

Signposts from Neuroscience and Psychology

At every level of neuroscience research, from single cells and their interactions to the functioning of whole integrated systems coordinating different centers of brain activity, one message is clear. There is interdependence between what is happening at the physical level of brain processes and at the levels of cognition and behavior. On that almost everyone today agrees.

The order of magnitude of the events occurring in the brain range from several centimeters in the case of long pathways and networks, down to molecular events occurring in changes in neurotransmitters. In chapters 2 and 3, Gareth Jones and I indicated the kinds of evidence that underline the ever-tightening links between brain and cognition. We gave examples illustrating what I called the bottom-up approach, moving up through the lower levels of molecular events at synapses to the higher levels of networks and systems.

One of the great contributions of the Nobel laureate neuroscientist Roger Sperry was his emphasis on the importance of paying full attention to the role of cognition in modifying brain processes. This he labeled a top-down effect. A recent vivid example of the power of top-down effects is the study of the ubiquitous placebo effect. Placebo analgesia is an important component in pain management.[3] The basic mechanisms that make it possible are poorly understood. It has long been believed that one important component of the effect is the body's endogenous opioid systems. Researchers used positron emission tomography to monitor activity in those brain areas known to be implicated in opioid analgesia. They discovered that activity in these areas resulting from the intake of a rapidly acting opioid was also activated, though slightly less so, under the placebo condition. In a word, *what the person believed* directly affected their brain activity, and in the same areas as those known to respond to administered opioids, though the placebo effect was slightly less than the effect when the opioids were ingested. The researchers concluded, "These findings indicate a related neural mechanism in placebo and opioid analgesia."[4]

As I indicated in my review of some of the relevant scientific evidence (chapter 2), the rate of progress in research indicating ever-tightening links between mind and brain continues to accelerate. There is much to discover and so many gaps in our present knowledge that there are ready-made opportunities for any such as John W. Cooper, who are committed to a body-soul dualism on other grounds, to say that "science does not justify an unqualified functional wholism."[5] He should note however that the gaps are steadily closing. In Cooper's brief treatment of brain science under the heading "Dualism and

Science," there is more than a hint, at times, of a God-of-the-gaps approach. He writes, "Many scientists operated with the assumption that brain science would eventually be able to map a one-to-one causal relation between particular states of the brain and specific states of mind. Some actually postulated the identity of mental states and brain states, assuming that science would vindicate that hypothesis. But science has not turned out that way."[6]

Cooper is certainly right in what he says about the detailed mapping of one-to-one causal relationships; however, any suggestion that the results of neuro-science fail to continue to accumulate evidence indicating closer links between brain states and mental states is simply untrue. For example, as recently as 1996 Grabowski and Damasio could write that "the imaging of the neural correlates of single and discreet mental events, such as one image or one word, remains a most desirable dream."[7] By the year 2000, O'Craven and Kanwisher could end their report by referring back to Damasio's comment and adding "that dream is now a reality."[8] This is perhaps a further warning of how dangerous it is to try to support Cooper's particular view, based upon what seemed at the time a current gap in our scientific knowledge. We face the same temptation here and therefore at no point argue from the science to a particular theology. Rather we point to the conclusions of biblical scholars as bringing into serious doubt belief in an intermediate state which for Cooper is a crucial doctrine requiring a substance dualist view of the human person. We believe there is a consonance between what biblical scholars are telling us about human nature and the emerging scientific portraits. We may both be wrong.

Signposts from Developmental Neurobiology

It is not enough to focus exclusively on mind-brain issues. By focusing only on those and their relevance to debates about the soul, dualism, and monism, we risk forgetting that, first and foremost, we are persons—not brains, not minds, not bodies, but persons. We constantly exercise our personal agency. Developmental neurobiologists remind us never to forget that a holistic approach to understanding human nature focuses on the person. Scientific developments in understanding neural plasticity and behavioral genetics underline the need to recognize and hold in proper balance, on the one hand, the biological and physical limits set to our capacities such as intellect and personality characteristics and, on the other hand, the pervasive influence of environmental and personal agency factors in shaping who we are and who we become. In chapter 3, Gareth Jones concluded, "It should now be clear why I categorically dismissed the 'brain as a machine' model. The classic view of machines is that they are manufactured according to certain specifications, so that they function in certain predetermined ways." He continued, "The human brain is entirely different from this. My brain was not designed to conform to some predetermined pattern. The personal model I am espousing reflects these ongoing interactions between what we are as people, the organization and plasticity of our brains, every facet of our environment, and all the relationships of which we are a part."

Whether we are considering aggressive behavior or sexual behavior, the fact that we know something of the genetic, neural, and hormonal substrates of each can help but not decide how we are to set limits to the expression of aggression or sexuality. Decisions about what is morally and ethically right or wrong, acceptable or unacceptable, cannot be derived from neurobiology. For Jones, agency and personal responsibility remain the primary concepts when talking about person-hood. At the same time our knowledge of neurobiology can and should inform our understanding of ourselves and hold back our proneness, at times, to make knee-jerk reactions in understanding and judging the actions of others.

Mind-Brain Interdependence

How can we best characterize the ubiquitous evidence of interdependence between what is happening at the physical level of brain processes and at the level of cognition and consciousness? Contributors to this book have their preferred ways of doing it. William Hasker offers emergent dualism (chapter 8), Stuart Palmer prefers Philip Clayton's emergent monism (chapter 12), while Virginia Todd Holeman refers to nonreductive physicalism. With shared Christian beliefs, they each seek to do justice to their understanding of the relevant science and their interpretation, helped by the biblical scholars, of the scriptural evidence.

There are no knock-down arguments ruling out dualism if one is com-mitted to it on other grounds. For example, the late Sir John Eccles, another neu-roscientist Nobel laureate, advocated strongly some form of dualism of substance while at the same time recognizing the problems inherent in such a position. He wrote that consciousness "is dependent on the existence of a sufficient number of such critically poised neurones, and, consequently, only in such conditions are willing and perceiving possible. However, it is not necessary for the whole cor-tex to be in this special dynamic state." He continued, "On the basis of this con-cept (of activity of the cortex) we can face up anew to the extraordinary problems inherent in a strong dualism. Interaction of brain and conscious mind, brain receiving from conscious mind in a willed action and in turn transmitting to mind in a conscious experience." He viewed mental events as acting causally on the brain, at times preceding the corresponding brain activity, and urged, "Let us be clear that for each of us the primary reality is our consciousness—every-thing else is derivative and has a second order reality. We have tremendous intel-lectual tasks in our efforts to understand baffling problems that lie right at the centre of our being."[9]

Roger Sperry echoed Edelman's concern over reductionism in presenting his preferred formulation of the mind-brain relationship, arguing that it was simplistic to try to reduce humans to "nothing but" physio-chemical machines. He wrote, "The new model adds downward to the traditional upward microdeterminism and is claimed to give science a conceptual foundation that is more adequate, valid and comprehensive."[10] Others chose simply *to identify mind with brain*, yet others argue that mental events are products of physical events that have no causal efficacy, the so-called *epiphenomenalist* view. Yet others argue that the best way of thinking about mind-brain links is *psychophysiological parallelism*. On this view there are two parallel streams of events. Physical events cause the physical events and mental events cause further mental events. The physical and mental events are tightly coupled in time.

In thinking about mind, brain, and person the first and most immediate aspect of reality with which we have to deal must be the data of our own conscious experience, as Eccles affirmed. It is here that we confront the concept of self-conscious human agency.

Scientists are well aware of the ever-present temptation to opt for a slick solution that reduces mind to matter without remainder. It is, however, our conscious reflection that generates our challenging theories about ourselves. If there are problems, they are of our own making. The Nobel laureate biologist Gerald Edelman tells us that what he finds so daunting about consciousness "is that it does not seem to be a matter of behaviour. It just *is*—winking on with the light, multiple and simultaneous in its modes and objects, ineluctably ours. It is a process and one that is hard to score. We know what it is for ourselves but can only judge its existence in others by inductive inference. As James put it, it is something the meaning of which 'we know as long as no one asks us to define it.'" Edelman recognizes that there is a mystery but is careful to identify what sort it is. He writes that " . . . there is no more mystery in our inability as scientists to give an explanation of an individual consciousness than there is in our inability to explain why there is something rather than nothing. There is a mystery perhaps, but it is not a scientific one." We share Gerald Edelman's view that "everything in scientific inquiry should be exposed to remorseless criticism" and strongly endorse his further comment that "the evolutionary assumption implies that consciousness is efficacious—that it is not an epiphenomenon."[11] Consciousness is primary and it is part of the world and the reality with which we have to deal. There is no place here for a simplistic reductionism.

Roger Sperry tells us that "consciousness is conceived to be a dynamic emergent property of brain activity, neither identical with nor reducible to, the neural events of which it is mainly composed"; "consciousness exerts potent causal effects in the interplay of cerebral operations" and "in the position of top command of the highest levels in the hierarchy of brain organisation, the subjective properties were seen to exert control over the biophysical and chemical activities at subordinate levels." Finally, he emphasizes "that consciousness phenomena are not conceived as nothing but neural events"—while admitting that the term he uses—"interaction," a psychophysical relation—is perhaps not the best descriptor.[12] To these views we can add the view of the distinguished mathematician Sir Roger Penrose, that "consciousness is the phenomena whereby the universe's very existence is made known."[13]

It is thus self-conscious human agency that is the primary ground with which we have to do, rather than mind or matter. We may project this concept of human agency onto the outside world in terms of an image of brain events or may take the standpoint of the agents themselves experiencing mental events. Many have suggested that these two are best seen as complementary descriptions and it is a distortion of reality to say that they are nothing but the one or nothing but the other. There is here then an intrinsic duality about the reality with which we have to deal, but this does not need to be taken to the extreme of dualism. We share with the interactionist and the materialist a desire to hang on to whatever is the real truth about our human nature. The materialist recognizes and emphasizes our physical embodiment and the benefits of analyzing it in the same physical terms of the rest of the material world. The interactionist has no doubt that the aspect of reality we call conscious agency is much richer than anything that can be described in material or even mental terms alone.

We regard mental activity and correlated brain activity as inner and outer aspects of one complex set of events *that together constitute conscious human agency*. The two accounts that can be written about such a complex set of events, the mental story and the brain story, demonstrate logical complementarity. In this way the irreducible duality of human nature is given full weight, but it is a duality of aspect rather than a duality of substance. This way of thinking about it views mental activity as embodied in brain activity rather than as being identical with brain activity.[14] To go beyond that and to adopt what is called a monist identity view is, we believe, to confuse categories that belong to two different logical levels. There is nothing within brain science or psychology to justify a monist identity view or to argue that it is any more compatible with the evidence than the view we have outlined here.

William Hasker's emphasis (chapter 8) on the importance of recognizing the role of the conscious experiencing individual echoes the insistence in my earlier chapter of the key concept of personal agency in understanding personhood and the interconnections between mind and brain. There seems a close similarity between the "emergent dualism" of William Hasker and my suggestion of characterizing the mind-brain relationship in terms of an intrinsic irreducible interdependence depending upon a duality but without dualism.

What Then Is a Human Being?

The anthropological question asked by scientists may be posed in the theological context. In some circles, it appears that efforts to redefine the soul become tantamount to getting rid of "soul talk." But "soul talk," says Patrick Miller in chapter 5, is a timely reminder that "there is something in the human reality that transcends the most complete analysis of the physiology and neurology of the human brain." The question remains, what is this something? Exegesis of key scriptural passages where the question is asked, "What is a human being . . . ?" reminds us that first and foremost in Scripture this is a relational question. The question is not asked abstractly but in the context of the author in each instance addressing his or her maker and affirming that it is the person whom "you regard, you care for, you think of, you test, you visit."

Our insignificance in the vastness of the universe as shown by cosmology is balanced from within science by the anthropic principle, suggesting as it does that the universe has been fine-tuned for human life. The debate over the validity and implications of the anthropic principle will continue but in the theological context our potential insignificance before the universe remains: "What is a speck of dust before the one who created that vast cosmos?" For Miller, the implicit claim made in Scripture is "that being human means to be the recipient of God's attention, to be noticed and regarded by the Creator of the universe." He observes that "it seems to belong to the nature of God to care about the human." But there is more, and this becomes evident in the appropriation of Psalm 8 in the New Testament. Here, says Miller, "there is an incarnational answer to the anthropological question," underscored where the New Testament makes Psalm 22 "the interpretive key to understanding the passion and death and resurrection of Jesus Christ." Miller concludes, "What therefore is to be said about the human cannot be confined to general statements about humanity apart from God. It cannot be said apart from the discovery that in Jesus Christ we see who we are and we also see God for us."

For those wishing to argue that dualism is clearly taught in Scripture, appeal is often made to certain key Old Testament passages. The first is Genesis 2:7— which classically, in the King James Version, reads "And the Lord God formed man of the dust of the ground, and breathed into his nostrils the breath of life; and man became a living soul." The second is 1 Samuel 28:3-19, where, as Bill Arnold observes in chapter 6, "a *prima facie* reading may result in the conviction that Samuel's 'soul' was present at Endor and that this text therefore has troubling implications for any monist anthropology." Stone (chapter 4) and Arnold (chapter 6) examine these passages in detail but do not find in them clear support for a dualist view.

Stone points out that " possessing a soul" is argued by some to distinguish humanity uniquely from the rest of creation and is moreover seen as an essential property in defining the image of God in humanity. Thus, as the title of his chapter suggests, Genesis 2:7 has been seen as dealing with "the genesis of human nature." He notes that "if the dualisms fail here, they forfeit their status as a privileged Christian view and scientific denials of dualism appear less controversial"—but, "if the immortality of the soul and, hence, dualism are essential to

Christian thought, then the church should be bracing for an encounter with science far overshadowing debates about creation and evolution." For Stone, however, the encounter with neuroscience should be regarded much more positively; indeed it should inspire a closer reading of the text. As he does this he arrives at several important conclusions:

- the text's focus on physicality as the vital center of human personhood strongly suggests that we may not separate the physical from the "spiritual";
- whatever human personhood is, it emerges from encounter with the physical universe, and its trajectory decisively affects the physical universe;
- human personhood can only finally emerge as God intended through creation in the framework of relationship, not out of some inner possession or part of human nature;
- Genesis 2 joins Genesis 1 in defining human existence principally in terms of standing under the divine word. Humans receive commands that are clearly statements of vocation;
- whatever else humanity shares with the animal world, humanity alone can look into the face of the Creator and say, "No, thanks"; and
- if the Bible does not in fact demand, nor even support, a classically dualist reading of human nature as "matter" and "spirit," perhaps this is a mercy. We would not be scandalized by discovering that depressed people can grow spiritually when they take medication.

Lawson Stone makes clear that there is thus no case for dualism from a careful exegesis of Genesis 2:7.

Bill Arnold reminds us that, in interpreting any text of scripture, we do well to pay attention to the history of interpretation before we undertake a contemporary examination of the exegetical issues of the text. He does this and describes how believers in antiquity read the account of Samuel's appearance at Endor. Against that background he explores the implications of this text and of the data from the Hebrew Scriptures generally for the current debate about human nature. In answer to the question he poses, whether the text portrays a disembodied human soul, he replies that "those who assumed a resuscitated physical body rather than a disembodied soul are closer to the original aim of this passage." Indeed, "if ancient Israelites were faced with the question before us, I believe they would respond, 'Of course there is no existence apart from the physical!'"

Moving on to ask what a contemporary reading of the text would look like in the light of today's "new biblical hermeneutics," he concludes that "this text represents a vestige of the customs and religious practices of Canaanites and some Israelites, despite the disapproval of normative Old Testament religion." At no point does Arnold suggest that a new exegesis provides a knock-down argument in favor of either dualism or monism. He notes, rather, "Like other data from the Hebrew Scriptures, this passage must ultimately remain inconclusive in matters of Christian anthropology, although the concept of physical resuscitation is suggestive." He concludes:

- although a superficial reading of 1 Samuel 28 may lead today's Christians to interpretations that appear to refute a monist anthropology, believers from earliest times have disagreed about this difficult text, and no consensus can possibly emerge from here defending a traditional dualism; and

- we should give closer attention to the Bible's phenomenological language with reference to the nature of human beings. When the text smakes reference to the process of human thought, there is a conspicuous absence of "brain" language, and perhaps it is instructive to point out that biblical Hebrew has no word for "brain."

In a recent essay published in *Science and Christian Belief*, Joel Green links the supposed dualism of Scripture with belief in an intermediate state. He writes, "From the theological side of the argument, one of the primary pillars in the argument for some form of dualistic portrayal of the human person has been the presumption of the centrality to biblical eschatology of a disembodied intermediate state."[15] In this he no doubt has in mind writers such as John Cooper, for whom "the main pillar on which our case for dualism rests is the claim that New Testament eschatology teaches a sequence of an intermediate state and resurrection. There is an interval, a period of time between death and resurrection, during which persons exist without bodies."[16] In his contribution to *Science and Christian Belief*, and more tersely in chapter 7 of this volume, Green asks whether the biblical materials in fact anticipate a waiting period of disembodied existence, experienced by the dead person, between death and resurrection. Having focused on three strands of evidence typically viewed as pivotal in discussions of an intermediate state—the concept of Sheol and the nature of the "shades" that inhabit Sheol, the significance of the Lukan parable of the rich man and Lazarus and account of Jesus' exchange with the criminal on the cross, and Paul's concerns in 2 Corinthians 5:1-10—Green concluded "*I have demonstrated the fallacy of this presumption.*" He continued,

> One might wish to argue that other texts can be brought to bear on this issue, texts that would mitigate the results of this exploration, but, in the face of the data already surveyed, at some point one would have to face the reality that a coherent "biblical" eschatology, in which a disembodied, intermediate state plays a central role, is actually an extra-biblical construct against which the biblical evidence must be set. Without the support of these crucial strands of

evidence, it is no longer possible to insist on a pattern of biblical eschatology requiring an intermediate state, much less one in which disembodied personal existence is integral.[17]

Resurrection and Personal Identity

If I have no immortal soul, how can I expect any kind of personal continuity after my physical death? How can my personal identity from death to life-after-death be guaranteed? It is here that Joel Green (chapter 7) reminds us that, for many, the hope of resurrection depends upon a dualist anthropology: mortal body and immortal soul. Beginning with Israel's Scriptures, he invites us to consider how talk of the resurrection might have been understood in the world of the New Testament.

The understanding of resurrection in the Old Testament Scriptures was the realization that is to be seen as profoundly theocentric, focused on Israel's covenant relationship with God. Thus resurrection signals the entire restoration of Israel when it will triumph over its enemies. It is the time when at last injustice and wickedness will not have the final word but will be decisively repudiated. Most important, it reminds us that ancient Jewish perspectives on life-after-death emphasized the human person as a psychosomatic unity. Belief in resurrection in Israel's Bible did not entail thought of liberating an immortal soul from a mortal body. Resurrection was not the reconstitution of the molecules of the deceased body, and resurrection hope had nothing to do with a "spirit" being.

Jewish thought at the time of Jesus was more variegated, however, and it remains difficult not to think of the disciples' reactions to Jesus after his resurrection as presuming some sort of dualist anthropology. Jesus' postresurrection bodily existence was out of the ordinary, but they were not encountering a disembodied spirit. Indeed, Jesus flatly contradicts their view, demonstrating that he is no ghost. He declares, "Look at my hands and my feet; see that it is I myself. Touch me and see; for a ghost does not have flesh and bones as you see that I have" (Luke 24:39). Here we have a transformed materiality, a fully bodily resurrection. The scene at the meal described in Luke's Gospel further emphasizes this, but it also helps to underline the postmortem persistence of Jesus' personal identity. This he does by reestablishing Jesus' fellowship with his disciples at the table. And all of this, Jesus reminds them, is part of God's whole story. "Then he said to them, these are my words that I spoke while I was still with you that everything written about me in the law of Moses, the prophets, and the psalms must be fulfilled" (Luke 24:44).

Thus according to the witness of both Luke and Paul as outlined by Green, "Personal identity is found in an historical narrative within which people live, in relation to the divine location given that people." "Resurrection is not soul flight but the exclamation point and essential affirmation that Jesus has placed on display for all to see his life of service, even the service of life-giving death, and that this life carries with it the divine imprimatur, actualizing as it does God's own redemptive project."

Turning to Paul, Green reminds us that the apostle's theological concerns arose from the situation in Corinth. His letter to the Corinthians was first and foremost written to restore unity. To do this he needed to represent the Christian belief in resurrection with enough sophistication to communicate effectively with those of both high and low status. In so doing he deals with both the what and the how of resurrection. The continuity between life in this world and life everlasting has to do with embodied existence. To share in life eternal this present body must be transformed. The images offered come from the natural world and from Christ's own resurrection. As it was with Christ's body so it will be with ours. It was the same yet not the same: transformed for life with God forever. Paul had no doubt that nothing in the created human being is intrinsically immortal. Resurrection and embodied afterlife are God's divine gift and his doing alone.

Moving on to the questions of our personhood Green first and foremost reminds us that we need to refocus and recognize that our personhood is "in Christ"; both now and in the life to come all depend on God's mercy. Paul locates the problem as a continuing "mystery" and emphasizes that the preservation of our personhood depends on a relationship each of us has "to Christ" and "with Christ." Green concludes, "This suggests that the relationality and narrativity that constitute who I am are able to exist apart from neural correlates and embodiment only insofar as they are preserved in God's own being, in anticipation of new creation." In death, according to Paul, the person really does die. Without divine intervention no part of us, no aspect of our personhood can survive death. There must be a reembodiment. We are not intrinsically capable of moving from life to life after death. The possibility of an afterlife is not a property of humanity but a divine gift.

Though described by Joel Green as an excursus, one aspect of his chapter addresses what is for many Christians a central question: What happened to Jesus between Friday afternoon and dawn on Sunday? Where was Jesus between his death and resurrection? In so doing Green formed a natural link with Charles Gutenson's discussion of space and time (chapter 9). Green's answer was simple. Where was Jesus? Jesus was with God.

Dualism and the Intermediate State

For some, the claim that Scripture teaches that there is an intermediate state between physical death and resurrection is a decisive factor in resolving the dualism-monism debate in favor of dualism. Indeed, John Cooper has no doubt that the key issue to which Christians must return is the question, What happens when we die? He heads one of his key sections, "An Intermediate State Presupposes Dualism."[18] He has already, according to his reading of the biblical literature, concluded that an intermediate state is a necessary view to be held by Christians.

It is also crucial to remember that any discussion of an intermediate state implies ideas about the nature of time and eternity. In his contribution, Gutenson reminded us of the three positions normally discussed. First, he calls attention to the commonsense position—namely, the view that God takes up a temporal location much as humans do. There is, second, Augustinian timelessness, according to which God exists outside of time in what is often called a timeless realm, from where he is able to observe all time in undivided wholeness. A third position is often conflated with the preceding position, creating the illusion that there are only two theories; this third is labeled the "eternalist" position, which can be traced back at least to Plotinus. Gutenson argued for the superiority of the eternalist position and considered how this would influence any speculation about the necessity for affirming an intermediate state.

> Recall that the eternalist conceives God's experience of time such that the entire course of universal history stands before him in undivided wholeness. For God, the general resurrection is just as present to him as the moment of anyone's death, and thus from God's perspective there is no interim time period between one's death and the general resurrection. The eternalist does not assert that the passage of time as experienced by humans is an illusion any more than the physicist who notes the experience of time is different for persons in different frames of reference. So, God's experience of time and eternity is *real* as is the human experience, though they are quite different.

Bringing these thoughts together, Gutenson notes that "to those taken up into the divine eternity, the general resurrection would be just as present as the moment of their death. For them, there would be no interim period before the general resurrection, rather to die is to be present to the general resurrection, and thus, to be ready for participation in resurrected life. *Accordingly, then, there would be no need to posit an intermediate state.*"

We suggest that a careful scrutiny of the evidence by scholars such as Joel Green questions the exegesis of the key passages to which Cooper and others like him refer, and we have also noted that Old Testament scholars such as Arnold and Stone likewise find no convincing evidence for an intermediate state. We also observe that the philosopher and theologian Gutenson has noted that any talk about an intermediate state implies certain assumptions about time and eternity, and he has argued that the necessity to posit an intermediate state is not required by an "eternalist" understanding of time and eternity. We concur with these conclusions. In short, as regards an intermediate state, we propose that there are no clear-cut biblical grounds for such a belief and that it misrepresents the nature of time and eternity, and therefore belief in such an intermediate state should not be retained. We readily acknowledge that questions remain. One which we discussed earlier concerns the nature of personal identity and the bridge by which such human identity crosses from this life to the next. On this topic, however, Joel Green has noted that the biblical writers have little of a specific nature to offer. "Paul himself speaks of the transformation from a body fit for this world to one fit for the world to come as a mystery (1 Corinthians 15:51-57)."[19]

The unavoidable problems inherent in using terms like dualism are highlighted when we recall that William Hasker labels his position as "emergent dualism" (chapter 8). He, however, is careful to note that it is an *emergent* dualism, because the mental individual emerges from the organism and is sustained by it; it is not (as in traditional dualism) a separate element added to the organism from outside by divine fiat. The chief difference from traditional dualism lies in the fact that the "conscious field" (as Hasker sometimes calls it) is generated and sustained by the biological organism, not "added to" the organism from outside. The key difference from Cartesian dualism on this point is that there is no presumption, for emergent dualism, that the conscious mind should be able to operate on its own independently of what goes on in the body and the brain. Thus emergent dualism does not lend itself to a doctrine of natural immortality. But if the assumption that Scripture teaches an intermediate state is wrong, as our biblical scholars unanimously affirm, then Cooper's case for dualism collapses.

Moving from a dualist view of the soul, however, does indeed have widespread implications not only for Christian doctrines such as eschatology, discussed above, but also for missiology and for Christian practices such as counseling. We now turn to these.

Missiology: "Saving Souls" or "Putting on Christ"?

It is not only within science that we need to be alert to the temptation of turning a wholistic view of the person, which emphasizes our psychosomatic unity, into a reductionist position, which says that we are "nothing but" a physical being, "nothing but" a material body. While recognizing the intrinsic interdependence of the mind and the brain, we may emphasize duality without accepting dualism. It could be argued that a plain reading of some of our favorite and best-loved hymns would suggest that we have slipped into a reductionist position in our theology. So great is the emphasis on "soul" that we appear to have forgotten that we are embodied. In its extreme form this amounts to saying that ultimately, in terms of eternity, we are "nothing but" souls. The body has become an encumbrance rather than "the temple of the Holy Spirit" (1 Cor. 6:19). As

Patrick Miller reminded us, "soul talk" remains an essential part of our Christian heritage. What is required is to endow it with a fully biblical meaning rather than one that owes more to the pervasive influence of Western philosophy. We need to recapture the view developed by Michael Rynkiewich that "the human person is not a body (substance) but a body-in-relationship" (chapter 10).

Many of our favorite hymns embody a tacit belief in the "soul" as some separate part of us. It is my "soul" that is saved as I personally receive Christ as Savior and Lord. It is my "soul" that, with all the other redeemed "souls," will gather round the throne of grace in heaven to continue our praise and worship. Thus it was the "saving of souls" that motivated those wonderful pioneering missionaries of past generations. Michael Rynkiewich urges that it is that which for many remains a primary motivation in their contemporary sacrificial missionary discipleship. Nevertheless, in recent years there has been sustained effort to underline as part of the essential missionary paradigms "the centrality of holism—life, deed, word, and sign." John Zizioulas, a leading Orthodox theologian cited by Rynkiewich, has written, "The first and most important characteristic of the Church is that she brings man into a kind of relationship with the world which is not determined by the laws of biology."[20] Rynkiewich avers that, "if there is only body-mind, and within it neural networks that link to personal and cultural hermeneutic systems, then it is impossible to be in mission to the mind-soul without being in mission to the body." He concludes, "A dualism that allows missionaries to separate evangelism and social justice is contrary to the *missio Dei*."

So imbued are we with the premises of Western ideology about persons—namely, that they are ontologically prior to relationships, that individuals are prior to society—that our social sciences devote a great deal of energy to asking how a person relates to groups such as the family (psychology), to others (sociology), to leaders and followers (political science), and as producers and consumers (economics). It is only by listening to missionaries that we are forced to remember that other cultures have other assumptions, that personhood is conceptualized differently in other cultures. Is there, for example, the same autonomous individual in all cultures who can make a decision and come forward alone to register that decision; or must conversion be conceived in a different way? Would conversion be the giving of oneself to receive from God in order to establish a new relationship; or is it just the acquisition of some new knowledge? Some missiologists have argued that the real issue is relationship, not knowledge, not scholarship. Rynkiewich urges us to remember that "our mission is not to convince the world that we have the truth with regard to the construction of personhood, but to introduce Christ as a person seeking relationship, to invite people to receive God's grace, and to enter into a new community through the Holy Spirit."

Rynkiewich provocatively goes even further, suggesting that, perhaps "many Protestant missionaries seem to think that the job is to impart words, knowledge, and creed." But this, he says, "is a pale reflection of 'the word became flesh and lived among us.'" Rather, he emphasizes, "The incarnation involved God

185

coming to humans in a recognizable form so that those who embrace the message may have fellowship with us; and truly our fellowship is with the Father and with his Son Jesus Christ." Are we in danger, he wonders, of reifying and deifying our own culture?

Personhood and Counseling with and without a Soul

Does it really matter whether we think we have a thing called a "soul," which is given by God when we are conceived and which remains attached to us or inside us somewhere until we die and then goes off again back to God? Does it really matter if we are "nothing but" a physical object, albeit a living one like the rest of the physical universe? In short, does the view that we hold about ourselves and about the nature of persons have any wider implications for how we live, how we treat ourselves, how we treat others in sickness and in health? Several contributors give a resounding "yes" to these questions.

Virginia Todd Holeman considers the very widespread practice, especially in North America, of offering and receiving counseling (chapter 11). But is there such a thing as Christian counseling? If so, how is it defined and how is it different from other forms of counseling? Holeman observes that, over the last one hundred years, the situation has changed dramatically through the development of psychology and more recently of neuroscience. She notes that "the view of personhood that takes the tightening in mind-brain links seriously leads to a particular understanding of the metapurpose of Christian counseling with specific attention to the role of the Holy Spirit in general and the counseling relationship in particular." In support of her view, she cites the evidence from a study by Lambert and others showing that there are four common factors that contribute to therapeutic success regardless of the theoretical orientation of the therapist.[21] Lambert notes, for example, that the rate of spontaneous recovery is about 40 percent, while use of a particular therapeutic technique ranked far down the list of things that bring about a change, estimated at about 15 percent. Holeman raises the question, If techniques matter so little in comparison with client factors, might it not suggest that specifically "Christian" techniques, while they would be nice, are not absolutely necessary for Christian counseling to occur? She concludes, "It is not the external strategies that define Christian counseling, but the agency of the kingdom of God in the lives of counselors who seek to bring this healing reality to bear upon the lives of clients. The person of the therapist-in-relation-to-God brings the Christian into Christian counseling. In effect, Christian counseling is less about technique and more about relationality."

Drawing on Clayton's emergent monism model, Stuart Palmer traces his views of pastoral care and counseling "without a soul" (chapter 12). He believes that any dualistic conception of "soul" is unnecessary for the existence and vitality of the field of pastoral counseling, and he believes this view is supported not only by consideration of the evidence from neuroscience but is also backed by a serious consideration of the implications and benefits of a trinitarian theology.

It is not only some scientists who are reductionist. In offering pastoral care, traditionally described as "soul care," there are hidden assumptions about the basic makeup of persons. Some act as if expressions of spirituality are reducible without remainder to psychological phenomena. Others believe that the psychological dynamics of life can be reduced without remainder to spiritual explanations. Neither, argues Palmer, does justice to the relevant evidence. People are physical beings, vulnerable to changes in their biology, including such changes as those in concentrations of neurotransmitters and, at times, associated depression. People are social beings. We need horizontal relationships. We need community support. People are made by God and for God. Though finite creatures we are invited into a vertical relationship with the infinitely divine Creator. These are assertions that Palmer believes are inherent in trinitarian theology.

Relatedness: A Key Concept and Pervasive Theme

In seeking to answer the question, *What is a human being?* Green observed that

> it is crucial that we recognize that the Old and New Testament do not define the human person in essentialist but above all in relational terms. Put differently, the Bible's witness to the nature of human life is at once naive and profound. It is naive not in the sense of gullibility or primitiveness, but because it has not worked out in what we may regard as a philosophically satisfying way the nature of physical existence in life, death, and afterlife. It is profound in its presentation of the human person fundamentally in relational terms, and its assessment of the human being as genuinely human and alive only within the family of humans brought into being by Yahweh and in relation to the God who gives life-giving breath.

For Green "the hope of any persistence of personal identity is to be seen profoundly *in relational terms*." It is because we are "in Christ" that we are "with Christ." In addition, our identity is embedded not only in relationality, but also in the whole narrative of our life histories. As Green has put it, "our personhood is inextricably bound up in our physicality, and so is inextricably tied to the cosmos God has created, and in the sum of our life experiences and relationships."

Gutenson underlined repeatedly the importance of relatedness. For example, he wrote that "to exist as a human person *is to exist in a complex web of relationships:* relationships with Father, Son, and Spirit, as well as with other personal and non-personal creatures." Later, in his discussions of personal identity, he again emphasized how this is intimately connected with the totality of one's life experiences in which the relationships with others is a key component. *"Personhood,"* he declared, *"is rooted in relationality,* and therefore, personal identity must be similarly rooted." He concluded that "a specifically Christian concept of personal identity involves God's revelation of his own tri-personal nature and corresponding relations to the world of creatures."

For a Christian, the primary relationship in which we exist is a relationship with Father, Son, and Holy Spirit. "What is it, then," asks Gutenson, "that makes some person in resurrected life the very same person that existed in this life? It is to be (re?)created by Father, Son, and Spirit as one who exists in and has been *formed by the very same relations."*

The practical implications of these views and this emphasis on relationships was further underlined by, for example, Virginia Todd Holeman, who, having adopted a monist model of mind-brain relations, commented that this view "proposes that soul care is less about technique and more about relationality." She later comments, "If relational capacities are indeed the essence of our soulishness, then perhaps counselor education, training, and supervision should invest more energy in developing counselors with godly character who work with clients to create therapeutic relationships that may bring about hope and healing. Here one finds heart and soul in Christian counseling."

A similar emphasis was endorsed by Stuart Palmer, who adopted an "emergent monist" position of mind-brain relations. He commented that Warren Brown, who holds a nonreductive physicalist view, agrees with his emergent monism in emphasizing that "the Christian idea of 'soulishness' can be retained if it is understood as a brain emergent human capacity for experiencing personal relatedness."[22] Palmer later adds that "persons develop and evolve in a context of relatedness—with animals, with fellow humans and with God."

This emphasis on the key role of relationships does not take the emphasis on the human capacity for relationship out of the realm of biology; these relationships are not disembodied. For example, Warren Brown, who has described what he calls human "soulishness" as a capacity for deep and rich experiences of personal relatedness, has been careful to point out that there are neurological conditions such as Capgras syndrome where this capacity to enter into loving relationships even with members of one's own family may be severely compromised, and that this results from defective neurological mechanisms. The current excitement today about mirror neurons and their role in the development and maintenance of inter-organism relationships has further underlined the neurobiological basis of the capacity for social relatedness. It is also the degeneration of this fundamental capacity for human relatedness that produces some of the most convincing evidence of the tightness of the links between brain and spirituality. How many Christians have agonized when, as helpless bystanders, they watch the changes taking place as devout Christians move into the later stages of Alzheimer's disease. Mind and brain are indeed fundamentally and intimately interdependent aspects of the human person.

All of this emphasis on the importance of relationships underlines what both Old Testament and New Testament scholars say repeatedly, that humans, unlike other parts of creation, whether animate or inanimate, are created by God "in his own image," and as such *are offered the relationship of* being God's partners. Communion or relationship is thus emphasized as central to the image of God and the capacity for relatedness is seen as a key feature of the image of God in humankind.

NOTES

1. Body and Soul? Questions at the Interface of Science and Christian Faith

1. Thomas Metzinger, "Introduction: Consciousness Research at the End of the Twentieth Century," in *Neural Correlates of Consciousness: Empirical and Conceptual Questions*, ed. Thomas Metzinger (Cambridge: MIT Press, 2000), 6.

2. References to these attributes are taken from Isaac Asimov, *I, Robot* (New York: Doubleday, 1950), 5, 9, 14, 23, 57, 59, 66, 69.

3. Are souls created by God *ex nihilo* at the moment of their infusion into the body (Lactantius, Aquinas, Peter Lombard)? Are body and soul formed together (Tertullian, Luther)? Are souls pre-existent (Origen)?

4. E.g., H. Wheeler Robinson, *The Christian Doctrine of Man*, 3rd ed. (Edinburgh: T&T Clark, 1926); and, more recently, Paul K. Jewett, *Who We Are: Our Dignity as Human: A Neo-Evangelical Theology*, ed. Marguerite Shuster (Grand Rapids: William B. Eerdmans, 1996). Cf. the much earlier work of Thomas Aquinas (1225–1274)—esp. *On Human Nature*, ed. Thomas S. Hibbs (Indianapolis/Cambridge: Hackett, 1999).

5. On the relation of science and faith in these matters, see the helpful surveys in Malcolm A. Jeeves, *Human Nature at the Millennium: Reflections on the Integration of Psychology and Christianity* (Grand Rapids: Baker, 1997); David G. Meyers and Malcolm A. Jeeves, *Psychology Through the Eyes of Faith*, rev. ed. (San Francisco: Harper SanFrancisco, 2002); Malcolm A. Jeeves and R. J. Berry, *Science, Life, and Christian Belief: A Survey of Contemporary Issues* (Grand Rapids: Baker, 1998).

6. E.g., Karl Barth, *Church Dogmatics*, vol 3: *The Doctrine of Creation*, part 1 (Edinburgh: T&T Clark, 1958).

7. Andrew Cunningham, "Sir Thomas Browne and His *Religio Medici*: Reason, Nature and Religion," in *Religio Medici: Medicine and Religion in Seventeenth-Century England*, ed. Ole Peter Grell and Andrew Cunningham (Aldershot, UK: Scolar, 1996), 12-61.

8. Jon Parkin, *Science, Religion and Politics in Restoration England: Richard Cumberland's De legibus naturae*, Studies in History New Series (Woodbridge, UK: Boydell, 1999).

9. Robert Boyle, *A Free Inquiry into the Vulgarly Received Notion of Nature*, ed. Edward B. Davis and Michael Hunter, Cambridge Texts in the History of Philosophy (Cambridge, Mass: Cambridge University Press, 1996 [1686]).

10. Thomas Willis, *The Anatomy of the Brain and Nerves*, trans. Samuel Pordage, ed. William Feindel; The Classics of Medicine Library (Birmingham: McGill-Queens University Press, 1978 [1681]), 51-52.

11. Alister E. McGrath, *A Scientific Theology*, vol. 1: *Nature* (Grand Rapids: William B. Eerdmans, 2001).

12. Cf. Joel B. Green, "Science, Religion, and the Mind-Brain Problem: The Case of Thomas Willis (1621–1675)," *Science & Christian Belief* 15 (2003): 165-85.

13. Richard Swinburne, *The Evolution of the Soul*, rev. ed. (Oxford: Clarendon, 1997); David J. Chalmers, *The Conscious Mind: In Search of a Fundamental Theory* (Oxford: Oxford University Press, 1996); John W. Cooper, *Body, Soul, and Life Everlasting: Biblical Anthropology and the Monism-Dualism Debate*, 2nd ed. (Grand Rapids: William B. Eerdmans, 2000); idem, "Biblical Anthropology and the Body-Soul Problem," in *Soul, Body, and Survival*, ed. Kevin Corcoran (Ithaca: Cornell University Press, 2001), 218-28; William Hasker, *The Emergent Self* (Ithaca: Cornell University Press, 1999); idem, "Persons as Emergent Substances," in *Soul, Body, and Survival*, 107-19; Kevin Corcoran, "Persons and Bodies," *Faith & Philosophy* 12 (1995): 324-39; idem, "Physical Persons and Postmortem Survival without Temporal Gaps," in *Soul, Body, and Survival*, 201-17; Lynne Rudder Baker, "Need a Christian Be a Mind/Body Dualist?" *Faith & Philosophy* 12 (1995): 489-504; idem, *Persons and Bodies: A Constitution View*, Cambridge Studies in Philosophy (Cambridge: Cambridge University Press, 2000); Philip Clayton, "Neuroscience, the Person, and God: An Emergentist Account," in *Neuroscience and the Person*, ed. John R. Russell, et al.; Scientific Perspectives on Divine Action (Vatican City State: Vatican Observatory, 1999), 181-214; Nancey Murphy, "Nonreductive Physicalism: Philosophical Issues," in *Whatever Happened to the Soul? Scientific and Theological Portraits of Human Nature*, ed. Warren S. Brown et al.; Theology and the Sciences (Minneapolis: Fortress, 1998), 127-48.

14. Francis Crick, *The Astonishing Hypothesis: The Scientific Search for the Soul* (New York: Simon & Schuster, 1994), 3.

15. See Warren S. Brown, "Reconciling Scientific and Biblical Portraits of Human Nature," in *Whatever Happened to the Soul?*, 213-28.

16. E.g., Klaus Berger, *Identity and Experience in the New Testament* (Minneapolis: Fortress, 2003); David Booth, "Human Nature: Unitary or Fragmented? Biblical Language and Scientific Understanding," *Science & Christian Belief* 10 (1998): 145-62; Warren S. Brown and Malcolm A. Jeeves, "Portraits of Human Nature: Reconciling Neuroscience and Christian Anthropology," *Science & Christian Belief* 11 (1999): 139-50; Brown et al., eds., *Whatever Happened to the Soul?*; Brian Edgar, "Paul and the Person," *Science & Christian Belief* 12 (2000): 151-64; Joel B. Green, "Eschatology and the Nature of Humans: A Reconsideration of the Pertinent Biblical Evidence," *Science & Christian Belief* 14 (2002): 33-50; idem, "Monism and the Nature of Humans in Scripture," *Christian Scholar's Review* 29 (2000): 731-43; idem, "Scripture and the Human Person: Further Reflections," *Science & Christian Belief* 11 (1999): 51-63; Philip Hefner, *The Human Factor: Evolution, Culture, and Religion*, Theology and the Sciences (Minneapolis: Fortress, 1993); Stanley

B. Marrow, "ΑΘΑΝΑΣΙΑ/ΑΝΑΣΤΑΣΙΣ: The Road Not Taken," *New Testament Studies* 45 (1999): 571-86; Russell et al., eds., *Neuroscience and the Person.*

17. Nancey Murphy, "Science and Society," in *Systematic Theology,* vol 3: *Witness,* by James William McClendon Jr., with Nancey Murphy (Nashville: Abingdon Press, 2000), 99-131 (126).

18. Wolfhart Pannenberg, *Systematic Theology,* vol. 2 (Grand Rapids: William B. Eerdmans, 1994), 181-202.

2. Mind Reading and Soul Searching in the Twenty-first Century

1. K. N. Laland and G. R. Brown, *Sense and Nonsense: Evolutionary Perspectives on Human Behavior* (Oxford: Oxford University Press, 2002), 291.

2. Kenan Malik, *Man, Beast, and Zombie: What Science Can and Cannot Tell Us about Human Nature* (New Brunswick, N.J.: Rutgers University Press, 2000), 37.

3. Francis H. Crick, *The Astonishing Hypothesis: The Scientific Search for a Soul* (London: Simon & Schuster, 1994), 261.

4. Dava Sobel, *Galileo's Daughter* (London: Fourth Estate, 2000), 180.

5. K. S. Lashley, "In Search of the Engram," in *Symposia of the Society of Experimental Biology IV: Physiological Mechanisms in Animal Behavior* (Cambridge: Cambridge University Press, 1950), 454-82.

6. D. I. Perrett, P. A. J. Smith, D. D. Potter, A. J. Mistlin, A. S. Head, A. D. Milner, and M. A. Jeeves, "Neurons Responsive to Faces in the Temporal Cortex: Studies of Functional Organisation, Sensitivity to Identity and Relation to Perception," *Human Neurobiology* 3 (1984): 197-208.

7. N. J. Emery, "The Eyes Have It: The Neuroethology, Function and Evolution of Social Gaze," *Neuroscience and Behavioral Reviews* 24 (2000): 581-604.

8. A. D. Baddeley, *Human Memory: Theory and Practice,* 2nd ed. (Hove, UK: Psychology Press, 1997).

9. C. Frith, "Images of Memory," *MRC News* (Summer 1994).

10. S. W. Anderson, A. Bechara, A. Damasio, D. Tranch, and A. R. Damasio, "Impairment of Social and Moral Behaviour Related to Early Damage in Human Prefrontal Cortex," *Nature Neuroscience* 2 (1999): 1032-37.

11. 19 October 1999.

12. Frans de Waal, *Good Natured: The Origin of Right and Wrong in Humans and Other Animals* (Cambridge: Harvard University Press, 1997), 216-17.

13. C. B. Gesch, S. M. Hammond, S. E. Hampson, A. Eves, and M. J. Crowder, "Influence of Supplementary Vitamins, Minerals and Essential Fatty Acids on the Antisocial Behaviour of Young Adult Prisoners," *British Journal of Psychiatry* 181 (2002): 22-28.

14. C. S. L. Lai, S. E. Fisher, J. A. Hurst, F. Vargha-Khadem, and A. P. Monaco, "A Forkhead-domain Gene Is Mutated in a Severe Speech and Language Disorder," *Nature* 413 (2001): 519-23.

15. N. Sadato, A. Pascual-Leone, J. Grafman, M. P. Deiber, V. Ibanez, and M. Hallett, "Neural Networks for Braille Reading by the Blind," *Brain* 121 (1998): 1213-29. See also A. Pascual-Leone and F. Torres, "Plasticity of the Sensorimotor Cortex Representation of the Reading Finger in Braille Readers," *Brain* 116 (1993): 39-52.

16. E. A. Maguire, D. G. Gadian, I. S. Johnsrude, C. D. Good, J. Ashburner, R. S. J. Frackopwiak, and C. Frith, "Navigation-related Structural Change in the Hippocampi of Taxi Drivers," *Proceedings of the National Academy of Sciences* 97 (2000): 4398-403.

17. J. A. Yesavage, M. S. Mumenthaler, J. L. Taylor, L. Friedman, R. O'Hara, J. Sheikh, J. Tinklenberg, and P. J. Whitehouse, "Donepezil and Flight Simulator Performance: Effects on Retention of Complex Skills," *Neurology* 59 (2002): 123-25.

18. K. Matthews, J. W. Dalley, C. Matthews, Tung Hu Tsai, and T. W. Robbins, "Periodic Maternal Separation of Neonatal Rats Produces Region- and Gender-specific Effects on Biogenic Anime Content in Postmortem Adult Brain," *Synapse* 40 (2001): 1-10.

19. K. M. O'Craven and N. Kanwisher, "Mental Imagery of Faces and Places Activates Corresponding Stimulus-specific Brain Regions," *Journal of Cognitive Neuroscience* 12 (2000): 1013-23.

20. T. J. Grabowski and A. R. Damasio, "Improving Functional Imaging Techniques: The Dream of a Single Image for a Single Mental Event," *Proceedings of the National Academy of Sciences* 93 (1996): 14302-03.

21. A. Karmiloff-Smith, "Elementary, My Dear Watson, the Clue Is in the Genes . . . or Is It?" *Proceedings of the British Academy* 117 (2002).

22. S. Pinker, *Words and Rules: The Ingredients of Language* (London: Wiedenfeld and Nicholson, 1999), 262.

23. P. J. Bowler, *Reconciling Science and Religion: The Debate in Early-Twentieth-Century Britain* (Chicago: University of Chicago Press, 2001).

24. G. Rizzolatti, L. Fadigo, V. Gallese, and L. Fogassih, "Premotor Cortex and the Recognition of Motor Actions," *Cognitive Brain Research* 3 (1996): 131-41.

25. V. S. Ramachandran, "Mirror Neurons and Imitation Learning as the Driving Force Behind 'The Great Leap Forward' in Human Evolution," *Edge* 69 (1 June 2000); http://www.edge.org/documents/archive/edge69.html.

26. J. Tooby and L. Cosmides, "The Psychological Foundations of Culture," in *The Adapted Mind: Evolutionary Psychology and the Generation of Culture*, ed. J. H. Barkow et al. (Oxford: Oxford University Press, 1992), 19-36.

27. R. W. Byrne and A. Whiten, *Machiavellian Intelligence: Social Expertise and the Evolution of Intellect in Monkeys, Apes and Humans* (Oxford: Clarendon Press, 1988).

28. A. Whiten and R. W. Byrne, *Machiavellian Intelligence II: Extensions and Evaluations* (Cambridge: Cambridge University Press, 1997), 1.

29. N. K. Humphrey, "The Social Function of Intellect," in *Growing Points in Ethology*, ed. P. P. G. Bateson and R. A. Hinde (Cambridge: Cambridge University Press, 1976), 303-17.

30. D. Premack and G. Woodruff, "Does the Chimpanzee Have a Theory of Mind?" *Behavioral and Brain Sciences* 1 (1978): 515-26.

31. Whiten and Byrne, *Machiavellian Intelligence II*, 150.

32. S. Baron-Cohen, *Mindblindness: An Essay on Autism and Theory of Mind* (Cambridge: MIT Press, 1997).

33. A. Whiten, "The Place of 'Deep Social Mind' in the Evolution of Human Nature," in *Human Nature*, ed., M. Jeeves (in press).

34. J. Call, "Chimpanzee Social Cognition" (in press).

35. Warren Brown, "Cognitive Contributions to Soul," in *Whatever Happened to the Soul?*, ed. Warren S. Brown, Nancey Murphy, and H. Newton Maloney (Minneapolis: Fortress, 1998), 99-125.

36. J. Polkinghorne, *The Way the World Is* (London: SPCK 1983), 55.

37. See T. J. Crow, ed., *The Speciation of Modern Homo Sapiens* (Oxford: Oxford University Press, 2003).

38. A. Damasio, *Descartes' Error: Emotion, Reason and the Human Brain* (New York: Grosset/Putnam, 1994), 40.

39. R. E. Kendell, "The Distinction Between Mental and Physical Illness," *The British Journal of Psychiatry* 178 (2001): 490-93.

40. D. MacKay, *Behind the Eye* (Oxford: Blackwell, 1991), 61.

41. P. F. Strawson, *Individualism: An Essay in Descriptive Metaphysics* (London: Methuen, 1959), 1.3.78-116.

3. A Neurobiological Portrait of the Human Person

1. Mario Moussa and Thomas Shannon, "The Search for the New Pineal Gland: Brain Life and Personhood," *Hastings Center Report* 22 (1992): 30-37.

2. Teresa Iglesias, "What Kind of a Being Is the Human Embryo?" in *Embryos and Ethics*, ed. M. Nigel de S. Cameron (Edinburgh: Rutherford House, 1987), 58-73.

3. Oliver O'Donovan, *Begotten or Made?* (Oxford: Clarendon, 1984).

4. Gilbert Meilaender, *Bioethics: A Primer for Christians* (Grand Rapids: William B. Eerdmans, 1996).

5. M. Flower, "Neuromaturation and the Moral Status of Human Fetal Life," in *Abortion Rights and Fetal Personhood*, ed. E. Doerr and J. Prescott (Long Beach: Crestline, 1989), 71-85.

6. Leon Eisenberg, "Would Cloned Humans Really Be Like Sheep?" *The New England Journal of Medicine* 340 (1999): 471-75.

7. Stephen Dunnett and Anders Björklund, "Prospects for New Restorative and Neuroprotective Treatments in Parkinson's Disease," *Nature* 399 (1999): A32-39.

8. Dunnett and Björklund, "Prospects. "

9. Thomas B. Freeman et al., "Neural Transplantation in Parkinson's Disease," *Parkinson's Disease*, Advances in Neurology 86, ed. Donald Calne and Susan Calne (Philadelphia: Lippincott Williams and Wilkins, 2001), 435-45.

10. D. Gareth Jones and Sharon Sagee, "Xenotransplantation: Hope or Delusion?" *Biologist* 48 (2001): 129-32.

11. For a review see D. Gareth Jones and Kerry A. Galvin, "The Brave New World of CNS Regeneration," *New Zealand Medical Journal* 114 (2001): 340-42.

12. Kerry A. Galvin and D. Gareth Jones, "Adult Human Neural Stem Cells for Cell-Replacement Therapies in the Central Nervous System," *Medical Journal of Australia* 177 (2002): 316-18.

13. G. Maguire and Ellen McGee, "Implantable Brain Chips? Time for Debate," *Hastings Center Report* 29 (1999): 7-13.

14. Board for Social Responsibility of the Church of England, *Cybernauts Awake!* (London: Church Publishing House, 1999).

15. Donald M. MacKay, "The Ethics of Brain Manipulation," in *Oxford Companion to the Mind*, ed. Richard L. Gregory (Oxford: Oxford University Press, 1987), 113-14.

16. Donald M. MacKay, "Brain Science and the Soul," in *Oxford Companion to the Mind*, 723-25.

17. Christopher M. Filley and Bette K. Kleinschmidt-DeMasters, "Neurobehavioral Presentations of Brain Neoplasms," *The Western Journal of Medicine* 163 (1995): 19-24.

18. V. Mark and F. Ervin, *Violence and the Brain* (New York: Harper & Row, 1970).

19. Vernon H. Mark and William A. Carnahan, "Organic Brain Disease: A Separate Issue," in *The Psychosurgery Debate*, ed. Elliot S. Valenstein (San Francisco: W. H. Freeman, 1980), 129-38.

20. Elliot S. Valenstein, *Brain Control* (New York: John Wiley and Sons, 1973).

21. Kenneth Tardiff, "Unusual Diagnoses among Violent Patients," *The Psychiatric Clinics of North America* 21 (1998): 567-76.

22. Arthur Caplan, "Open Your Mind," *Economist* (25 May 2002): 73-75.

23. V. Arango et al., "Serotonin 1A Receptors, Serotonin Transporter Binding and Serotonin Transporter mRNA Expression in the Brainstem of Depressed Suicide Victims," *Neuropsychopharmacology* 25 (2001): 892-903.

24. Masoud Kamali, Mario A. Oquendo, and J. John Mann, "Understanding the Neurobiology of Suicidal Behavior," *Depression and Anxiety* 14 (2001): 164-76.

25. Carol Ezzell, "The Neuroscience of Suicide," *Scientific American* (February 2003): 33-39.

26. Ezzell, "Neuroscience of Suicide."

27. Ibid.

28. S. Le Vay, "A Difference in Hypothalamic Structure between Heterosexual and Homosexual Men," *Science* 253 (1991): 1034-37.

29. L. S. Allen, and R. A. Gorski, "Sexual Orientation and the Size of the Anterior Commissure in the Human Brain," *Proceedings of the National Academy of Sciences* 89 (1992): 7199-7202.

30. Nuffield Council on Bioethics, *Genetics and Human Behaviour* (London: Nuffield Council on Bioethics, 2002).

31. Nuffield Council on Bioethics, *Genetics and Human Behaviour*, 73.

32. Nuffield Council on Bioethics, *Genetics and Human Behaviour*, 74. See M. J. Chorney et al., "A Qualitative Trait Locus Associated with Cognitive Ability in Children," *Psychological Sciences* 9 (1998): 159-66; P. J. Fisher et al., "DNA Pooling Identifies QTLs on Chromosome 4 for General Cognitive Ability in Children," *Human Molecular Genetics* 8 (1999): 915-22; R. Plomin et al., "A Genome-Wide Scan of 1847 DNA Markers for Allelic Associations with General Cognitive Ability: A Five Stage Design using DNA Pooling," *Behavior Genetics* 31 (2001): 497-509.

33. H. G. Brunner et al., "Abnormal Behavior Associated with a Point Mutation in the Structural Gene for Monoamine Oxidase A," *Science* 262 (1993): 578-80.

34. A. Caspi et al., "Role of Genotype in the Cycle of Violence in Maltreated Children," *Science* 297 (2002): 851-54.

35. D. H. Hamer et al., "A Linkage between DNA Markers on the X Chromosome and Male Sexual Orientation," *Science* 261 (1993): 321-27.

36. S. Hu et al., "Linkage between Sexual Orientation and Chromosome Xq28 in Males but Not in Females," *Nature Genetics* 11 (1995): 248-56.

37. G. Rice et al., "Male Homosexuality: Absence of Linkage to Microsatellite Markers at Xq28," *Science* 284 (1999): 665-67.

38. Nuffield Council on Bioethics, *Genetics and Human Behaviour*, 125.

39. John Eccles, *The Human Mystery* (Heidelberg: Springer International, 1979), 189-90; idem, *The Human Psyche* (Heidelberg: Springer International, 1980), 18-19, 167-72.

40. MacKay, "Brain Science and the Soul."

41. Ibid.

4. The Soul: Possession, Part, or Person?

1. For a review of the relevant research in a format convenient to theologically interested readers, see Malcolm Jeeves, *Human Nature at the Millennium: Reflections on the Integration of Psychology and Christianity* (Grand Rapids: Baker, 1997).

2. John Calvin, *Institutes of the Christian Religion*, vol. 1.5.5. (Grand Rapids: William B. Eerdmans, 2001), 1:53-54.

3. James Barr makes this argument in *The Garden of Eden and the Hope of Immortality* (Minneapolis: Fortress, 1992).

4. Citation of the technical literature, where possible, is avoided in preference to generally accessible surveys of scholarship. For the exegetical issues and literature, cf. Claus Westermann, *Genesis 1–11: A Commentary* (Minneapolis: Augsburg, 1984), 178-278; Gordon J. Wenham, *Genesis 1–15* (Word Biblical Commentary; Waco: Word, 1987), 41-91.

5. For example, they debated whether the soul was created prior to insertion in the body. A selection of patristic comments can be found in Andrew Louth, ed., *Genesis 1–11*, Ancient Christian Commentary on Scripture 1 (Downers Grove, Ill.: InterVarsity, 2001), 47-53.

6. The view is as old as Aristophanes's encomium on love; cf. *The Great Dialogues of Plato* (New York: Mentor, 1956), 85-89. This interpretation, repeated in midrashic traditions, was rejected in the eleventh century by Rashi; cf. *Pentateuch with Targum Onkelos, Haphtaroth, and Rashi's Commentary* (New York: Hebrew Publishing, 1965), 1:7. It was revived by Phyllis Trible in *God and the Rhetoric of Sexuality* (Philadelphia: Fortress, 1978).

7. Brevard S. Childs, *Old Testament Theology in a Canonical Context* (Philadelphia: Fortress, 1986), 188-92.

8. Theodore J. Lewis, "Dead, Abode of the," in *Anchor Bible Dictionary*, ed. David Noel Freedman et al. (New York: Doubleday, 1992), 2:101-5; Roy E. Hayden, "עפר" in *New International Dictionary of Old Testament Theology and Exegesis*, 5 vols., ed. Willem A. VanGemeren (Grand Rapids: Zondervan, 1997), 3:472-73.

9. Cf. H. Seebass, "נפש," in *Theological Dictionary of the Old Testament*, vol. 9, ed. G. Botterweck, H. Ringgren, and H. J. Fabry (Grand Rapids: William B. Eerdmans, 1998), 497-519; Daniel C. Fredericks, "נפש," in *New International Dictionary of Old Testament Theology and Exegesis*, 3:133-4; C. A. Briggs, "The Use of npsh in the Old Testament," *Journal of Biblical Literature* 16 (1897): 17-30.

10. While the preposition *neged* appears over 500 times in the Old Testament, it never appears with the prefixed preposition *k*- outside of Genesis 2.

11. *Pentateuch . . . with Rashi's Commentary*, 1:10.

12. John Calvin, *Genesis* (Edinburgh: Banner of Truth, 1965 [1554]), 1:112.

13. Calvin, *Institutes*, 1:53-54.

14. Fredericks, "נפש,"133. Cf. also R. Eduard Schweizer, "Body," in *Anchor Bible Dictionary*, 1:767-72; William C. Robinson Jr., "Exegesis on the Soul," in *Anchor Bible Dictionary*, 2:688-89.

15. Seebass, "נפש," 510-11.

16. For summaries, see Charles A. Kennedy, "Dead, Cult of the," in *Anchor Bible Dictionary*, 2:105-8; Richard Bauckham, "Descent to the Underworld," in *Anchor Bible Dictionary*, 2:145-59.

17. Mark S. Smith, "Rephaim," in *Anchor Bible Dictionary*, 5:674-76.

18. *Epistle of Barnabas* 6:9, *Apostolic Fathers 1*, ed. Kirsopp Lake, Loeb Classical Library (Cambridge: Harvard University Press, 1935), 361.

5. What Is a Human Being?

1. In this essay, I am significantly dependent upon two sources that have helped me think about this topic: James L. Mays, "What Is a Human Being? Reflections on Psalm 8," *Theology Today* 50 (1994): 511-20 (available online at http://theologytoday. ptsem. edu/); and Brevard S. Childs, *Biblical Theology in Crisis* (Philadelphia: Westminster, 1969), 150-63. An earlier form of the essay was presented as one of the Ryan Lectures for 2002 at Asbury Theological Seminary.

2. Karl L. Popper and John C. Eccles, *The Self and Its Brain* (New York: Springer, 1977).

3. For further elaboration of this point, see P. D. Miller, "Whatever Happened to the Soul?" *Theology Today* 50 (1994): 507-19 (also available online at http://theologyto-day.ptsem.edu/).

4. Karl Barth, *Church Dogmatics* (Edinburgh: T&T Clark, 1961), III/4, 386.

5. John Eccles tells of a distinguished musician who told his doctor that he had lost all appreciation of music, that while he could still play the piano, "it means nothing to me. I have no thrill, no emotion, no feeling. I've lost the sense of beauty, of value." Eccles reports that this loss of "the sense of beauty, of value" was due to a not very extensive vascular lesion in the superior temporal lobe on the right side of the musician's brain (*The Self and Its Brain*, 483).

6. Mays, "What Is a Human Being?" 513.

7. See P. D. Miller, *They Cried to the Lord: The Form and Theology of Biblical Prayer* (Minneapolis: Fortress, 1994), 173-77.

8. Mays, "What Is a Human Being?" 514.

9. James Wharton, *Job*, Westminster Bible Companion (Louisville: Westminster John Knox, 1999), 50-51.

6. Soul-Searching Questions About 1 Samuel 28

1. So, e.g., Thomas O. Figart rejects the idea that a "psychological" ecstatic trance was involved (perhaps with the use of hallucinogenic narcotics), but assumes instead the view that Samuel's "spirit" appeared ("Saul, the Spiritist, and Samuel," *Grace Journal* 11 [1970]: 13-29, esp. 19-21).

2. Fortunately we have available two studies of this very topic. I have benefited most from K. A. D. Smelik, "The Witch of Endor: 1 Samuel 28 in Rabbinic and Christian Exegesis till 800 A.D.," *Vigiliae Christiane* 33 (1977): 160-79. The article by Figart is quite general in its scope, and of little value for this study ("Saul, the Spiritist, and Samuel").

3. Pionius, the third-century martyr, supposedly regarded the Jews as dangerous for Christians because they taught that Jesus' resurrection was the result of necromancy and therefore his divinity should be denied. Apparently Jews of Pionius's day had appealed to

1 Samuel 28 as a parallel to Jesus' resuscitation, which they alleged took place also by means of necromancy. Pionius, not unlike Tertullian, countered that Samuel's appearance was demonic, and therefore not parallel to Jesus' resurrection. (The exegesis of early Rabbinic and Christian thinkers was not necessarily always in conflict, as this single case might lead us to believe—a point emphasized by Smelik, "Witch of Endor," 160-61.)

4. Figart, "Saul, the Spiritist, and Samuel," 19-21. We may recall here the use of such practices by the Delphic oracle in Greek history.

5. Justin Martyr, *Dialogus cum Tryphone*, 105.

6. Dracontius, *Carmen de Deo*, 248.

7. For the evolution of Augustine's views on this topic, see Smelik, "Witch of Endor," 173.

8. Augustine, *De octo dulcitii quaestionibus*, 6.1-4.

9. As defined, among others, by Adele Berlin, who has boldly outlined several elements of this new hermeneutics ("A Search for a New Biblical Hermeneutics: Preliminary Observations," in *The Study of the Ancient Near East in the Twenty-first Century*, ed. J. S. Cooper and G. M. Schwartz (Winona Lake, Ind.: Eisenbrauns, 1996], 195-207, esp. 201-7).

10. This is the *locus classicus* for any examination of necromancy in the Hebrew Bible, although there are others. For details, see especially Theodore J. Lewis, *Cults of the Dead in Ancient Israel and Ugarit*, Harvard Semitic Monographs 39 (Atlanta: Scholars, 1989), 104-17.

11. For overview of this topic, see Bill T. Arnold, "Religion in Ancient Israel," in *The Face of Old Testament Studies*, ed. David W. Baker and Bill T. Arnold (Grand Rapids: Baker, 1999), 391-420, esp. 414-15; Patrick D. Miller, *The Religion of Ancient Israel* (Louisville: Westminster John Knox, 2000), 71-73. For a slightly different approach, see Philip Johnston, "The Underworld and the Dead in the Old Testament," *Tyndale Bulletin* 45 (1994): 415-19; idem, *Shades of Sheol: Death and Afterlife in the Old Testament* (Downers Grove, Ill.: InterVarsity, 2002). Thorough analysis of the evidence for an Israelite cult of the dead may be found in Karel van der Toorn, *Family Religion in Babylonia, Syria and Israel: Continuity and Change in the Forms of Religious Life*, Studies in the History and Culture of the Ancient Near East 7 (Leiden: E. J. Brill, 1996), 206-35. For archaeological evidence, see Elizabeth Block-Smith, *Judahite Burial Practices and Beliefs about the Dead*, Journal for the Study of the Old Testament Supplement Series 123 (Sheffield: Sheffield Academic Press, 1992).

12. Others have argued that interest in the dead developed first in the Neo-Assyrian empire, and entered Israel only in the late eighth and seventh centuries BC due to Assyrian influence. See Brian B. Schmidt, *Israel's Beneficent Dead: Ancestor Cult and Necromancy in Ancient Israelite Religion and Tradition* (Tübingen: J. C. B. Mohr [Paul Siebeck], 1994). However, in order to explain the evidence of 1 Samuel 28, Schmidt is forced to argue for its late or post-deuteronomistic origins (pp. 201-20), which moves in the opposite direction of the literary evidence.

13. For more on what follows, see Bill T. Arnold, "Necromancy and Cleromancy in 1 and 2 Samuel," forthcoming.

14. Saul's specific imperative to the woman (NRSV's "*consult* a spirit for me," *qosômî*) is a *terminus technicus* for divination generally, which is not limited to necromancy but applies to all forms of divination. Thus, "divine for me" or "consult by divination." See L. Koehler et al., *The Hebrew and Aramaic Lexicon of the Old Testament*, 4 vols. (Leiden: E. J. Brill, 1994–99), 3:1115; Malcolm J. A. Horsnell, "קסם" in *New International Dictionary of Old Testament Theology and Exegesis*, 5 vols., ed. W. A. VanGemeren (Grand

Rapids: Zondervan, 1997), 3:945-951. Thus we may translate as "divine for me using necromantic rituals" (compare NJPS's "please divine for me by a ghost").

15. Philip S. Johnston, "'Left in Hell?' Psalm 16, Sheol and the Holy One," in *The Lord's Anointed: Interpretation of Old Testament Messianic Texts*, ed. P. E. Satterthwaite et al. (Carlisle: Paternoster, 1995), 213-22, esp. 216-21.

16. Othmar Keel, *The Symbolism of the Biblical World: Ancient Near Eastern Iconography and the Book of Psalms* (New York: Seabury, 1978), 16-60; Douglas A. Knight, "Cosmogony and Order in the Hebrew Tradition," in *Cosmogony and Ethical Order: New Studies in Comparative Ethics*, ed. R. W. Lovin and F. E. Reynolds (Chicago: University of Chicago Press, 1985), 133-57, esp. 138-40; J. Edward Wright, "Biblical Versus Israelite Images of the Heavenly Realm," *Journal for the Study of the Old Testament* 93 (2001): 59-75.

17. One recent commentary is structured around the concept of 1 and 2 Samuel as "witness to the Torah" (Robert D. Bergen, *1,2 Samuel*, New American Commentary 7 [Nashville: Broadman and Holman, 1996], esp. 43-55), which, however helpful at certain points, goes considerably beyond what I will propose here.

18. Arnold, "Necromancy and Cleromancy," forthcoming; and see P. Kyle McCarter Jr., *I Samuel*, Anchor Bible 8 (New York: Doubleday, 1980), 421-23.

19. For details of the Hebrew collocation "inquire of YHWH/God" used in connection with the practice of Israelite lot-casting, see Arnold, "Necromancy and Cleromancy," forthcoming.

20. I am grateful to John H. Walton for this example and his helpful discussion on this topic in general (*Genesis*, NIVAC [Grand Rapids: Zondervan, 2001], 87-88).

21. As in modern Hebrew's *moah*, "brain."

22. So Walton observes that the Egyptians extracted the brain during the process of mummification, and discarded it as so much trash, while carefully preserving the heart (Walton, *Genesis*, 88).

23. For a helpful survey of the anthropological perceptions in the Hebrew Scriptures, see Mark S. Smith, "The Heart and Innards in Israelite Emotional Expressions: Notes from Anthropology and Psychobiology," *JBL* 117.3 (1998): 427-36.

24. See the paper by Lawson G. Stone, chapter 4 in this collection.

25. Michael A. Knibb, "Life and Death in the Old Testament," in *The World of Ancient Israel: Sociological, Anthropological and Political Perspectives*, ed. R. E. Clements (Cambridge: Cambridge University Press, 1989), 395-415, esp. 397-402. Newer studies have merely confirmed the monistic reading of Walther Eichrodt, *Theology of the Old Testament* (trans. J. A. Baker; Philadelphia: Westminster, 1967), 2:147-50.

7. Resurrection of the Body

1. Caroline Walker Bynum, *The Resurrection of the Body in Western Christianity, 200–1336* (New York: Columbia University Press, 1995). She concludes that "a concern for material and structural continuity showed remarkable persistence even where it seemed almost to require philosophical incoherence, theological equivocation, or aesthetic offensiveness. . . . The materialism of [traditional Christian] eschatological expressed not body-soul dualism but rather a sense of self as psychosomatic unity" (11).

2. See, e.g., Mark 15:46; John 19:40.

3. This problem was grasped by Augustine, who wrote, "For all the flesh which hunger has consumed finds it way into the air by evaporation, whence . . . God almighty can recall it. That flesh, therefore, shall be restored to the [one] in whom it first became human flesh. For it must be looked upon as borrowed by the other person, and, like a pecuniary loan, must be returned to the lender" (*City of God*, 22.20). Augustine's proposal breaks down, of course, when the full extent of our biological interrelatedness is understood.

4. On these questions, see the important discussion in Kevin Corcoran, ed., *Soul, Body, and Survival: Essays on the Metaphysics of Human Persons* (Ithaca: Cornell University Press, 2001). It might be argued that Christian belief in an intermediate state, some sort of personal existence between death and resurrection, likewise requires an anthropological dualism (so John W. Cooper, *Body, Soul, and Life Everlasting: Biblical Anthropology and the Monism-Dualism Debate*, 2nd ed. [Grand Rapids: William B. Eerdmans, 2000]). I will not be addressing this question in this chapter for two reasons. Most important, with or without recourse to an intermediate state, whether the passage from death to life-after-death is instantaneous or delayed, the question of continuity of personal identity is equally pressing. Second, belief in a disembodied intermediate state is problematic on exegetical grounds—cf. Joel B. Green, "Eschatology and the Nature of Humans: A Reconsideration of the Pertinent Biblical Evidence," *Science & Christian Belief* 14 (2002): 33-50; Brian Edgar, "Biblical Anthropology and the Intermediate State," *Evangelical Quarterly* 74 (2002): 27-45, 109-21.

5. Cf. Anthony Harvey, "'They discussed among themselves what this "rising from the dead" could mean' (Mark 9.10)," in *Resurrection: Essays in Honour of Leslie Houlden*, ed. Stephen Barton and Graham Stanton (London: SPCK, 1994), 69-78.

6. Kevin L. Anderson, "The Resurrection of Jesus in Luke-Acts" (Ph.D. diss.; Brunel University, 2000), 111.

7. For orientation, see Jan Assmann, "Resurrection in Ancient Egypt," *Resurrection: Theological and Scientific Assessments*, ed. Ted Peters, Robert John Russell, and Michael Welker (Grand Rapids: William B. Eerdmans, 2002), 124-35; Edwin Yamauchi, "Life, Death, and the Afterlife in the Ancient Near East," in *Life in the Face of Death: The Resurrection Message of the New Testament*, ed. Richard N. Longenecker, McMaster New Testament Studies (Grand Rapids: William B. Eerdmans, 1998), 21-50; Peter G. Bolt, "Life, Death, and the Afterlife in the Greco-Roman World," in *Life in the Face of Death*, 51-79; and Richard Bauckham, "Life, Death, and the Afterlife in Second Temple Judaism," in *Life in the Face of Death*, 80-95.

8. Cf. the helpful, summary remarks in Kent Harold Richards, "Death: Old Testament," in *Anchor Bible Dictionary*, 6 vols., ed. David Noel Freedman (New York: Doubleday, 1992), 2:108-10; and the more expansive Philip S. Johnston, *Shades of Sheol: Death and Afterlife in the Old Testament* (Downers Grove, Ill.: InterVarsity, 2002).

9. Cf. e.g., Psalms 9:18; 16:10; 30:4; 31:18; 49:16; 55:16; 86:13; 88:6; Isaiah 5:14; Job 24:19; et al.; also Desmond Alexander, "The Old Testament View of Life after Death," *Themelios* 11 (1986): 41-46 (43-44); Philip Johnston, "The Underworld and the Dead in the Old Testament," *Tyndale Bulletin* 45 (1994): 415-19 (416).

10. See further, Stanley B. Marrow, "ΑΘΑΝΑΣΙΑ/ΑΝΑΣΤΑΣΙΣ: The Road Not Taken," *New Testament Studies* 45 (1999): 571-86.

11. I have developed this further in "Restoring the Human Person: New Testament Voices for a Wholistic and Social Anthropology," in *Neuroscience and the Person*, ed.

Robert John Russell, Nancey Murphy, Theo C. Meyering, and Michael A. Arbib, *Scientific Perspectives on Divine Action* 4 (Vatican City State: Vatican Observatory; Berkeley, California: Center for Theology and the Nature Sciences, 1999), 3-22. See also Robert A. Di Vito, "Old Testament Anthropology and the Construction of Personal Identity," *Catholic Biblical Quarterly* 61 (1999): 217-38.

12. Cf. Leviticus 11; Numbers 19; Hans Walter Wolff, *Anthropology of the Old Testament* (London: SCM, 1974), 102-5.

13. Bauckham, "Life, Death, and Afterlife," 86. For the continuity of Old and New Testaments with regard to the message of resurrection, see also Frank Crüsemann, "Scripture and Resurrection," in *Resurrection: Theological and Scientific Assessments*, 89-123.

14. Josephus, *Jewish War* 2.8.14 §165; see also Matthew 22:23; Mark 12:18; Luke 20:27.

15. Nevertheless, we should recognize that this period of theological development spawned a variety of eschatological beliefs—some related more to the immortality of the soul, or the resurrection of the spirit, or the resurrection of the person understood as a unity, or to no afterlife whatsoever. See John J. Collins, "The Afterlife in Apocalyptic Literature," in *Judaism in Late Antiquity*, part 4: *Death, Life-after-Death, Resurrection and the World-to-Come in the Judaisms of Antiquity*, ed. Alan J. Avery-Peck and Jacob Neusner, Handbook of Oriental Studies—1: The Near and Middle East 49 (Leiden: E. J. Brill, 2000), 119-39; George W. E. Nickelsburg, "Judgment, Life-after-Death, and Resurrection in the Apocrypha and the Non-Apocalyptic Pseudepigrapha," in *Death, Life-after-Death, Resurrection, and the World-to-Come*, 141-62; Philip R. Davies, "Death, Resurrection, and Life after Death in the Qumran Scrolls," in *Death, Life-after-Death, Resurrection, and the World-to-Come*, 189-211; Lester L. Grabbe, *Judaic Religion in the Second Temple Period: Belief and Practice from the Exile to Yavneh* (London: Routledge, 2000), 257-70.

16. More broadly, see Robert H. Gundry, "The Essential Physicality of Jesus' Resurrection According to the New Testament," in *Jesus of Nazareth: Lord and Christ: Essays on the Historical Jesus and New Testament Christology*, ed. Joel B. Green and Max Turner (Grand Rapids: William B. Eerdmans, 1994), 204-19.

17. On the connections of this material with angelophanies, see Crispin H. T. Fletcher-Louis, *Luke-Acts: Angels, Christology and Soteriology*, Wissenschaftliche Untersuchungen zum Neuen Testament 2:94 (Tübingen: Mohr Siebeck, 1997), 62-70. Fletcher-Louis helpfully analyzes Luke's presentation of Jesus in these scenes as both more divine than angels and more human.

18. David Goodman, "Do Angels Eat?" *Journal of Jewish Studies* 37 (1986): 160-70.

19. See the helpful analysis of this scene in John Paul Heil, *The Meal Scenes in Luke-Acts: An Audience-Oriented Approach*, Society of Biblical Literature Monograph Series (Atlanta: Society of Biblical Literature, 1999), 219-26.

20. Jürgen Moltmann, *God in Creation: A New Theology of Creation and the Spirit of God*, The Gifford Lectures 1984–1985 (San Francisco: Harper & Row, 1985), 244-75 (citation from 245).

21. For this and other traditional readings, see Gerald Bray, ed., *James, 1–2 Peter, 1–3 John, Jude*, Ancient Christian Commentary on Scripture 11 (Downers Grove, Ill.: InterVarsity, 2000), 106-8.

22. Its one clear reference to a human being in the New Testament comes in Heb. 12:23, where "spirit" is qualified with the adjective "righteous. "

23. E.g., Paul J. Achtemeier, *1 Peter* (Minneapolis: Fortress, 1996), 252-62; John H. Elliott, *1 Peter: A New Translation with Introduction and Commentary*, Anchor Bible 37B (New York: Doubleday, 2000), 647-63.

24. Charles E. Gutenson, "Time, Eternity, and Personal Identity: The Implications of Trinitarian Theology," in this volume.

25. See Andrew T. Lincoln, *Paradise Now and Not Yet: Studies in the Role of the Heavenly Dimension in Paul's Thought with Special Reference to His Eschatology*, Society for New Testament Studies Monograph Series 43 (Cambridge: Cambridge University Press, 1981), 77-84.

26. Cf. 2 Esdras 4:7-8; *Testament of Abraham* (B), 10:3.

27. Cf. *1 Enoch* 37-71 (which most scholars now date to the late first century CE).

28. E.g., 2 Esdras 7:36; 8:52; *2 Apocalypse of Baruch* 51:11; *Testament of Levi*, 18:10-11. See the summary in James H. Charlesworth, "Paradise," in *Anchor Bible Dictionary*, 5:154-55.

29. Cf. Joel B. Green, "'Witnesses of His Resurrection': Resurrection, Salvation, Discipleship, and Mission in the Acts of the Apostles," in *Life after Death*, 227-46.

30. Dale B. Martin, *The Corinthian Body* (New Haven: Yale University Press, 1995). This is true even if his understanding of the nature of the resurrection body is problematic.

31. See further the chapter by Lawson Stone in this volume, "The Soul: Possession, Part, or Person? The Genesis of Human Nature in Genesis 2:7."

32. See Alan G. Padgett, "The Body in Resurrection: Science and Scripture on the 'Spiritual Body' (1 Cor. 15:35-58)," *Word & World* 22 (2002): 155-63.

33. Richard Lattimore, *Themes in Greek and Latin Epitaphs*, Illinois Studies in Language and Literature 28.1-2 (Urbana: University of Illinois Press, 1942), 35 (see 32-35).

34. Anderson, "Resurrection of Jesus," 59-60, 102. On the association of stars with heavenly beings, cf. Dan. 8:10; Judges 5:20; Job 38:7. On the association of eternal life with angelic existence, cf. *1 Enoch* 39:5; 104:2-6; *2 Bar.* 51:10-11; *T. Mos.* 10:9; cf. 4 Ezra 7:97, 125. On the regnant connotations of star imagery, cf. Num. 24:17; Judges 5:20; Isa. 14:12-13; Dan. 8:10; Wis. 13:2; 2 Macc. 9:10. For the enthronement motif, cf. Isa. 14:12-14; *Ps. Sol.* 1:5; *T. Levi.* 18:3; *T. Jud.* 24:1.

35. Anthony C. Thiselton, *The First Epistle to the Corinthians: A Commentary on the Greek Text*, New International Greek Testament Commentary (Grand Rapids: William B. Eerdmans, 2000), 1276-81.

36. See further, Murray J. Harris, "Resurrection and Immortality in the Pauline Corpus," in *Life in the Face of Death*, 147-70; Richard N. Longenecker, "Is There Development in Paul's Resurrection Thought?" *Life in the Face of Death*, 171-202.

37. See the similar reflections in Peter Lampe, "Paul's Concept of a Spiritual Body," in *Resurrection: Theological and Scientific Assessments*, 103-14. Lampe, however, presumes that, with this language, Paul introduces an intermediate state, but this is not at all clear (cf., e.g., Markus Bockmuehl, *The Epistle to the Philippians*, Black's New Testament Commentary [London: A. & C. Black, 1998], 91-93).

38. See Elizabeth Gould and Charles G. Gross, "Neurogenesis in Adult Mammals: Some Progress and Problems," *Journal of Neuroscience* 22 (2002): 619-23.

39. Joseph LeDoux, *Synaptic Self: How Our Brains Become Who We Are* (New York: Viking Penguin, 2002), 3; cf. Susana Cohen-Cory, "The Developing Synapse: Construction and Modulation of Synaptic Structures and Circuits," *Science* 298 (25 October 2002): 770-76.

40. Nancey Murphy, "The Resurrection Body and Personal Identity: Possibilities and Limits of Eschatological Knowledge," in *Resurrection: Theological and Scientific Assessments*, 202-18; Charles E. Gutenson, "Time, Eternity, and Personal Identity. " Cf. the fascinating argument of Caroline Walker Bynum concerning the coalescing of (bodily) shape and (embodied) story in personal identity (*Metamorphosis and Identity* [New York: Zone, 2001]).

8. Emergent Dualism

1. Antonio R. Damasio, "How the Brain Creates the Mind," *Scientific American Special Edition: The Hidden Mind* (2002): 9.
2. It will be recognized that my account of dualism, here and elsewhere, is focused on the Cartesian version. The other leading candidate is Thomistic dualism, which is discussed in my *The Emergent Self* (Ithaca: Cornell University Press, 1999), 161-70.
3. For a more extensive presentation, see my *Emergent Self*, 147-61.
4. Charles Taliaferro, *Consciousness and the Mind of God* (Cambridge: Cambridge University Press, 1994).
5. Letter to the Marquis of Newcastle, in David M. Rosenthal, ed., *Materialism and the Mind-Body Problem* (Englewood Cliffs, N.J.: Prentice-Hall, 1971), 21.
6. For a more extensive critique of Cartesian dualism, see my *Emergent Self*, 148-61.
7. In Jaegwon Kim, *Supervenience and Mind: Selected Philosophical Essays* (Cambridge: Cambridge University Press, 1991).
8. Warren S. Brown, Nancey Murphy, and H. Newton Malony, eds, *Whatever Happened to the Soul? Scientific and Theological Portraits of Human Nature* (Minneapolis: Fortress, 1998).
9. See Nancey Murphy, "Nonreductive Physicalism: Philosophical Issues," in *Whatever Happened to the Soul?* 127-48 (page references in the text are to this article).
10. There may, of course, be laws that are not yet known, or corrections may be needed to some presently accepted laws. This will not matter for our argument, so long as the revised laws are of the same *kind* as those already accepted. (They will not, for example, involve primitive teleology or intentionality.)
11. This terminology is less than completely accurate, given the element of indeterminacy that is held to exist at the quantum level. This indeterminacy may however be unimportant in practice, since statistical laws ensure that the behavior of larger-scale objects (including neurons) is effectively deterministic.
12. See her "Response to Cullen," in *Science & Christian Belief* 13 (2001): 161-63.
13. See, for instance, her "Giving the Nonreductive Physicalist Her Due: A Response to Hasker's *The Emergent Self*," *Philosophia Christi* 2 (2000): 167-73; for my response see "Reply to My Friendly Critics," *Philosophia Christi* 2 (2000): 197-207.
14. R. W. Sperry, "Psychology's Mentalist Paradigm and the Religion/Science Tension," *American Psychologist* 43 (1988): 609.
15. Roger Sperry, "In Defense of Mentalism and Emergent Interaction," *Journal of Mind and Behavior* 12 (1991): 235-36.
16. Ibid.
17. This formulation may be preferable because it does not suggest, as the phrase "emergent laws" may suggest, that the system with its emergent powers must function deterministically.

18. See Timothy O'Connor, "Emergent Properties," *American Philosophical Quarterly* 31 (1994): 91-104; also his *Persons and Causes: The Metaphysics of Free Will* (New York: Oxford University Press, 2000), ch. 6.

19. Gottfried Wilhelm Leibniz, *Monadology* 17; in Nicholas Rescher, G. W. *Leibniz's Monadology: An Edition for Students* (Pittsburgh: University of Pittsburgh Press, 1991), 19.

20. For a more extensive development of this argument, see my *The Emergent Self*, 122-46.

21. For further development of the ideas in this section, see *The Emergent Self*, 211-31.

22. It is not an answer to this to assert that God, being good, would not (and perhaps *could* not) create such duplicates or near-duplicates. What is needed for the objection to go through is only the metaphysical possibility of a situation in which the appropriate atoms are arranged in the right configuration. It is hardly a necessary truth that only God would be able to do this.

23. It needs to be pointed out that there is a materialist version of the resurrection that is not subject to this objection. Peter van Inwagen has proposed that God, at the time of death, surreptitiously removes either the entire body or some crucial portion thereof (such as the central nervous system), and replaces it with a simulacrum. The resurrection occurs when the body that has been removed is reanimated, at the same time being transformed into its exalted, resurrected state ("The Possibility of Resurrection," *International Journal for Philosophy of Religion* 9 [1978]: 114-21). So far as I can see, this suggestion is conceptually coherent, but as an account of how God actually proceeds it leaves a great deal to be desired.

24. For a more extensive exposition, see my *The Emergent Self*, ch. 7.

25. For further discussion of this point see Keith Yandell, "Mind-Fields and the Siren Song of Reason," *Philosophia Christi* 2 (2000): 183-95; and my "Reply to My Friendly Critics. "

26. For more on this, see my *The Emergent Self*, 94-109.

27. See my *The Emergent Self*, 192.

28. Richard Feynman, *QED: The Strange Theory of Light and Matter* (Princeton: Princeton University Press, 1985), 10.

9. Time, Eternity, and Personal Identity

1. David Braine, "God, Time, and Eternity: An Essay in Review of Alan G. Padgett, *God, Eternity, and the Nature of Time*," *Evangelical Quarterly* 66 (1994): 340.

2. I must admit some displeasure with the marginally felicitous phrase "undivided wholeness." However, creaturely language tends to be tinged with finitude, and, consequently, such language tends to be best suited for what I have called the "commonsense" view. What I am trying to avoid is the covert smuggling of limiting, temporal concepts back into the discussion. One could speak of God's experience of time "all at once" or "simultaneously." However, the introduction of either reintroduces temporality in an unintended way—suggesting, for example, that all of time "happens at once." The focus both here and in the subsequent position is upon the fact that all of history stands before God in fullness, in completion, in undivided wholeness, not upon the "simultaneity" of happenings. Plotinus long ago recognized the difficulty in *The Enneads* when he denied temporal weight to certain terms that he went on to use for the sake of convenience. More

contemporarily, William P. Alston has used "specious present" to get at the divine experience of time without smuggling in temporality ("Hartshorne and Aquinas: A *Via Media*," in William P. Alston, *Divine Nature and Human Language* [Ithaca: Cornell University Press, 1989], 136).

3. I realize, of course, there is some debate on the proper way to take the divine omnipresence. The position I defend here is laid out in more detail by Wolfhart Pannenberg, *Systematic Theology*, 3 vols. (Grand Rapids: William B. Eerdmans, 1988–97), 1:337-448.

4. Nelson Pike, *God and Timelessness* (New York: Schocken, 1970).

5. Eleonore Stump and Norman Kretzmann, "Eternity, Awareness, and Action," *Faith and Philosophy* 9 (1992): 463-82 (463).

6. Pannenberg's objection here, to be fully grasped, must be set within the context of his deployment of a metaphysical, rather than mathematical, conception of the Infinite. See his discussion in *Systematic Theology*, 1:1-61, 337-448.

7. Stanley J. Grenz and Roger E. Olson, *Twentieth-Century Theology: God and the World in a Transitional Age* (Downers Grove: InterVarsity, 1997).

8. Pannenberg explores these matters in some detail in *Systematic Theology*, 1:259-448.

9. Note that my language has changed from that of an intermediate "state" to that of an intermediate "place." The change is not insignificant, since whatever else one can say about this reality, one must affirm the physicality of it. There are physical locations; Lazarus has fingers; and the rich man has a tongue upon which he wishes to receive a drop of water. Clearly, this is not a place peopled by disembodied souls.

10. See Brian Edgar, "Biblical Anthropology and the Intermediate State," *Evangelical Quarterly* 74 (2002): 27-45, 109-21.

11. Some have raised the "duplicate problem" (the problem that arises in speculating that God might create duplicate persons so that we would be unable to tell which one is the "real" person), and suggested that it is decisive in rebuttal of the recreationist position. I fail to see why this is the case. One simply need note that God, as the God of truth, actually *could not* participate in such deception. Here, *could not* is to be taken in the strongest sense, i.e., I am claiming that the so-called duplicate scenario is not logically possible, for it would be logically impossible for God to engage in such deceit.

12. It might be argued that biblical revelation trumps these considerations by requiring an intermediate state. This, at least, is the argument of John W. Cooper, *Body, Soul, and Life Everlasting: Biblical Anthropology and the Monism-Dualism Debate*, 2nd ed. (Grand Rapids: William B. Eerdmans, 2000); idem, "Biblical Anthropology and the Body-Soul Problem," in *Soul, Body, and Survival: Essays on the Metaphysics of Human Persons*, ed. Kevin Corcoran (Ithaca: Cornell University Press, 2001), 218-28. Cf., however, Edgar, "Biblical Anthropology"; Joel B. Green, "Eschatology and the Nature of Humans: A Reconsideration of the Pertinent Biblical Evidence," *Science & Christian Belief* 14 (2002): 33-50.

13. Colin E. Gunton, *The Promise of Trinitarian Theology* (Edinburgh: T&T Clark, 1991), 113.

14. Ibid.

15. Ibid., 114.

16. Here I am indebted to insights from an unpublished essay by Laurence Wood.

17. Frank Tipler, "The Omega Point as Eschaton," *Zygon* 24 (1989): 217-53. I recognize that it is disputable whether Tipler's position is best considered a "physicalist" theory. I

have taken it as such because of the focus upon physical aspects of human existence and the corresponding physical remnants.

18. Miroslav Volf, *Exclusion and Embrace* (Nashville: Abingdon, 1996), 66.

19. As Volf says, "For without boundaries there would be no discrete identities, and without discrete identities there could be no relation to the other" (*Exclusion and Embrace*, 67).

20. T. F. Torrance, *The Christian Doctrine of God* (Edinburgh: T&T Clark, 1996), 105.

21. Catherine LaCugna, *God for Us* (San Francisco: Harper Collins, 1991), 266.

22. Torrance, *Christian Doctrine of God*, 160.

23. Wolfhart Pannenberg, "Person," in *Die Religion in Geschichte und Gegenwart: Handwörterbuch für Theologie und Religionswissenschaft*, vol. 5, 3rd ed. (Tübingen: Mohr Siebeck, 1957), 231-32. Here, Pannenberg is noting that Scotus sees humans as constituted as persons only in relationship with God. However, the point I appropriate is merely that one cannot escape being constituted as person in relationship with God, although I see creatures as also having a role in the constitution of human persons.

10. What About the Dust?

1. In this volume, see Malcolm Jeeves, "Mind Reading and Soul Searching in the Twenty-first Century: The Scientific Evidence"; and D. Gareth Jones, "A Neurobiological Portrait of the Human Person: Finding a Context for Approaching the Brain."

2. In this volume, see Joel B. Green, "Resurrection of the Body: New Testament Voices Concerning Personal Continuity and the Afterlife"; also, idem, "What Does It Mean to Be Human? Another Chapter in the Ongoing Interaction of Science and Scripture," in *From Cells to Souls: Changing Portraits of Human Nature*, ed. Malcolm A. Jeeves (Grand Rapids: William B. Eerdmans, 2004), forthcoming.

3. Ralph Winter, approvingly quoted by David Hesselgrave, "Redefining Holism," *Evangelical Missions Quarterly* 35 (1999): 278-84 (278).

4. Thus, Hesselgrave makes a telling statement: "as summarized in Luke 4:18-19—a favored passage of liberals" ("Redefining Holism," 279).

5. John R. W. Stott, *Christian Mission in the Modern World* (Downers Grove, Ill.: InterVarsity, 1975).

6. Hesselgrave, "Redefining Holism," 280.

7. Ibid., 282.

8. Ibid., 284.

9. Bryant Myers, "Another Look at 'Holistic Mission,'" *Evangelical Missions Quarterly* 35 (1999): 285-87 (286).

10. Ibid., 286-87.

11. See, e.g., Joel Matthews, "Biblical Holism and Secular Thought in Christian Development," *Evangelical Mission Quarterly* 35 (1999): 290-98; Roger S. Greenway, *Together Again: Kinship of Word and Deed* (Monrovia, Calif.: MARC, 1998); Bruce Bradshaw, *Bridging the Gap: Evangelism, Development and Shalom* (Monrovia, Calif.: MARC, 1993); and Andrew Kirk, *The Good News of the Kingdom Coming* (Downers Grove, Ill.: InterVarsity, 1983).

12. John D. Zizioulas, *Being as Communion: Studies in Personhood and the Church* (Crestwood, N.Y.: St. Vladimir's Seminary Press, 1985).

13. Ibid., 39.

14. Stanley J. Grenz, *Theology for the Community of God* (Nashville: Broadman and Holman, 1994), 93.

15. Zizioulas, *Being as Communion*, 46.

16. Ibid., 50.

17. Ibid., 54.

18. Ibid., 56.

19. Thus, "the Lamb was slain from the foundation of the world" (Rev. 13:8), not before the foundation of the world, shows us that reaching out in loving relationship in creation was costly mission for the triune God.

20. "Here is the question to be pondered: does Piper's attitude reflect piety at its best or is it deeply at odds with God's character revealed in scripture? Interestingly, the title of Piper's article we cited is 'How does a sovereign God love?' We believe Piper has the question backwards and that his article reflects just that unfortunate subordination of love to will that Gunton identifies. Given the full revelation of God in scripture, the question we should be asking is: how would a God of perfect love express his sovereignty?" (Jerry Walls, *Why I Am Not a Calvinist* [Downers Grove, Ill.: InterVarsity, forthcoming]).

21. James M. Houston, "Modernity and Spirituality," in *Faith and Modernity*, ed. Philip Sampson et al. (Oxford: Regnum, 1994), 199.

22. Joseph LeDoux, *The Emotional Brain* (New York: Simon & Schuster, 1996).

23. Steven Johnson, "The Brain and Emotions," *Discover* (March 2003): 33-39.

24. Johnson, "Brain and Emotions," 38.

25. Ibid., 39.

26. Stephen P. Reyna, *Connections: Brain, Mind, and Culture in a Social Anthropology* (London: Routledge, 2002), 97.

27. Joaquin M. Fuster, *Memory in the Cerebral Cortex* (Cambridge: MIT Press, 1999).

28. Reyna, *Connections*, 114.

29. Ibid., 118. Franz Boas (1858–1942), who has been called "The Father of American Anthropology," founded the first department of anthropology at Columbia University and trained the whole first generation of anthropologists (Alfred Kroeber, Ruth Benedict, Margaret Mead, and others).

30. *The Works of John Wesley*, vol. 8, Bicentennial ed. (Nashville: Abingdon, 1984), 644.

31. Rebekah L. Miles, "The Instrumental Role of Reason," in *Wesley and the Quadrilateral: Renewing the Conversation*, W. Stephen Gunter, Scott J. Jones, Ted A. Campbell, Rebekah L. Miles, and Randy L. Maddox (Nashville: Abingdon, 1997), 103.

32. Reyna, *Connections*, 143.

33. Elaine Storkey, "Modernity and Anthropology," in *Faith and Modernity*, 139.

34. Wilbert R. Shenk, "The Training of Missiologists for Western Culture," in *Missiological Education for the 21st Century: The Book, the Circle and the Sandals*, ed. J. Dudley Woodberry et al. (Maryknoll, N.Y.: Orbis, 1996), 37.

35. Marilyn Strathern, *The Gender of the Gift: Problems with Women and Problems with Society in Melanesia* (Berkeley: University of California Press, 1988), 12.

36. See Paul G. Hiebert, "The Category *Christian* in the Mission Task," in *Anthropological Reflections on Missiological Issues* (Grand Rapids: Baker, 1994), 107-36.

37. Dan P. McAdams, "What Do We Know When We Know a Person?" *Journal of Personality* 63 (1995): 365-96 (382).

38. Jacques Derrida, *Positions* (Chicago: University of Chicago Press, 1982), 41.

39. James Scherer, *Gospel, Church and Kingdom: Comparative Studies in World Mission Theology* (Minneapolis: Augsburg, 1987), 235-36.

40. An interesting presentation of Old Testament theologies of land is found in Norman C. Habel, *The Land Is Mine: Six Biblical Land Ideologies* (Minneapolis: Fortress, 1995).

41. Ilaitia S. Tuwere, *Vanua: Towards a Fijian Theology of Place* (Suva, Fiji: Institute of Pacific Studies, University of the South Pacific; Auckland: College of St. John the Evangelist, 2002), 61.

42. Ibid., 62.

43. Ibid., 101.

44. Storkey, "Modernity and Anthroplogy," 139.

45. Harold A. Netland, "Truth, Authority and Modernity: Shopping for Truth in a Supermarket of Worldviews," in *Faith and Modernity*, 98.

46. C. P. Snow, *The Two Cultures and the Scientific Revolution* (New York: Cambridge University Press, 1959).

47. Rodney Clapp, *Border Crossings: Christian Trespasses on Popular Culture and Public Affairs* (Grand Rapids: Brazos, 2000), 32.

48. Miriam Adeney, "Mission Theology from Alternate Centers," in *The Good News of the Kingdom: Mission Theology for the Third Millennium*, ed. Charles van Engen et al. (Maryknoll, N.Y.: Orbis, 1993), 183.

49. John 12:32; Acts 3:19-21; Rom. 8:18-25; Rev. 21:1; Matthews, "Biblical Holism."

11. The Neuroscience of Christian Counseling?

1. Psychology and counseling are intimately related but not identical disciplines. Psychology studies all aspects of human nature including, but not limited to, perception, sensation, cognition, social interaction, human development, organizational behavior, etc. Counseling, on the other hand, focuses attention on theories and techniques that intend to relieve suffering caused by psychological and emotional disorders and relational problems.

2. See, for example, Antonio R. Damasio, *Decartes' Error: Emotion, Reason, and the Human Brain* (New York: Quill, 1994); Harold G. Koening, ed., *Research News and Opportunities in Science and Theology* (Trentwood, N.J.); Nancy S. Duvall, ed., "Special Issue: Perspectives on the Self/Soul," *Journal of Psychology and Theology* 26 (1998); Warren S. Brown, Nancey Murphy, and H. Newton Malony, eds., *Whatever Happened to the Soul? Scientific and Theological Portraits of Human Nature* (Minneapolis: Fortress, 1998); Louis Cozolino, *The Neuroscience of Psychotherapy* (New York: W. W. Norton, 2002).

3. For the purpose of this essay, I define professional counseling as that work which seeks to ameliorate pain caused by emotional and mental disorders as defined by the DSM-IV TR. Professional counseling is usually governed by rules set forth in state licensure laws. These laws pertain either to psychiatrists, psychologists, counselors, marriage and family therapists, or social workers. While pastoral care and counseling indeed may wrestle with the issues presented here, the relationship between pastoral counseling and "soul care" historically has been assumed. This is not so for professional counseling.

4. For more expanded discussions see Eric L. Johnson and Stanton L. Jones, "A History of Christians in Psychology," in *Psychology and Christianity*, ed. Eric L. Johnson and Stanton L. Jones (Downers Grove, Ill.: InterVarsity, 2000), 11-53.

5. A profession "is typically defined as a vocational activity having (1) an underlying body of theoretical and research knowledge, (2) an identifiable set of effective skills and activities, and (3) a publicly professed, voluntarily self-imposed set of behavioral guidelines" (P. J. Wittmer and Larry C. Loesch, "Professional Orientation," in *An Introduction to the Counseling Profession*, ed. Michael D. Lewis et al. [Itasca, Ill.: Peacock, 1986], 103). Professional Christian counseling draws upon the theoretical and research knowledge of psychology, counseling, theology, and biblical studies. Professional counselors employ counseling skills consistent with their level of academic training and state licensure. The Association of Christian Counselors and the Christian Association for Psychology Studies offer ethical guidelines for their members.

6. Johnson and Jones, "A History of Christians in Psychology. "

7. For masters-level programs, e.g., Asbury Theological Seminary, Ashland Theological Seminary, Denver Seminary, and Trinity Evangelical Divinity School. For doctoral-level programs in psychology, e.g., Biola University, Fuller Theological Seminary, and Wheaton College.

8. See, e.g., Kenneth I. Pargament, *The Psychology of Religion and Coping: Theory, Research and Practice* (New York: Guilford, 1997). The appendices refer to 268 studies that explore relationships between religious and psychological variables. See also P. S. Richards and Alan E. Bergin, *A Spiritual Strategy for Counseling and Psychotherapy* (Washington, D.C.: APA, 1997).

9. See, e.g., Johnson and Jones, eds., *Psychology and Christianity*; Robert C. Roberts and Mark R. Talbot, eds., *Limning the Psyche* (Grand Rapids: Eerdmans, 1997).

10. E.g., Martin Bobgan and Diedre Bobgan, *Psychoheresy: The Psychological Seduction of Christianity* (Santa Barbara, Calif.: East Gate, 1987); idem, *The End of "Christian Psychology"* (Santa Barbara, Calif.: East Gate, 1997).

11. E.g., Neil T. Anderson, *Helping Others Find Freedom in Christ* (Ventura, Calif.: Regal, 1995); Edward M. Smith, *Beyond Tolerable Recovery*, 2nd ed. (Campbellsville, Ky.: Family Care Ministries, 1997).

12. E.g., Neil Anderson et al., *Christ-Centered Therapy* (Grand Rapids: Zondervan, 2000); Gary R. Collins, *The Rebuilding of Psychology: An Integration of Psychology and Christianity* (Wheaton, Ill.: Tyndale, 1977); Mark McMinn, *Psychology, Theology and Spirituality in Christian Counseling* (Wheaton, Ill.: Tyndale, 1996). See also Johnson and Jones, ed., *Psychology and Christianity*, for a comparison of four views of integration.

13. See, e.g., Brown, Murphy, and Maloney, eds., *Whatever Happened to the Soul?*; Francis Crick, *The Astonishing Hypothesis: The Scientific Search for the Soul* (New York: Simon & Schuster, 1994); Damasio, *Descartes' Error*; William Hasker, *The Emergent Self* (Ithaca: Cornell University Press, 1999); Malcolm A. Jeeves, *Human Nature at the Millennium: Reflections on the Integration of Psychology and Christianity* (Grand Rapids: Baker, 1997).

14. Nancey Murphy, "Human Nature: Historical, Scientific, and Religious Issues," in *Whatever Happened to the Soul?*, 1-29 (25).

15. This is not to deny the biological basis of neurobiological brain disorders, such as major depression, schizophrenia, and the like, nor am I suggesting an anti-medication stance. Rather, I am proposing that a reductive materialist would view the problem as *nothing but* problematic brain events and that a pharmacological remedy provides a necessary and sufficient cure.

16. See, e.g., Mary Stewart Van Leeuwen, *The Person in Psychology: A Contemporary Christian Appraisal* (Grand Rapids: Eerdmans, 1985).

17. Murphy, "Human Nature," 24.

18. Hasker, *Emergent Self*, 115.

19. Murphy, "Human Nature," 25.

20. Ibid., 24.

21. J. P. Moreland, "Restoring the Substance to the Soul of Psychology," *Journal of Psychology and Theology* 26 (1998): 29-43 (35).

22. Anderson et al., *Christ-Centered Therapy*, 36.

23. See, e.g., Anderson, *Helping Others Find Freedom*; Smith, *Beyond Tolerable Recovery*.

24. See, e.g., Bobgan and Bobgan, *End of Christian Psychology*; idem, *Psychoheresy*.

25. E.g., Jay E. Adams, *More Than Redemption* (Phillipsburg, N.J.: Presbyterian and Reformed, 1979); David Powlison, "A Biblical Counseling View," in *Psychology and Christianity*, 196-225; Edward Welch, "How Theology Shapes Ministry: Jay Adams's View of the Flesh and an Alternative," *The Journal of Biblical Counseling* 20 (3, 2002): 16-25.

26. Various monistic theories have been proposed, including nonreductive physicalism (see various contributions to Brown, Murphy, and Maloney, eds., *Whatever Happened to the Soul?*) and emergent monism (Philip Clayton, "Neuroscience, the Person, and God: An Emergentist Account," *Neuroscience and the Person*, ed. Robert John Russell et al., Scientific Perspectives on Divine Action [Berkeley, Calif.: Center for Theology and the Natural Sciences; Vatican City State: Vatican Observatory, 1999], 191-214). It is beyond the scope of this essay to describe the distinctive features of these perspectives.

27. Ray S. Anderson, "On Being Human: The Spiritual Saga of a Creaturely Soul," in *Whatever Happened to the Soul?*, 175-94 (177; italics added).

28. Warren S. Brown, "Cognitive Contributions to Soul," in *Whatever Happened to the Soul?*, 99-126.

29. Ibid., 102.

30. Although brain traumas may limit our human experience of God, God is not bound by such limitations. In "asymmetric relatedness" Warren Brown notes that "one person with greater relational capacity can uphold and sustain relationalness, or 'soulishness'. . . of another person. I think we stand that way in relationship to God. We're all in some ways autistic in the sense that God is extending to us asymmetrically a relatedness that we only barely reciprocate. So, in that sense—in any absolute sense—our differences in abilities or capacities are not nearly as critical as the fact that God is extending to us and relating" (Doug Hardy, "Theologians of a Kind: Trinity Church Conference Speakers on What It Is to Be Human," *Research News & Opportunities in Science and Theology* 2 [1, 2001]: 24-25 [24]).

31. This is not to deny that sinful choices can contribute to creating contexts in which major depression, understood as chemical imbalances of the brain, is triggered. It is to argue that major depression is not caused by sin.

32. Daniel J. Siegel, *The Developing Mind* (New York: Guildford, 1999).

33. Robert O. Piehl, "Marbles, Clocks, and the Postmodern Self," *Journal of Psychology and Theology* 26 (1998): 83-100.

34. Cf. Joel B. Green, "'Bodies—That Is, Human Lives': A Re-examination of Human Nature in the Bible," in *Whatever Happened to the Soul?*, 149-73; idem, "Monism and the Nature of Humans in Scripture," *Christian Scholar's Review* 29 (2000): 731-43; idem, "Scripture and the Human Person: Further Reflections," *Science & Christian Belief* 11 (1999): 51-63.

35. E.g., Stanley J. Grenz, *The Social God and the Relational Self: A Trinitarian Theology of the Imago Dei* (Louisville, Kentucky: Westminster John Knox, 2001); Stanley J. Grenz and John R. Franke, *Beyond Foundationalism: Shaping Theology in Postmodern Context* (Louisville, Ky.: Westminster John Knox, 2001).

36. Cf. Piehl, "Marbles, Clocks, and the Postmodern Self. "

37. On the notion of top-down influence, see Brown, "Cognitive Contributions," 102.

38. Cf. Siegel, *Developing Mind.*

39. Thomas C. Oden, *The Transforming Power of Grace* (Nashville: Abingdon, 1993).

40. Michael J. Lambert, "Implications of Outcome Research for Psychotherapeutic Integration," in *Handbook of Psychotherapy Integration*, ed. J. C. Cross and M. R. Goldfried (New York: Basic, 1992), 94-129.

41. Oden, *Transforming Power*, 47.

42. The nature of the therapeutic relationship accounts for 30 percent of the variance. Clients' hopeful and expectant outlook on therapy and counselors' model/techniques each account for 15 percent. For support of Lambert's conclusions, see Mark A. Hubble, Barry L. Duncan, and Scott D. Miller, *The Heart and Soul of Change: What Works in Therapy* (New York: Guilford, 1999).

43. Barry L. Duncan, Mark A. Hubble, and Scott D. Miller, *Psychotherapy with Impossible Cases: Efficient Treatment of Therapy Veterans* (New York: Norton, 1997).

44. Michael J. Lambert, David A. Shapiro, and Allen E. Bergin, "The Effectiveness of Psychotherapy," in *Handbook of Psychotherapy and Behavior Change*, 3rd ed., ed. Sol L. Garfield and Allen E. Bergin (New York: Wiley, 1986), 157-212.

45. Karen Tallman and Arthur C. Bohart, "The Client as a Common Factor: Clients as Self-Healers," in *Heart and Soul of Change*, 91-132 (117).

46. Murphy, "Nonreductive Physicalism: Philosophical Issues," in *Whatever Happened to the Soul?*,127-48.

47. Grenz and Franke, *Beyond Foundationalism*, 215.

48. Piehl, "Marbles, Clocks, and the Postmodern Self," 96.

49. I am indebted to Bonnie Crandall for this descriptive phrase.

50. Alexander Bachelor and Adam Horvath, "The Therapeutic Relationship," in *Heart and Soul of Change*, 133-78 (139; italics added).

51. Ibid., 152.

52. Warren S. Brown, "Nonreductive Physicalism and Soul: Finding Resonance Between Theology and Neuroscience," *American Behavioral Scientist* 45 (2002): 1812-21 (1820).

12. Pastoral Care and Counseling Without the "Soul"

1. See, e.g., Francis H. Crick, *The Astonishing Hypothesis: The Scientific Search for a Soul* (London: Simon & Schuster, 1994); Antonio R. Damasio, *Descartes' Error: Emotion, Reason and the Human Brain* (New York: Grosset/Putnam, 1994); idem, *The Feeling of What Happens: Body and Emotion in the Making of Consciousness* (New York: Harcourt, 1999); Joseph LeDoux, *The Emotional Brain: The Mysterious Underpinnings of Emotional Life* (New York: Simon & Schuster, 1996); idem, *Synaptic Self* (New York: Simon & Schuster, 2002).

2. See, e.g., Warren S. Brown, Nancey Murphy, and H. Newton Malony, eds., *Whatever Happened to the Soul? Scientific and Theological Portraits of Human Nature* (Minneapolis:

Fortress, 1998); John W. Cooper, *Body, Soul, and Life Everlasting: Biblical Anthropology and the Monism-Dualism Debate*, 2nd ed. (Grand Rapids: William B. Eerdmans, 2000); Kevin Corcoran, ed., *Soul, Body, and Survival: Essays on the Metaphysics of Human Persons* (Ithaca: Cornell University Press, 2001); William Hasker, *The Emergent Self* (Ithaca: Cornell University Press, 1999); J. P. Moreland and Scott B. Rae, *Body and Soul: Human Nature and the Crisis in Ethics* (Downers Grove, Ill.: InterVarsity, 2000).

3. See Philip Clayton, "Neuroscience, the Person, and God: An Emergentist Account," in *Neuroscience and the Person*, Scientific Perspectives on Divine Action, ed. Robert John Russell, Nancey Murphy, Theo C. Meyering, and Michael A. Arbib (Berkeley, Calif.: Center for Theology and the Natural Sciences; Vatican City State: Vatican Observatory Publications, 1999), 181-214.

4. Malcolm Jeeves, "Brain, Mind, and Behavior," in *Whatever Happened to the Soul?*, 79.

5. Ibid., 81.

6. For reductive materialism, see Crick, *Astonishing Hypothesis*; for a strong dualism, see John C. Eccles, ed., *Brain and Conscious Experience* (Berlin: Springer, 1966).

7. See, e.g., James Gleick, *Chaos: Making a New Science* (New York: Penguin, 1987); Stuart Kaufman, *At Home in the Universe: The Search for the Laws of Self-Organization and Complexity* (New York: Oxford University Press, 1995); Daniel Siegel, *The Developing Mind: How Relationships and the Brain Interact to Shape Who We Are* (New York: Guilford, 1999); M. Mitchell Waldrop, *Complexity: The Emerging Science at the Edge of Order and Chaos* (New York: Simon & Schuster, 1992).

8. Louis Cozolino, *The Neuroscience of Psychotherapy: Building and Rebuilding the Human Brain* (New York: Norton, 2002); Bryan Kolb and Ian Q. Whishaw, "Brain Plasticity and Behavior," *Annual Review of Psychology* 49 (1998): 43-64; Allan N. Schore, *Affect Regulation and the Origin of the Self: The Neurobiology of Emotional Development* (Hillsdale, N.J.: Erlbaum, 1994).

9. Siegel, *Developing Mind*.

10. See, e.g., Damasio, *Descartes' Error*; idem, *The Feeling of What Happens*; LeDoux, *Emotional Brain*; idem, *Synaptic Self*.

11. See, e.g., Warren S. Brown, "Cognitive Contributions to Soul," in *Whatever Happened to the Soul?*, 99-126; Todd E. Feinberg, *Altered Egos: How the Brain Creates the Self* (Oxford: Oxford University Press, 2001); Jeeves, "Brain, Mind, and Behavior."

12. Hasker, *Emergent Self*.

13. See the discussion in Nancey Murphy, "Human Nature: Historical, Scientific, and Religious Issues," in *Whatever Happened to the Soul?*, 1-29.

14. Cf., e.g., Kevin Corcoran, "Physical Persons and Postmortem Survival Without Temporal Gaps," in *Soul, Body, and Survival*, 201-17; Trenton Merricks, "How to Live Forever Without Saving Your Soul," in *Soul, Body, and Survival*, 183-200.

15. By "pastor," I refer to ordained clergy in a congregational setting. This is not to suggest that pastoral care and counseling are the exclusive domain of the clergy, but that ordained pastors have a unique role in providing leadership, care, and counsel so as to empower laity to function in ministries such as care and counseling. The ordained pastor is "a priest to the priests," "a servant to the servants of God" (see William Willimon, *Pastor: The Theology and Practice of Ordained Ministry* [Nashville: Abingdon, 2002]). On the long tradition of "soul care," see, e.g., David G. Benner, *Care of Souls: Revisioning Christian Nurture and Counsel* (Grand Rapids: Baker, 1998); William Clebsh and Charles Jaekle, *Pastoral Care in Historical Perspective* (Northvale, N.J.: Jason Aronson, 1964);

E. Brooks Holifield, *A History of Pastoral Care in America* (Nashville: Abingdon, 1983); Thomas Oden, *Care of Souls in the Classic Tradition* (Philadelphia: Fortress, 1984); Orlo Strunk Jr., "A Prolegomenon to a History of Pastoral Counseling," in *Clinical Handbook of Pastoral Counseling*, ed. Robert J. Wicks, Richard D. Parsons, and Donald E. Capps (New York/Mahwah: Integration, 1985), 14-25.

16. I have borrowed this taxonomy from David G. Benner, *Psychotherapy and the Spiritual Quest* (Grand Rapids: Baker, 1988).

17. These labels are suggested in Murphy, "Human Nature," 24-25.

18. See, e.g., Benner, *Psychotherapy*; Kenneth J. Collins, "What Is Spirituality? Historical and Methodological Considerations," *Wesleyan Theological Journal* 31 (1992): 76-94; Donald Evans, *Spirituality and Human Nature* (Albany: State University of New York Press, 1992).

19. Harold G. Koenig, Michael E. McCollough, and David B. Larson, *Handbook of Religion and Health* (New York: Oxford University Press, 2001).

20. The terms "soul" and "spirituality" are of particular concern because they are so tainted by the Western influence of Cartesian "dualism." Maybe we should call a moratorium on the use of these particular terms until they are not so tightly bound to a dualistic perspective.

21. William Willimon, *Worship as Pastoral Care* (Nashville: Abingdon, 1979); idem, *Pastor*.

22. David G. Benner, *Strategic Pastoral Counseling: A Short-term Structure Model* (Grand Rapids: Baker, 1992); Brian Childs, *Short-term Pastoral Counseling* (Nashville: Abingdon, 1990); Philip Culbertson, *Caring for God's People: Counseling and Christian Wholeness* (Minneapolis: Fortress, 2000); John Patton, *Pastoral Care in Context: An Introduction to Pastoral Care* (Louisville: Westminster/John Knox, 1993).

23. See, e.g., Benner, *Strategic Pastoral Counseling*; Paul W. Pruyser, *The Minister as Diagnostician: Personal Problems in Pastoral Perspective* (Philadelphia: Westminster, 1976); Nancy J. Ramsay, *Pastoral Diagnosis: A Resource for Ministries of Care and Counseling* (Minneapolis: Fortress, 1998).

24. Benner, *Care of Souls*; Mark A. Hubble, Berry L. Duncan, and Scott D. Miller, *The Heart and Soul of Change: What Works in Therapy* (New York: Guilford, 1999).

13. Human Nature

1. Thomas Metzinger, "Introduction: Consciousness Research at the End of the Twentieth Century," in *Neural Correlates of Consciousness: Empirical and Conceptual Questions*, ed. Thomas Metzinger (Cambridge: MIT Press, 2000), 6.

2. Francis H. Crick, *The Astonishing Hypothesis: The Scientific Search for the Soul* (London: Simon & Schuster, 1994), 3.

3. Predrag Petrovic, Eija Kelso, Karl Magnus Petersson, and Martin Ingvar, "Placebo and Opioid Analgesia—Imaging a Shared Neuronal Network," *Science* 295 (2002): 1737-40.

4. Petrovic et al., "Placebo and Opioid Analgesia," 1737.

5. John W. Cooper, *Body, Soul and Life Everlasting: Biblical Anthropology and the Monism-Dualism Debate* (Grand Rapids: William B. Eerdmans, 1989).

6. Cooper, *Body, Soul and Life Everlasting*, 225.

7. T. J. Grabowski, and A. R. Damasio, " Improving Functional Imaging Techniques: The Dream of a Single Image for a Single Mental Event," *Proceedings of the National Academy of Sciences* 93 (1996): 14302-03.

8. K. M. O'Craven and N. Kanwisher, "Mental Imagery of Faces and Places Activates Corresponding Stimulus Specific Brain Regions," *Journal of Cognitive Neuroscience* 12 (2000): 1013-23.

9. John C. Eccles, ed., *Brain and Conscious Experience* (Berlin: Springer, 1996), 327.

10. Roger W. Sperry, "American Psychological Association," *Psychological Science Agenda* (1994): 10-13. See G. Edelman, *Bright Air and Brilliant Fire: On the Matter of the Mind* (London: Penguin, 1992).

11. Edelman, *Bright Air and Brilliant Fire*, 111.

12. Roger W. Sperry, *Essays in Honor of Roger W. Sperry*, ed. C. Trevarthen (Cambridge: Cambridge University Press, 1990), 312, 384.

13. Roger Penrose, *The Emperor's New Mind* (Oxford: Oxford University Press, 1989), 580.

14. Donald M. MacKay, *Behind the Eye* (Oxford: Blackwell, 1991).

15. Joel B. Green, "Eschatology and the Nature of Humans: A Reconsideration of Pertinent Biblical Evidence," *Science and Christian Belief* 14 (2002): 33-50 (50).

16. Cooper, *Body, Soul and Life Everlasting*, 210.

17. Green, "Eschatology and the Nature of Humans," 50.

18. Cooper, *Body, Soul and Life Everlasting*, 116.

19. Green, "Eschatology and the Nature of Humans," 50.

20. John D. Zizioulas, *Being as Communion: Studies in Personhood and the Church* (Crestwood, N.Y.: St. Vladimir's Seminary Press, 1985), 56.

21. Michael J. Lambert, "Implications of Outcome Research for Psychotherapeutic Integration," in *Handbook of Psychotherapy Integration*, ed. J. C. Cross and M. R. Goldfried (New York: Basic 1992), 94-129.

22. Warren S. Brown, "Cognitive Contributions to Soul," in *Whatever Happened to the Soul? Scientific and Theological Portraits of Human Nature*, ed. Warren S. Brown, Nancey Murphy, and H. Newton Maloney (Minneapolis: Fortress Press, 1998), 99-125.

CONTRIBUTORS

Bill T. Arnold (Ph.D., Hebrew Union College) is Professor of Old Testament and Semitic Languages, Asbury Theological Seminary.

Joel B. Green (Ph.D., University of Aberdeen) is Dean of Academic Affairs and Professor of New Testament Interpretation, Asbury Theological Seminary.

Charles E. Gutenson (Ph.D., Southern Methodist University) is Associate Dean for Distributed Learning, School of Theology, and Associate Professor of Philosophical Theology, Asbury Theological Seminary.

William Hasker (Ph.D., University of Edinburgh) is Emeritus Professor of Philosophy, Huntington College.

Virginia T. Holeman (Ph.D., Kent State University) is Associate Dean of the School of Theology and Professor of Counseling, Asbury Theological Seminary.

Malcolm Jeeves (Ph.D., University of Cambridge) is Honorary Research Professor of Psychology, University of St. Andrews.

D. Gareth Jones (D.Sc., University of Western Australia) is Professor of Anatomy and Structural Biology, Otago School of Medical Sciences, University of Otago, New Zealand.

Patrick D. Miller (Ph.D., Harvard University) is Charles T. Haley Professor of Old Testament Theology, Princeton Theological Seminary.

Stuart L. Palmer (Psy.D., Fuller Theological Seminary) is Associate Professor of Pastoral Counseling, Asbury Theological Seminary.

Michael A. Rynkiewich (Ph.D., University of Minnesota) is Professor of Anthropology, Asbury Theological Seminary.

Lawson G. Stone (Ph.D., Yale University) is Professor of Old Testament, Asbury Theological Seminary.

AUTHOR INDEX

Whitehouse, P. J., 194
Whiten, A., 26, 194
Wicks, R. J., 214
Willimon, W., 213-14
Willis, T., 9, 192
Winter, R., 207
Wittmer, P. J., 210
Wolff, H. W., 202
Wood, L., 206
Woodberry, J. D., 208

Woodruff, G., 26-27, 194
Wright, J. E., 200

Yamauchi, E., 201
Yandell, K., 205
Yesavage, J. A., 194

Zizioulas, J. D., 135, 185, 207-8, 215
Zuehlke, J. S., 151
Zuehlke, T. E., 151

SCRIPTURE INDEX